BELZONI

BELZONI

THE GIANT ARCHAEOLOGISTS LOVE TO HATE

IVOR NOËL HUME

University of Virginia Press

CHARLOTTESVILLE AND LONDON

University of Virginia Press
© 2011 by the Rector and Visitors of the University of Virginia
All rights reserved
Printed in China

First published 2011

9 8 7 6 5 4 3 2 1

LIBRARY OF CONGRESS CATALOGING-IN-PUBLICATION DATA
Noël Hume, Ivor.
    Belzoni : the giant archaeologists love to hate / Ivor Noël Hume.
        p.   cm.
    Includes bibliographical references and index.
    ISBN 978-0-8139-3140-1 (cloth : acid-free paper)
    1. Belzoni, Giovanni Battista, 1778–1823. 2. Belzoni, Giovanni Battista, 1778–1823—
Travel—Egypt. 3. Belzoni, Mrs. (Sarah), 1783–1870—Travel—Egypt. 4. Archaeologists—
Italy—Biography. 5. Archaeologists—Egypt—Biography. 6. Egyptologists—Biography.
7. Excavations (Archaeology)—Egypt. 8. Egypt—Antiquities. 9. Egypt—Description
and travel. I. Title.
    DT76.9.B4N64 2011
    932.0072'02—dc22
    [B]   2011000693

Frontispiece: Sarah Belzoni's own copy of her 1824 memorial engraving in tribute to her
husband and his discoveries. (© Bristol Museums, Galleries & Archives)

Contents

Preface

Given that condemning one's predecessors for their mistakes or general incompetence is an established archaeological sport, why else, you might ask, would a twenty-first-century archaeologist set out to write about an Egyptologist who died in 1823? But criticism is not my intent. On the contrary, I feel a certain affinity for Giovanni Belzoni, who began his career as a stage performer and by accident found himself at the forefront of Egyptian archaeology at a time when very little was known about it and no teachers existed to show him what to do.

Like Belzoni, my own career began in the English theater while learning to be a playwright. By accident, again like Belzoni, I became involved in archaeology, albeit of the British seventeenth and eighteenth centuries. Just as classicists thought nothing of Belzoni's Egyptian treasures, when I began, almost all professional archaeologists were focusing on the Roman and Saxon centuries. But, unlike Belzoni, I did have a tutor, though one who left London's Guildhall Museum two weeks after I joined his two-man staff. Thenceforth I was on my own. I made mistakes, as did Belzoni, and was criticized by my elders for making statements to the press that made me appear more knowledgeable than I was. So did Belzoni. Nevertheless, he was doing the best he could with what he had and made contributions to the British Museum's Egyptian collections that have never been equaled. He was an Anglophile whose driving desire was to give something worthwhile to the British nation. It never thanked him for doing so. In that respect, I was more fortunate. While it is true that my discoveries have not matched the stature of his seven-ton Young Memnon, my interpretive goal has been the same.

Throughout the book, I have retained spellings as written by Belzoni and his contemporaries. Some of these may be construed as offensive to modern readers, to whom I apologize.

I am frequently asked how one becomes an archaeologist. I answer that the day you discover that finding is less satisfying than finding out is when you can don the mantle. It is my opinion, therefore, that Belzoni's lone efforts to do that made him a bona fide archaeologist—as these chapters will attest.

Acknowledgments

Once having embarked on writing a book, it is a good idea to finish it while the people who helped are still alive. Unfortunately, this one has been stretched over forty years, and so most of them are not. However, that sad reality in no way relieves me of my duty to give thanks where thanks are due. Two old friends head the list: my literary agent Marilyn Marlow, who encouraged me to finish the book, and the Egyptologist Dr. Veronica Seton Williams, who inspired me to start it. I am grateful, also, to the courier Maureen Tracey (known only as "Tracey"), who ministered to my wounded wife one night at Luxor when she should have been out looking for our lost boat. Much more recently, Dr. Sally Anne Ashton, curator of Egyptian Antiquities at the Fitzwilliam Museum at Cambridge, United Kingdom, has helped look for a missing mummy, as had the Egyptologist Dylan Bickerstaffe, who made sense of Belzoni's disputed sarcophagus lids. In Brussels, Mrs. Jeannine Johnson Maia did much-appreciated legwork in pursuit of Sarah Belzoni's mummy, and Dr. Dirk Huyge, curator of Egyptian antiquities for the Belgian Royal Museums of Art and History, kindly provided some of the answers. At Sir John Soane's Museum in London, the librarian Christina Scull provided me with a wealth of documents relating to the sale of the Seti sarcophagus. At the Bristol City Museum, the archaeological assistant Susan Giles and documentation assistant for foreign archaeology Amber Druce sent me copies of pages from Sarah Belzoni's notebook that included her last letter to her husband, copied by the previous curator, Robert Stanton, with whom my wife worked as a student. The Bristol Museum also put me in touch with Amanda Harris, who was independently working on the museum's collection of Belzoni drawings. In my failing efforts to locate Sarah's grave site, I was generously helped by Mrs. Joan Porter of the Jersey Wildlife Preservation Trust as well as by the Jersey archaeologist James Hibbs. Anthony Mitchell, the Historic Buildings representative for Wessex, assisted me in pursuing the history of the Bankes obelisk at Kingston Lacy. At the University of California at Santa Barbara, the Egyptologist Stuart Tyson Smith did his best to guide me through the Cave of Sokar and the primordial waters of Nun. I am no less grateful to Kent R. Weeks, the director of the Theban Mapping Project, for his thoughts on the mystery tunnel then being excavated beyond the tomb of Seti I. I owe more than I can say to my late wife, Audrey, whose enthusiasm for sailing the Nile was as buoyant as my own, and who, throughout my archaeological career, provided me with the support and wisdom of a latter-day Sarah.

Wherever possible I have worked from original sources, all of which are cited in the bibliography, several of them relatively recent reprints and of inestimable value. Stanley Mayes's 1959 book *The Great Belzoni* has been an important cross-checking resource, as has been Warren R. Dawson and Eric P. Uphill's *Who Was Who in Egyptology*. Patricia Usik's highly readable and authoritative *Adventures in Egypt and Nubia* (2002) has opened the doors to the William John Bankes archive at Kingston Lacy. In Charlottesville, Virginia, the literary researcher Susan Broadwater has been incredibly generous in sharing her notes and knowledge of Giovanni and Sarah Belzoni. Without Susan, I would never have found the valuable references in contemporary antipodean newspapers. I am grateful, too, to fellow author Wilford Kale, who posed as a general reader of the manuscript (which he is not) and made numerous valuable suggestions. Most rewarding of all, however, has been the pleasure of possessing my own copy of Belzoni's intensely personal and provocative 1821 *Narrative of the Operations and Recent Discoveries within the Pyramids, Temples, Tombs, and Excavations in Egypt and Nubia; and a Journey to the Coast of the Red Sea, in Search of the Ancient Berenice; and Another to the Oasis of Jupiter Ammon*—without which Giovanni and Sarah Belzoni would long ago have been forgotten.

When relevant I have relied on my own on-site photographs (and any uncredited illustrations are my own photographs or from my collection), but this is Belzoni's story and not mine. So it is only proper that his images as well as those credited to his wife, Sarah, should be the most prominent. That they are reproduced in color is due to the generosity of my friend and neighbor Bill Harrison of Four Mile Tree, Virginia, and

Corpus Christi, Texas. For the nineteenth-century peripheral engravings and paintings, I am most grateful to Peter Thornton, who, apart from being a distinguished scholar, is the leading expert on what one might term Belzoniana.

Finally, I lack the words to express my gratitude to my wife, Carol, whose review of the manuscript in its many stages kept me on track, and to copy editor Susan Murray, who ensured that all those multichoice spellings of ancient Egyptian and Arab names were properly synchronized.

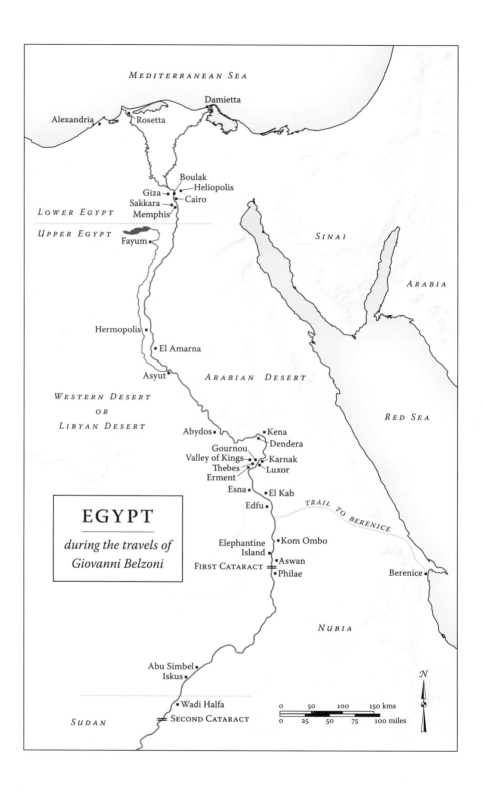

MEDITERRANEAN SEA

Damietta

Alexandria ▪   Rosetta ▪

Boulak
Heliopolis
Giza ▪ ▪ Cairo
Sakkara ▪
Memphis ▪

LOWER EGYPT
UPPER EGYPT
Fayum ▪

SINAI

ARABIA

Hermopolis ▪

▪ El Amarna

Asyut ▪   ARABIAN DESERT

WESTERN DESERT
OR
LIBYAN DESERT

RED SEA

Abydos ▪   ▪ Kena
Dendera
Gournou
Valley of Kings ▪ Karnak
Thebes ▪ ▪ Luxor
Erment
Esna ▪   ▪ El Kab
Edfu ▪   TRAIL TO BERENICE

Elephantine ▪ Kom Ombo
Island
FIRST CATARACT ▪ Aswan
▪ Philae   Berenice ▪

EGYPT

*during the travels of
Giovanni Belzoni*

NUBIA

Abu Simbel ▪
Iskus ▪

N

▪ Wadi Halfa
SECOND CATARACT

SUDAN

0   50   100   150 kms
0   25   50   75   100 miles

About Egypt I shall have a great deal more to relate because of the number of remarkable things which the country contains, and because of the fact that more monuments which beggar description are to be found there than anywhere else in the world.

HERODOTUS, ca. 454 BC

PROLOGUE

A BABOON AND A BABY BULL have shared the same home for more than 150 years. Concealed within yellowed and brittle bandages, they reside in the Mummy Room of the British Museum. Few tourists pay them much attention. Packaged animals cannot compete with the linen-wrapped corpses of ancient Egyptian dignitaries and friends of pharaohs. Nevertheless, these pathetic animals from another world once played their part in one of archaeology's most contentious chapters. Nothing in their labeling tells us that, but the evidence is there: Printed on their wrappings in neatly inked letters are the date 1821 and the name "SALT."

Downstairs in the Egyptian sculpture gallery sits a black basalt statue of Amenophis III (1417–1379 BC, also known as Amenhotep), still quizzically eyeing his subjects after close on 3,400 years. The figure was sculpted to grace the king's mortuary temple at Thebes, and everyone knew who he was. But the temple no longer survives, so today he needs a curator's label to let the museum's tourists and art students know that this is the face of the man who captured Babylon, built the city of Thebes, had the Colossi of Memnon erected in his honor, was the first living Egyptian king to be worshiped as a god, and married his own daughter. Without the label, however, the uninitiated might think him an Italian, for carved deep into the plinth beside his left heel they can read the name "BELZONI."

Just as the baboon's label says nothing about Salt, so that of Amenophis ignores Belzoni; yet they and the British army were the fathers of the museum's Egyptian collections. The army's contributions were the unexpected spoils of war with Napoleon; but Giovanni Belzoni's coups were premeditated and often won in single mind-to-mind combat with his sinister French rival, Bernardino Drovetti—a man no more French than Belzoni was British.

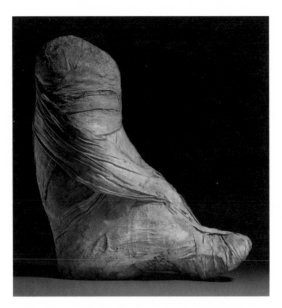

Animal mummy in the British Museum, marked "SALT 1821" and believed to contain the bones of a baboon. (© The Trustees of the British Museum)

Basalt statue of Amenophis III found in the remains of the king's mortuary temple at Thebes, inscribed "BELZONI" (see p. 264). (© The Trustees of the British Museum)

In 1929, the president of the Archaeological Institute of America declared: "When the modern scientific archaeologist reads about Belzoni, of Beelzebubish memory, who in 1817 began the search for buried Pharaohs across from Thebes, he becomes a human chameleon. He turns absolutely green with envy, then red with shame, then white with rage."[1] Later, an American professor who writes excellent textbooks condemned Belzoni "as the greatest plunderer of them all," while a writer-editor for the National Geographic Society got in a few licks of her own, calling him "the most notorious tomb robber Egypt has ever known."

The archaeological critics forget that most of the key objects in the world's great museums were found by amateur antiquaries or by chance. However, there is no denying that had twenty-first-century technology and experience been available 280 years earlier, much more would have been learned. Instead, Giovanni Belzoni did as best he could, and if the wagging finger of blame must be pointed, it should be aimed at the gentleman scholars, curators, and collectors who hired him, profited from him, and eventually abandoned him. Leaving him to take the heat alone, Belzoni's mentor and patron, Henry Salt, has been allowed to melt into the shadows of historical oblivion.

As a professional archaeologist, I have found the wrongs done to the ill-fated Italian as fascinating as they were deplorable. The tragedy of Signor Belzoni and Mr. Salt, though played out in the crowded streets of London, in the halls of the British Museum, and amid the vast set-pieces of ancient Egypt, was as intimate as two minds could make it. It grew from a mutual search, not only for "old rocks," as Belzoni told dubious Arabs, but for respect. One man wanted to be larger than his station had made him, and the other yearned to be recognized for his ability rather than his size. Both wanted to be wanted—Salt seeking social status and Belzoni scholarly acceptance. Instead, each ended his days further from his goal than he had begun. Salt wasted his inheritance ingratiating himself with the noble and wealthy, only to be dismissed by them for being a dealer and a poor poet. Belzoni, who briefly earned the fickle favor of London society, would be pursued through its streets by a mob and arrested by the Bow Street Runners for allegedly crashing a benefit party for the Irish poor. Two years later, he would die alone in a West African village whose inhabitants remembered the fever-ridden stranger only for his prodigious size.

Here is a story of naiveté, ambition, duplicity, avarice, and poverty worthy of Charles Dickens or Henry James, differing only in that it happens to be true. At the same time, it is a tale of high adventure against settings that carry us from the squalor of English freak shows to Egypt and the Valley of Kings, and eventually back to Westminster Abbey and the coronation of George IV. This sad history was not Belzoni's alone; he shared it with his faithful and long-suffering wife. Throughout it all, Sarah, his one-time circus assistant, battled fleas, sand, blindness, Arab robbers, and the difficulties of making Christmas dinner in a tomb, with a stoicism that placed her at the head table of feminism thirty years before it earned a name.

I dare hope that having read the story of Giovanni and Sarah, you will be inspired to travel the Nile, seek out Belzoni's name, and visit the great hall at Karnak against whose yardstick all civilization's architectural achievements must be judged.

1 } SAMPSON & SARAH

GIOVANNI BATTISTA BELZONI was born in the Italian city of Padua on November 5, 1778—a simple sentence heralding the birth of a most uncommon boy. In an age wherein the height of an average male was 5'6", Giovanni would grow to be a foot taller. In modern basketball terms, his height raises few eyebrows, but in eighteenth-century Italy he was a giant.[1] Furthermore, he had the physique to match it, and unlike many of nature's oddities, he had a handsome face and a fertile brain. But being the son of a poor family—his father was a barber—the young Belzoni had no idea where his future lay, knowing only that living and dying in Padua held scant appeal.

Although Padua was a picturesque medieval city with a famed university that dated from 1222, and possessed more than enough churches to satisfy the spiritual needs of it citizens, its entrenched Venetian rulers and merchant class offered little to a young man with dreams of being better than a barber. Though a mere twenty-five miles away, Venice would only offer him more of the same. Besides, his parents were Romans and not Venetians, and Rome, therefore, was the portal to the future—whatever that might turn out to be.

Giovanni had three brothers, Antonio, Domenico, and Francesco, who was also of above-average height. They are reputed to have derived their physique from their mother, Teresa, who was described as "a woman of muscular strength and stature."[2] Together the boys worked in the family barber shop until Giovanni was sixteen and secured his father's reluctant permission to go to the fabled Rome to further his education. Although very little is known about him in those teenage years, Giovanni was both bright and good with his hands, thereby making him a better candidate for a trade school than a university. He had developed an interest in hydraulics, though how, when, and why, nobody now knows; but it is likely that such education as he acquired in Rome carried him further in that direction.

By the 1790s, Europe was in political turmoil. The short man from Corsica had seized most of it, and in 1796, Napoleon Bonaparte's army was in control of northern Italy, and a year later occupied Rome and forced the pope into exile. Perhaps fearing that his prodigious size would make him a target for French recruiters, Belzoni enrolled in a Capuchin monastery with the not entirely serious intention of becoming a monk. According to one probably apocryphal legend, his entry into the monastery was the result of being hired to dig an artesian well in its grounds. But true or not, Belzoni obtained anonymity there while Napoleon's troops sacked and rampaged through Rome. It allowed him time to wonder how long it would be before the sanctity of the monastery would be invaded, a prospect that soon persuaded him to set out on the long road north as a peddler of religious talismans. He would later make it clear that he had not chosen the life of an itinerant salesman but had only needed money to help him on his way.

On foot and hitchhiking on wagons, Belzoni traveled into the heart of the Napoleonic Empire, but what he did in France and how long he stayed is unrecorded. An oversized hydraulic engineer whose French was minimal was not in demand there, and his need for money to sustain his search for work reluctantly forced him to seek the help of his parents. "My family supplied me occasionally with remittances," he explained, "but as they were not rich, I did not choose to be a burthen to them, and contrived to live on my own industry, and the little knowledge I had acquired in various branches."[3] He admitted to suffering "many vicissitudes" in his search for a respectable living, but omitted any specifics. Indeed, when writing his book twenty years later, Belzoni avoided any discussion of his life in the fifteen years after leaving Rome. By 1820, he had become a national celebrity in England, and the city fathers of Padua had commissioned a medal to be struck in his honor. That was no time to recall his years of penury and the ignominy of the work he had been forced to do to keep bread on his table.

Just as in the twenty-first century the media can be relied on to keep one's past alive, so Belzoni's early adult years could never be entirely buried. Consequently, because he would not write about them himself, we have to rely on the printed recollections of others whose memories were often less than reliable. Unfortunately, for the months and years between 1800 and 1803, we are bereft even of those. Again penniless, he appears to have returned to Padua to take stock of his prospects, and there resolved to try his luck as a hydraulic engineer in the Netherlands. While it was true that Holland had a readier access to water than virtually any other country in Europe, it also had the greatest experience in controlling it. Giovanni's help was not needed, nor was that of his brother Francesco, who had elected to travel with him. Consequently, there were now two out-of-work Belzonis in Holland.

Since Giovanni had left Rome to Napoleon's soldiery, the European political landscape had appreciably changed. The first inkling that it was about to do so reached British spies in the spring of 1798. Something was afoot in the French port of Toulon. A huge fleet was being assembled in such secrecy that even those ordered aboard had no idea where they were going. In addition to three hundred troop transports, a battle fleet of thirteen ships of the line led by one of the largest afloat, the 120-gun *L'Orient*, was making ready to sail. The lading of hundreds of dismantled boats had made some observers conclude that Napoleon planned to carry them overland to the Red Sea as the first step to invading England's territories in India. Less easy to explain was the embarking of a large printing press and scores of civilians that included astronomers, artists, naturalists, engineers, and professors of Arabic, Persian, and Turkish.

It turned out that Napoleon's first target was the island of Malta, which had been ruled by the Knights of St. John of Jerusalem since the sixteenth century, and ever since had been at war with the Ottoman Turks, to whose destruction they had dedicated themselves. But the knights were an old and motley lot, two hundred of whom were Frenchmen. It came as no surprise, therefore, that the island capitulated with very few shots being fired. Napoleon landed at Valetta on June 11, 1798, and having ordered the knights' religious treasure melted down into ingots and loaded aboard the *L'Orient*, by June 19 he was on his way to his primary destination.

The English still did not know what the French intended. But fearing that they meant to break out into the Atlantic and mount an invasion of Ireland, Lord Nelson was ordered to take the only available British warships into the Mediterranean to stop them—if he could find them. But after sailing by Toulon and Corsica without a sign of their sails, Nelson deduced that Napoleon was targeting the Levantine Turks in an attempt

Napoleon's Cairo Institute, 1799. (From Dominique Vivant Denon's Description de l'Égypte, *1809)*

to dominate the Middle East. In reality, Egypt was the prize, and Nelson eventually found the French armada at anchor in Aboukir Bay at the mouth of the Nile east of Alexandria. Taking the French by surprise, he attacked the moored ships, capturing or sinking most of them. The huge *L'Orient,* after taking numerous British broadsides, caught fire and eventually blew up, taking the Maltese gold down with it. The Battle of the Nile had been fought on the evening of August 1, and left Napoleon's vast army ashore at Alexandria with no means of escape should the Egyptians prove more formidable than he expected. They were, but fine horses and flashing sabers were no match for coordinated French firepower, and after the so-called Battle of the Pyramids, the Arab Mamelukes fled south into Upper Egypt.

With Cairo in French hands, Napoleon established an Egyptian Institute of Arts and Sciences—thus explaining the presence of the civilian scholars (savants) who were to staff it. Among them was Dominique Vivant Denon, who, before the Revolution, had been a curator of gems and medals for Louis XV. In Egypt, he was Napoleon's principal antiquary and gatherer of ancient objects worth taking home. Although Bonaparte's articles of instruction to the new institute made no mention of collecting exportable antiquities, squads of soldiers were detailed off to dig for relics, some of which were still only half uncovered when, in 1801, the French army surrendered to the British.

Previously, however, Napoleon's months as Egypt's new pharaoh had come to an abrupt end when Austria declared war on France, the Russians invaded Turin, Britain allied with the Turks, and his attempt to add Syria to his Middle East empire ended in costly failure. In August 1799, Bonaparte announced that, "in view of the news from Europe," he was leaving Cairo and his institute to return to France. A surprised but competent General Jean Baptiste Kléber thus found himself the civil and military ruler of Egypt. Less than a year later, he was assassinated by a student fanatic and was succeeded by General Jacques Menou, who was described as "an officer without merit . . . who in Egypt had rendered no service of any account." Nevertheless, at the end of May 1801, it fell to Menou to render the service of capitulating to the British expeditionary force, which had landed in Aboukir Bay on March 10. In what may have been his last letter to Napoleon, Menou wrote that he had kept the archaeological pieces, thinking that they were safer there than on a ship that might be

French troops at Rosetta, 1799. (From Dominique Vivant Denon's Description de l'Égypte, *1809)*

captured. He added that "these objects are in a sacred depository."[4] They almost certainly included a three-foot slab of inscribed reddish-brown basalt that a French officer named Pierre François Xavier Bouchard had unearthed near the delta town of Rosetta. Bouchard thought the inscriptions might be important—but not to the brothers Belzoni, who, in 1801, were trying to scratch out a living in Holland.

Although defeated and driven out of Egypt, Napoleon remained the dominant figure in Europe and no friend to Britain. Nevertheless, both sides needed to draw a breath, and in 1802 they called a halt to the hostilities and put their signatures to the document known as the Peace of Amiens. For the British, it meant no more dead soldiers or sailors and perhaps an antidote to growing unemployment. Staffordshire potters produced commemorative jugs and plates featuring a victorious Britannia with slogans like "George III for Ever" and "Down with Bonaparte." For his part, Napoleon cared not whether the despised English loved him or hated him. He needed time to be rid of opponents in the Assembly, to create a new constitution, and to become consul for life with the right to name his successor. It was the Revolution's year X (August 1802), in which the Napoleonic Empire was born. Paris was to be transformed into the new Imperial Rome, and its Caesar was ready to welcome the legates of the world—and also their tourists.

Through the 1790s, foreign travelers had been reluctant to risk their purses or their persons on brigand-infested European roads or to risk being swept aside in the clash and smoke of opposing armies. English gentlemen schooled in art and classical history stayed home, tapped their snuff boxes, and pored over their collections while waiting for better, safer touring days. With the Peace of Amiens, those days had come.

Tourists flocked across Europe bound first for Paris and then the Grand Tour of Italy and Greece. Having become aware of the new international traffic, Giovanni and his brother decided to go the other way. London and England's growing industrial towns had to be in need of hydraulic help. Unfortunately, the English were either unaware of this need or the media of the day (newspapers, broadsheets, and word of mouth) failed to embrace and promote the Italians. It took another Italian named Morelli, the prompter at the Sadler's Wells Theatre, to introduce the Belzonis to his manager, the famed Charles Dibdin Jr., whose real name was Charles Isaac Mungo Pitt.[5] In 1683, landowner Thomas Sadler had discovered a medicinal spring on what became the theater site, thus giving

A fanciful watercolor view of Belzoni's strong-man act by R. H. Norman, bearing the inscription, "drawn on Easter Monday, 1803." (Courtesy of Peter Clayton)

it its name. Whether it was that or the adjacent New River tributary of the Thames that attracted the Belzonis has gone unrecorded, but after they gained employment at the theater, in 1804 Dibdin installed a huge water tank on the stage and thus transformed Sadler's Wells into a home for entertainments he called "Aquatic Dramas." The first of them was the *Siege of Gibraltar,* complete with miniature men-of-war and a naval bombardment. Giovanni got no credit for the water show—and there is no assurance that any was due—but he quickly became as big a draw as the boats and the bangs. With a steel frame strapped to his waist, he was able to lift and carry as many as a dozen smallish men around the stage clinging to his torso and mounted on his shoulders. Giovanni Belzoni had become Charles Dibdin's "Patagonian Sampson." On May 9, 1803, his feats of strength were sandwiched between a pantomime titled *Fire and Spirit* and another called *Philip Quarl: or, The English Hermit,* in which Signor Belzoni played the part of a "Black Chief." As he had only recently arrived in England, it is safe to assume that he had no lines to speak. Nevertheless, he had his name, if not in lights, prominently on the Sadler's Wells playbill, where boxes cost four shillings, the pit two, the gallery one shilling, "with unadul'erate Wine at only 1s the pint."[6] Giovanni was now in show biz and would continue to perform onstage for the next twelve years.

Belzoni had arrived in England believing that his future lay in establishing himself as a bona fide hydraulic engineer, and in spite of his new employment, he still hoped to do so. Tom Ellar, an actor who knew him well, described him as "a man of gentlemanly but very unassuming manners, yet of great mind."[7] Consequently, the emotional strain of putting his mind to amusing crowds whose language was foreign to him must have been hard to bear. He was not born to be a clown, yet found himself in the company of the greatest of them all, Joe Grimaldi, who was currently the star of Dibdin's Sadler's Wells. Blacking his face to make himself a savage chief and wearing ridiculous costumes can only have gnawed at the dignity of a man whose stature alone should have been enough to warrant admiration, if not respect. Moviegoers who remember Emil Jannings in *The Blue Angel* may recall his descent from professor to lavatory attendant and see a similarity in Belzoni's degradation. He was, nevertheless, a realist, and pounds in his pocket were preferable to starving in the street. If Giovanni was embarrassed by his first appearances on the English stage, the stimulation of applause reassured him that he was a person of worth, at least in the eyes of theatrical managers. Being big at the box office gave

Left: *Promotional notice for Charles Dibdin's Sadler's Wells theater, 1803. (Courtesy of Peter Clayton).* Above: *The "Patagonian Sampson" at Sadler's Wells Theatre, 1803. (From R. Chambers's* Book of Days, *vol. 2, 1864)*

him leverage, and before long he was designing his own act, one that had more staying power than simply lifting people on his shoulders.

For reasons unknown, Belzoni left the Dibdin Company at the end of the summer and is next heard from in a booth at Smithfield's annual Bartholomew Fair. Smithfield (originally Smoothfield) covered ten acres outside the London city walls and had been a horse and cattle market since the twelfth century. Every year, beginning on the Feast of St. Bartholomew, it became a fairground for freaks, acrobats, card tricksters, wild-animal trainers, indeed, anyone with a talent to sell. One visitor wrote in 1685 that "the main importance of this fair is not so much for merchandise, and the supplying what people really want; but as a sort of Bacchanalia, to gratify the multitude in their wandering and irregular thoughts."

Belzoni was tall, but by no means the tallest to be stared at by fairground patrons. A famed Irish giant named Patrick Cotter stood 8'4" and died in 1804 at the age of forty-seven. The contemporary writer Robert Chambers noted that "the modern giants are generally a sickly, knock-kneed, splay-footed, shambling race, feeble in both mental and bodily organization."[8] But not so Belzoni. In the midst of the fairground mayhem, he proudly stood with four customers clinging like limpets to his person, there to be drawn by the satirical artist George Cruikshank. The gawkers embraced every level of society from princes to the penniless, the latter intent on improving their lot by picking the pockets of their betters. And then there was John Thomas Smith, the eminently respectable (if poorly paid) keeper of prints and drawings at the British Museum, who elected to "perambulate Bartholomew Fair" after wisely deciding to leave his watch at home. He was impressed by a magnificent man, standing 6'6". "The gorgeous splendour of his Oriental dress," wrote Smith, "was rendered more conspicuous by the immense plume of white feathers, which were like the noddings of an undertaker's horse, increased in their wavy graceful motion by the movements of the wearer's head." Before Belzoni's act was through, Smith had succumbed to paying his sixpence to be one among four men who had purchased the privilege of being hoisted and carried around the stage. "Sampson performed his task with an ease of step most stately," Smith added, "without either the beating of a drum, or the waving of a flag."[9] It can be no accident, therefore, that an 1804 drawing of the white-plumed "Patagonian Sampson" is housed in the Prints and Drawings collection at the British Museum.

Belzoni may have found reassurance in the fact that his was a class act amidst "others [who], if born in any monstrous shape, or have children that are such, here . . . celebrate their misery and by getting of money forget how odious they are made."[10] But Smithfield, even when the fairground roustabouts had dropped their tents and carted away the booths, was still among the foulest sinks in London. The meat market was described by Charles Dickens in *Oliver Twist.* "The ground," he wrote, "was covered, nearly ankle-deep, with filth and mire, a thick steam perpetually rising from the reeking bodies of the cattle." It was, he said, "a bewildering scene, which quite confounded the senses."

With the fair over, Belzoni next worked for John Astley at the Royalty Theatre, where he opened on Boxing Day (December 26) and for six nights as the "Patagonian Sampson" went "through his surprising Feats of Strength, accompanied by a Groupe of Savages" dramatically enhanced by "the five Pandean Minstrels from Vauxhall Gardens who contributed martial music, each playing on two instruments." The engagement that began on December 26, 1804, was a success, and in the following week Belzoni persuaded Astley to let him put on "a most curious Exhibition of Hydralicks" in which he created fountains of both water and flame, thereby introducing an element more suited to his hydraulic education. This, too, was deemed a success, and went with the strong-man act when the brothers Belzoni left London to tour the provinces, where audiences could be expected to be even more gullible and more easily amazed than those who had grown tired of him in London.

No records survive to define the role played by Francesco, but it is evident that he traveled with his brother and may have played supporting roles onstage and served as stage manager. Like so much else, details of their itinerary have not survived, but it seems to have started in the West Country and may have led him to Bristol, where he is said to have met Sarah Barre (or Banne), whom he soon married. He would then have been thirty and she five years younger.[11] *The Dictionary of National Biography* described her as being "of Amazonian proportions" and said that together the Belzonis "made a gigantic pair." However, there is no confirmation for either statement. Indeed, there is evidence to the contrary from the pen of Charles Dickens, who described her as a "pretty delicate-looking young woman."[12] If Dickens is to be believed, Sarah's size was not abnormal, but had it been, her appearances onstage beside her husband would have diminished his Sampsonian presence.

Sarah's early years remain as much a mystery as her husband's British travels. An essay on his life published in 1827 included a footnote stating that "Mrs. Belzoni is a native of Ireland," but neglecting to say where or when.[13] A later writer (perhaps drawing on the footnote) firmly stated that "Belzoni married in Ireland, and continuing his wandering life, exhibited in France, Spain, and Italy."[14] Nevertheless, some biographers have assumed that Giovanni met his wife while he was performing at Sadler's Wells. One has suggested that she was a rope dancer.[15] Such acts usually

A rope dancer in some distress at the Southwark Fair. (William Hogarth, detail from a painting engraved in 1733/4)

involved two or three performers, one walking a tight rope, another dancing on a slack rope, and the third a fiddler. However, there is no evidence that such a group was performing at Sadler's Wells while Belzoni was there.[16] It is entirely possible, therefore, that he met Sarah later at the Bartholomew Fair, where similar acts had been popular for more than a century. The Grub Street reporter Ned Ward was there in 1705 and watched "a couple of plump lasses" perform, to be followed by "a negro woman and an Irish Woman" who provoked much merriment among the "country fellows."[17]

Traders and acts setting up stalls and tents in Smithfield had to be licensed by the lord mayor, and surviving licenses issued for the fair in 1803 included rope dancing in the Exon booth.[18] "Exon" being an abbreviation for Exeter, it is likely that the rope dancers came from Devonshire and that Sarah was one of them.

The pursuit of happiness and entertainment in the early nineteenth century is hard for twenty-first-century readers and viewers to understand. It was not that our ancestors were stupid, only that they lived their lives within the framework of long-established traditions. The same was true of what would eventually become the music hall stage. They emerged out of medieval miracle and mumming plays, whose plots (such as they were) involved a good knight (St. George) battling a Turkish villain. When one or the other was killed, a doctor entered to bring him back to life. Audiences knew the lines and the plots by heart, and could shout out the rhyming couplets:

> I am King George, this noble knight
> Came from foreign lands to fight
> To fight that fiery dragon who is so bold
> And cut him down with his blood cold.

To this would be added an entirely different show derived from the Italian Renaissance commedia dell'arte that came to be known as the harlequinade. Its principal players were Harlequin, a dancer dressed in a costume of bright, diamond-shaped silk patches who was the suitor of the young tutu-attired Columbine. Her father, named Pantaloon, accompanied by his oafish servant, the clown, pursued the eloping lovers through numerous pratfalls and seriocomic incidents devised by the management or by the clown, who, at Sadler's Wells, was played by Grimaldi. His contemporary Tom Ellar was a famed harlequin portrayer who first saw Belzoni when he was back in the Bartholomew Fair in 1808, and again when they worked together at the Crow Street Theatre in Dublin. Ellar was performing in a pantomime called *The Mountain Witches* while Belzoni was simultaneously putting on one of his hydraulic exhibitions, which at one performance went disastrously wrong. The water flooded onto the stage and cascaded down into the orchestra pit, soaking the fleeing musicians. Ellar recalled ending the scene "in the midst of a splendid shower of fire and water,"[19] words suggesting that Belzoni was duplicating Charles Dibdin's Sadler's Wells harlequinade that he had titled *Fire and Spirit*.

Performing venues, be they in fully equipped theaters, small-town corn exchanges, or Masonic halls, were known to the profession as touring circuits. It seems likely, therefore, that Belzoni was linked to one of them. We know that he was in Plymouth early in 1810, where he got into a contract dispute with the theater manager and thereby came in contact with the editor of the *West Briton and Cornwall Advertiser.* The latter, Cyrus Redding, recalled that Belzoni was still accompanied by his brother Francesco who, said Redding, was 6'6" in height. But as the editor, in his published recollections thirty years later, wrote that Giovanni stood seven feet tall, one may forgive him for stretching his memory. Unfortunately, though Redding mentioned that Sarah was with her husband in Plymouth, he said nothing about her size or character.

By April, the Belzonis had moved on to Scotland, performing in both Edinburgh and Perth, where Giovanni not only exhibited his strength, did conjuring tricks, and played on musical glasses, but also played parts in conventional theatrical productions. Major figures of the professional stage played the Scottish circuit, and in October, Henry Siddons (the son of the great Sarah Siddons) was in Perth playing *Hamlet.* The next week Belzoni followed him in Shakespeare's footsteps with his own production of *Macbeth, King of Scotland.* Although Giovanni played the thane, it is unlikely that he was trying to emulate Henry Siddons (whom critics considered a poor actor), but rather that he was a mime in a production that was termed a *burletta.* These were comic pastiches of already familiar plays that avoided licensing laws and played havoc with the original scripts. However, even as a *burletta,* Belzoni must have been on risky ground playing a Scot to Scottish audiences. At the same time, it is evident that he had matured both as a performer and as an impresario. The production was significantly shorter than Shakespeare's because it shared the bill with a pantomime play called *Algerine Pirates; or, The Rock of the Seven Capes,* in which Belzoni played the lead pirate.[20]

Back in Edinburgh, where Henry Siddons managed the principal theater, Belzoni was engaged to play one of the two leads in a romantic drama titled *Valentine and Orson.* He was Orson. The play was French and was first produced in England around 1550; it featured a Byzantine queen whose son, Orson, was carried off by a bear and reared as a wild man, but was then saved by a dwarf with a magic wooden horse. The bear was shot by hunters and died in the arms of Orson. In this production, however, instead of an actor in a bear suit (this was called "skin work"), Belzoni used a real bear, and when it was slow to play dead, he slapped it. The Scottish audience was enraged and booed him off the stage. What Henry Siddons had to say about this debacle has gone unrecorded, but Giovanni and his troupe moved on into the shadows of forgotten time, performing here and there without any headline-grabbing pursuits by a bear or soakings of the orchestra.

Early in 1812, Belzoni was back in Ireland at the Patrick Street Theatre in Cork. His handbill promised that he would "introduce a feat of legerdemain, which he flatters himself will astonish the Spectators, as such a feat never was attempted in Great Britain or Ireland." The notice added: "After a number of Entertainments, he will CUT a Man's Head Off!!! And put it on Again!"[21] One must suppose that the act involved deceptive cabinetry of the kind used to saw a woman in half; yet it is hard to imagine what mere sleight of hand could be described as a feat capable of astonishing his spectators. Perhaps Giovanni had reached the limits of his wizardry along with the shrillness of his self-promotion. For want of evidence to the contrary, we must accept that all his traveling decisions were his own as was the content of his shows. But it remains a theatrical fact of life that mounting a production calls for many hands, from scenery designers, builders, and movers, to those who monitor each date's box-office management. Somebody had to write the scripts, make costumes and hire local bit-part talent, handle pre-opening promotion and keep the books. Knowing that Francesco was still with the show, perhaps it was he who shouldered some of those responsibilities. Or was it Sarah—Sarah who was always by Giovanni's side when he needed her?

We know that she long outlived her husband and was close to destitute when, in 1851, friends petitioned Prime Minister Lord Palmerston's government to grant her a small Civil List pension. That renewed public interest in the Belzonis may have prompted Charles Dickens to pick up their story. He was then the owner and chief contributor to a weekly periodical he called *Household Words.* It was widely read, and in May 1851, his Belzoni essay was reprinted in New York's *Harper's New Monthly Magazine.* Dickens never met Giovanni. He was only ten years old when, in 1822, the man known as "the great traveller" set out on his last disastrous expedition. Dickens had begun his literary career as a newspaper reporter and was wearing that hat when he sat down to describe the Belzonis' performance when their tour reached Edinburgh. As in so many of Dickens's famous books, he began by introducing a secondary character, one Henry Salt, whose name, he said, "had become so celebrated among the discoverers of Egyptian antiquities."[22]

Attracted by the clamor of a gathering crowd, Salt allegedly found the

Belzonis performing in the hope of gathering pennies from a Scottish audience not renowned for its generosity. Dickens described Giovanni as "a Hercules in tinsel" whose female assistant passed around a small wooden alms bowl. Dickens reported that when she showed her husband the meager take, "he hastened to terminate his performance."

Any modern newspaper editor would take a quizzical look at this copy. Why, he might ask, would Sarah be showing Giovanni the contents of the bowl *before* he had finished his show? Setting doubt aside, the famed reporter noted that "Mr. Salt pitied the poor fellow, and as the young woman was passing, said to her: 'you forgot to present your bowl for my contribution. Here it is.'" He then slipped a silver coin into her hand, a gesture which could have prompted the same suspicious editor to ask why Salt had not dropped his coin into the bowl? Nevertheless, the coin provided the introduction that enabled Salt to learn more about the giant from Padua, who told him:

> Six months ago, sir, if any man had told me that I should be reduced to earn my bread by exhibiting my strength in public, I should have been greatly inclined to knock him down. I came to England for the purpose of making known some hydraulic machines of my invention; but the spirit of routine and the love of ignorance, closed every avenue against me. Previously, before losing all my hopes of success, I married this young girl. Had I been alone in the world, I verily believe that the bitter destruction of my expectations would have rendered me careless of supporting life; but how could I leave her in misery?

Mr. Salt (as a typical Dickensian Good Samaritan) "not only relieved Belzoni of his immediate wants, but offered to recommend him and his wife to the manager of Astley's Circus in London." Their generous benefactor not only paid their fares from Edinburgh, but accompanied them in the coach to London. Once there, the manager of Astley's promptly recognized the Paduan Goliath's potential and hired both husband and wife "at a liberal salary." Soon after, Henry Salt had "the satisfaction of seeing Giovanni Belzoni appear on the stage, carrying twelve men on his arms and shoulders, while Madame, in the costume of Cupid, stood at the top, as the apex of the pyramid, and waving a tiny crimson flag."

From this, one would have to conclude that Sarah was no Amazon and that, had she been an oversized Cupid, would have looked dangerously precarious waving her flag from the top of the heap. There is, however, no evidence that Dickens ever met or saw Madame, or any assurance that she was of a size to fit a Cupid's costume. He had just published *David Copperfield* and was at work on *Bleak House* when he wrote his Belzoni essay, and fiction was his forte. Dickens had said that the meeting with Henry Salt took place in Edinburgh "one day in the beginning of 1803."[23] Had he checked, he would have found that, in 1802, Salt had set out as secretary to George Annesley, Viscount Valentia, on an extended tour of India and the Middle East and did not return for four years. Belzoni, of course, had no need of Salt's introduction to the manager of Astley's theater, having starred there *before* he set out on his provincial tour. How that tour ended and who paid for the Belzonis' return to London is yet another missing chapter, but it is certain that Henry Salt had no place in it. Instead, both men agreed that they first met in Egypt in 1816. In short, Dickens, true to his calling as a novelist, did not hesitate to make stuff up.

The Belzoni company's Cork engagement in February 1812 may have been pivotal in charting the brothers' future. Perhaps severing a man's head was the extent of Giovanni's inventiveness and thinning audiences were rendering the "get out" insufficient to cover the costs. Or maybe he was tired of incomprehensibly accented Irishmen and Scots asking him to explain his own Italian accent. Whatever the reason, he resolved to leave Britain and take his theatrical talents to Portugal and Spain. Neither Francesco nor Sarah was to go with him. Instead, they would pack up the act and return to London. Meanwhile, Belzoni had hired a young Irish lad (who may have been working for the Belzonis at Cork) named James Curtin to accompany him; James would later be described on Giovanni's passport as his servant.

The decision to choose Portugal and Spain was prompted in part by the news from Europe that the British under the Duke of Wellington had driven the French out of Madrid and the southern sector of Spain. Napoleon had pulled his troops back to embark on his disastrous campaign against Russia. In short, this looked like a good time to entertain Iberians and relieve them of their reals and with luck, their escudos.

In London, although Belzoni was probably unaware of it, an imposing new building was rising in Piccadilly to be called the London Museum, its façade designed by Peter Frederick Robinson. He was the design beneficiary of one of Napoleon's brightest and best, Dominique Denon, whose drawings and writing published in 1802 under the title *Description de l'Égypte* was widely read, lavishly praised, and had a profound impact

Denon at work using a paddle to block out the Egyptian sun, 1799. (Detail from Egypt, *1816, previously the frontispiece to Denon's* Description de l'Égypte, *1809)*

on contemporary European art from furniture design to architectural detail. Architect Robinson, therefore, gave his London Museum the façade of an Egyptian temple that remained a Piccadilly landmark known as the Egyptian Hall until it was demolished in 1905.

At the same time that surprised Londoners were watching masons carving weird Egyptian hieroglyphs on the portals of the new museum, farther east at the Lyceum Theatre audiences wishing to learn more about Egypt could be treated to an introduction to the "Arts, Manners and Mythology of Ancient Egypt—Part I." Part 2 opened the eyes of theatergoers to "A Sketch of Modern Egypt," while part 3 explored its "Society and Manners." Needless to say, that worthy enterprise did not long survive, and the Belzonis missed this educational opportunity. The loss, however, was of no consequence as neither Giovanni nor Sarah had any interest in Egypt or the Egyptians. Portugal was the goal and Lisbon the city waiting to be amazed, thrilled, and aghast at the strength and virtuosity of the Patagonian Sampson.

2] MOHAMMED'S MAN IN MALTA

PREVIOUS WRITERS HAVE CRITICIZED Belzoni for leaving his wife behind when he boarded a ship for Lisbon, but circumstantial evidence suggests that the decision was business-related and intended no unkindness to Sarah. Cork, in the province of Munster, was Ireland's most southerly port. It is likely, therefore, that Giovanni met the captain of a Portuguese ship, learned from him that Lisbon could be receptive to his kind of entertainment, and so took passage aboard it. After nine years of touring and building up his show, there had to have been a considerable investment in props, costumes, and scenery, the shipping of which would have been prohibitively expensive—particularly if the captain proved to be wrong. It made sense, therefore, to go on a brief scouting mission before risking all of the Belzoni eggs in one Portuguese basket. Giovanni settled instead for taking young James Curtin as his servant, part baggage handler and part proof of his master's importance. Meanwhile, Sarah and Francesco stayed behind to pack up the show and ship both it and themselves to Bristol. It is possible that they went there because Sarah had family in the town, but it is more likely that Bristol, the principal West of England port, had carters who could provide ready wagon transportation to London.

Giovanni was not gone long, and there is no evidence that he did anything more than make himself known to potential theater managements. In 1936, Professor Luigi Gaudenzio of Padua published a collection of Belzoni papers and letters, among them a passport issued at Cadiz in December 1812.[1] On January 27 of the following year, an endorsement showed that both Giovanni and James Curtin had gone on to Malaga. There being no evidence of what they were doing there, the passport entry is only significant as identifying their last stop in Spain before returning to England. A month later, perhaps responding to a date booked by Sarah or Francesco, Giovanni was performing at the Blue Boar Inn in Oxford for the enjoyment of "the Noblemen and Gentlemen of the University."[2] With an encore performance in the following week, this was a really big show that lasted two-and-a-half hours. Among the offerings was a scene titled "The Roman Hercules" that included "the celebrated Fighting Gladiators" and other groups. Clearly this was not a one-man production and had to have been culled from previous touring material. It seems evident, therefore, that Giovanni needed his strong and experienced brother to wield a sword and be part of the performance "uniting Grace and Expression with Muscular Strength."

The Blue Boar gig was the Belzonis' last recorded performance in England, and it seems probable that, with a return to Lisbon confirmed, Francesco decided to go home to Padua. At some time in the preparatory months that followed, Giovanni sought the help of his old mentor Charles Dibdin, having, as he said: "come expressly to England, to engage performers for Lisbon." In truth, he had come for his wife and to take with them whatever stage materials she had brought back from the theater in Cork. Although the record is thin, it would appear that no newly hired jugglers, acrobats, or gladiators had joined the company. Giovanni, Sarah, and James Curtin were the extent of it when the three of them set out on the odyssey that was to change their lives.

The decision to go first to Lisbon rather than to Madrid or Cadiz proved to have been wise. Lisbon had suffered a major earthquake in 1755 that had demolished its opera house,[3] and toward the end of the century a group of businessmen had resolved to build a new one. The Teatro Nacional de São Carlos had been completed in 1793 and so was still relatively new when Belzoni arrived in 1814. It could seat more than a thousand in five tiers and possessed one of the finest and largest royal boxes in Europe. Indeed, even today, its public relations promoters call the building "the 2nd most beautiful opera house in Europe," bowing only to La Scala, Milan, from which it took its design. Belzoni opened there with something tried and true, namely *Valentine and Orson,* in which he again played Orson, though perhaps not with a real bear. He was sufficiently well received to stay at the São Carlos long enough to perform as Sampson. But then what? Having played the Palladium, village halls were several steps backward, and by this time Giovanni was a star—at least in his own opinion.

Portugal lacked the small-town opportunities that had yielded him a livelihood in Britain. He had heard that the Mediterranean's theatrical Mecca was to be found among the gilded domes of Constantinople, and believing that to be so, the Belzoni show moved on, first to Madrid and then to Sicily. From Messina, Giovanni wrote to his parents, telling them that he was on his way to Malta, "and from there to Constantinople, and then to see dear Italy again."[4]

Since Belzoni left the Netherlands for Britain in 1803, the European chess game had made several historic moves. Napoleon's 550,000-strong army that had reached Moscow had lost all but 20,000 by the time it returned to Paris on December 18, 1812. At the close of 1813, Wellington had driven the French out of Spain, and by April of the next year, Napoleon had abdicated and been exiled to the Isle of Elba. He would, of course, be back, but for the time being, the feared French were contained. Their assault on Malta in 1798 had done them little good, and by the Peace of Amiens in 1802, the island was given back to the French-leaning Knights, who were detested by the Maltese peasantry. In 1814, therefore, at the Treaty of Paris, Malta became a British colony. Bubonic plague, which one usually associates with medieval Europe, often broke out in the Mediterranean countries, and did so in Malta in 1813. It lasted for almost eight months and killed thousands, and it was not until the spring of 1815 that Belzoni deemed it safe to sail for the island in the next step of his planned journey to the Great Porte. Malta was then governed by Lieutenant-General Sir Thomas Maitland, a no-nonsense soldier who has been described as masterful and was disparagingly known as "King Tom" by the British military. It was unlikely, therefore, that he was any more enamored of a large Italian showman with British pretensions than he was of the Maltese peasantry. But King Tom had installed a stable government and made its capital fortress of Valetta safe for foreign visitors to go about their business. Giovanni Belzoni went about his for approximately six months—though there is no record of what that was. Two blocks from the sixteenth-century palace of the Grand Masters stood (and still stands) the Teatru Manoel, a small gem of a theater erected in 1731 by Grand Master Antonio Manoel de Villena, which almost certainly beckoned Belzoni to its stage. Indeed, from its four tiers of boxes may have come the last "Bravos!" and the last applause he would ever hear. In a Valetta hotel, Giovanni met a man who introduced himself as Ishmael Gibraltar, a commercial agent for Egypt's Pasha Mohammed Ali.

It is doubtful that Giovanni and Sarah cared anything about Egypt or had even heard of Mohammed Ali, their destination being Constantinople and its fabled opportunities to entertain rich Turks. But Belzoni was ever anxious to tell his listeners that he had been educated to better things than portraying Orson the Wild Man or even Macbeth. He was an engineer—a hydraulic engineer.

"So," said Ishmael, "funny you should say that"—or words to that effect. "My master, the great Mohammed Ali has need of people like you." He went on to explain that Ali wanted to bring backward Egypt forward into the nineteenth century. The land, he explained, is dependent on the bounty of the River Nile, but the people's system of pivoting buckets (*shadoofs*) and simple waterwheels (*saquiahs*) was too primitive to allow year-round agriculture. What was needed was a modern system of distributing the water. Would Signor Belzoni be willing to go to Egypt and consult with the Great Pasha?

Ever since he had left Rome, Giovanni had waited to hear such words, and so with little or no hesitation he agreed to let the Great Porte wait, and sail, instead, for Alexandria. He, Sarah, and servant Curtin left Malta on May 19, 1815, and arrived off Alexandria on June 9. But there was a hitch; the bubonic plague that had kept them from Malta was now in Alexandria and required that all new arrivals be quarantined in what was called the French Occale, a complex of four houses in a square entered by a single gate. No one could touch another person, and no provisions were allowed in unless they had first passed through water. "The disease is so easily caught," wrote Belzoni, "that a piece of thread blown by the wind is quite sufficient to infect the whole country."[5] Such was the public's fear that any illness was promptly identified as the plague, and those so diagnosed were then ostracized and left to die untreated. Some who were barely ill at all were helped on their way by poisons administered by profit-seeking relatives. No cause of death needed to be recorded, the plague being reason enough.

During their days of semi-voluntary incarceration, both Sarah and her husband became seriously ill, but dared not let it be known lest they be hauled away as plague victims. In reality, the cause of their sickness was a simple gastric fever brought on by June's unaccustomed heat and the fetid atmosphere of the Nile delta. The Belzonis did not swelter alone. On June 9, another British traveler noted, "The thermometer is only one degree above yesterday, yet never do I remember having been so exhausted by heat before." He put it down to the east wind, which he described as "always hot and damp."[6]

Just as the plague's supposed scourge was combated with bizarre regulations by Egyptian officials, so its cessation was identified by fiat. On June 24, St. George's Day, the plague was officially over. By then the Belzonis had recovered, and on July 1, aboard a hired sailing barge called a *jerm*, they set oars and sail for Cairo accompanied by a young Englishman they had met in Alexandria. His name was William Turner, and we learn more from him about the journey to Cairo than we do from Giovanni. Turner was then twenty-three and employed at the British embassy in Constantinople; he spoke French and Greek, and was on the middle leg of a prolonged tour of the Middle East. His journal references specifically to Giovanni were few, though he was included as "we" throughout the journey upstream to Cairo. Surprisingly, for a man who wrote about so much at such length, Turner never mentioned that his companion was of above-average stature. Even when they swam together, he wrote only that "Mr. B, an English servant of his, and myself, bathed in the river. I swam or rather walked across it, and I was astonished at the shallowness of the Nile before its rise."[7] However, Turner's first mention of their meeting is

Typical Nile transportation, ca. 1816. (From Samuel Manning, Land of the Pharaohs, *1880)*

remarkably revealing: "Mr. Belzoni has devoted the last twelve years of his life to the study of mechanicks, and his professed object in coming here is to propose to the Pasha, to employ a machine he has brought with him for drawing up water from the Nile to the land round it, without the assistance of man or beast."[8] Mr. B was a new man with a new past, both designed for a different future. It seems likely, therefore, that after his meeting with Ishmael Gibraltar, he made a conscious decision to leave his old life—along with its props and scenery—behind in Malta. He would have no further use for tinsel, feathers, or tights—though one wonders whether he may have kept the costume he had worn at his last appearance in England, where he was billed as "The Grand Sultan of all the Conquerors."

Turner's statement that Belzoni had brought with him the machine that was to haul water without the help of man or beast has to be questioned. He may have built a small-scale model while in Valetta, but it is more likely that he had proceeded no further than a drawn set of specifications. Later, when it came time for Giovanni to make his demonstration, it was the use of manpower that would prove his undoing. Nevertheless, such caveats aside, William Turner was a congenial and informative traveling companion.

The journey upstream was not without its problems. The Nile was at its lowest, and the boat, though of shallow draft, frequently ran aground, requiring the crew to shed their robes and go over the side to push it free. Gusting and contrary winds contributed to the grounding and made the captain (*reis*) refuse to sail after dark. The high winds forced a halt at Aboukir, prompting Belzoni and Turner to go ashore, where, in 1801, the British under General Abercromby had landed and engaged the French. "Human bones," wrote Belzoni, "were scattered here and there." To his companion they "brought strongly to mind the contrast of the dead stillness that reigned here now, with the tumult of Nelson's battle. I picked up a small cannon ball," Turner added, "which had lain undisturbed since the day of the combat."[9] Aboukir lies at the western mouth of the Nile, and its harbor had long been the landing site for anyone wanting to attack Alexandria. After Nelson's naval victory of 1798, a Turkish army landed there in 1799 in an attempt to wrest Egypt from the French while Napoleon was away campaigning in Syria, followed by General Abercromby's assault of two years later. Turner's souvenir, like the scattered bones, therefore, could have been from any one of the land battles—but not from Nelson's assault on the French fleet. The point is small, but a useful reminder that events scarcely twenty years old can be incorrectly recalled even by educated chroniclers.

Neither Belzoni nor Turner mentioned Sarah in their accounts of the voyage to Cairo or of the wind-induced visit to the plains of Aboukir. They wrote about the fetid state of the river, about the mosquitoes, and even mentioned the *reis*'s shipboard parrot, but nary a word about the long-suffering Sarah. How did she handle her female necessities, and what was it like to endure the damp heat dressed in European clothes sitting hour upon hour in the stern of a mostly open boat? Nobody cared to tell us, or even note that she had an opinion. This was a male-dominated world and would become more evidently so when Europeans found themselves foreigners in the Realm of Islam.

Four days after leaving Aboukir, the boat moored alongside the teeming wharves of Boulak, that being the port a mile from the city of Cairo. Turner had a letter of introduction to the Christian fathers of the Convent of Terra Santa, who were happy to provide him with a room, but not so Belzoni, to whom they explained that by the terms of their order they could not permit women within their walls. Fortunately, he had another contact, namely Mohammed Ali's diplomatic conduit to his European guests. Joussef Boghos Bey[10] was a wealthy and influential Armenian from Smyrna who spoke Arabic, Turkish, Italian, and French and who lent the Belzonis a house, not in Cairo but in Boulak, amid the riverside warehouses and fellaheen slums. Although the house had numerous rooms, all were in an advanced stage of disrepair. The windows were shuttered with broken wooden rails, the staircase threatened to collapse, and the only furniture was a single mat in what Giovanni described as one of the best rooms. However, they had their own bedding from the boat; a trunk served as a table, and the floor substituted for chairs. The always useful James Curtin "brought us a set of culinary utensils. Such," wrote Belzoni, "was our accommodations."[11] Still no mention of Sarah, for whom sitting on the floor cannot have been either easy or decorous; nor did he explain how he renewed his acquaintanceship with the better-accommodated William Turner. But he did, and together they took the almost mandatory tourist trip to the pyramids. At that time, Giovanni explained, "my principal object was not antiquities," yet he could not restrain himself from going to see "the wonder of the world."

Turner had already been accepted by Muhammad Ali's courtiers as "an English nobleman" with all the right visas (*firmans*) to prove it, and so

Labeled The Egyptian Pyramids with a View of Part of the Nile, *this eighteenth-century watercolored engraving is representative of English visual knowledge of the Egyptian pyramids prior to Denon's publications.*

when Belzoni joined him on the trek to the pyramids, they had an escort of Turkish soldiers to protect them from beggars and bandits. Most Europeans' knowledge of the pyramids was drawn from fanciful engravings and woodcuts sketched by artists who had never been there that bore scant resemblance to the real Wonders of the World. The three principal pyramids at Giza stand in graduated sizes, the smallest from the reign of Mycerinus; the next, that of Chephren; and the largest, that of Cheops, known with irrefutable justification as the Great Pyramid. All three date from the Fourth Dynasty (ca. 2613–2494 BC), though the Arab interpreters *(dragomen)* who guided Belzoni would not have known the names and probably continued to identify the vast structures by their fanciful medieval name as "Pharaoh's granaries." In 1798, Napoleon, with the help of his surveyors, was said to have determined that the huge stones used to build the three pyramids could have encircled France with a wall ten feet high. Most of the outer surface stones had been robbed for Arab construction projects, leaving a rough staircase of three-foot-high steps up the face of the Great Pyramid, making the ascent possible but arduous. Modern guidebooks note that "it is not recommended to those who have no head for heights."[12] Neither Belzoni nor Turner was phased by the climb, and they elected to make it before the sun rose. "We were on the top of it long before the dawn of day," wrote Giovanni, adding that his written description could not begin to do justice to the view across the Nile Valley to the minarets of Cairo.

Like many a visitor before him, Belzoni followed Turner into the pyramid and clambered along the downward-sloping passage that measured scarcely four feet high or wide. It was not Sampson-sized, and Belzoni, having become stuck in it, had to be hauled and thrust along it by the Arab guides. It fell to Turner, therefore, to record that experience, Belzoni omitting to mention his discomfort and probable embarrassment. Three years later when writing his book, he evidently wanted posterity to see him in the best possible light. Being a figure of fun, even when stuck in a pyramid, would have taken him too close to his memories of Bartholomew Fair.

On their way back from disturbing the bats in the Great Pyramid, the two new friends took time to stare at the Sphinx and wonder at its age and purpose. Only the head and shoulders were visible above the blown sand. Although dug out by various conquerors across the millennia, the feet would not be uncovered again until 1818, this time by another Italian, Captain Giovanni Battista Caviglia, the owner of a Mediterranean trading vessel based at Malta. Though born at Genoa, Caviglia considered himself a British subject and would become a rival pyramidologist. But that was two years into the future, and the Genoese captain had not yet arrived on the Egyptological scene.

Had Napoleon's savants not been chased out by the British, they might very well have undertaken the Sphinx's reemergence. We know from contemporary engravings that they stood on its head and lowered plumb-bobs to measure it. However, the legend that an artillery officer ordered his gunners to test their aim by firing at its nose is declared to be apocryphal. In 1865, a Scottish astronomer named Piazzi Smyth declared that it had been "knocked off by a mediaeval Mohammedan dervish to prevent its ensnaring his countrymen by idolatrous beauty."[13]

Although Belzoni expressed only a casual tourist's interest in the ancient sites, he went with Turner on expeditions taking them short distances upstream to Sakkara and Dashur, and made intelligent, architecturally based notes on the pyramids of both. They also visited the ruins of Memphis, long the capital of Ancient Egypt and once as richly magnificent as Mesopotamia's Babylon. There, Giovanni regretted that he did not have time to visit the pits containing the embalmed mummies of birds, but was offered an earthen jar containing what he took to be the bones of a hawk. "The vase was so perfect," he recalled, "that we laughed at the Arab for his attempting to impose on us." That was a mistake. The trader smashed the jar "to show what connoisseurs we were of antiques." In hindsight, Giovanni admitted, "We overshot the mark this time; for the caution that had been given us, never to credit what an Arab says, made us disbelieve the truth."[14] Although Belzoni did not say so, the shattered jar was an early lesson in gauging the attitude of the contemporary Arabs toward their ancient inheritance; it was one that would stand him in good stead in the years ahead.

Two days later after returning to his lodging in Boulak, Belzoni received word from his landlord, Boghos Bey, that the Great Pasha was now ready to receive him. Riding astride an ass and wearing his best European clothes, he felt more than a little conspicuous, but being accompanied by so important an official as the Pasha's emissary, he thought it unlikely that he would be spat at or stoned. On their way to the Pasha's palace, they

The pyramids of Giza behind savants measuring the Sphinx, which, here, has ears substituting for the sides of his headdress. (After Denon, a watercolored engraving by W. M. Craig, 1832)

threaded their way through several of Cairo's principal streets crowded with Arabs, Turks, and assorted European foreigners whom Boghos (and everyone else) referred to as Franks—regardless of their nationalities. Belzoni noted that in contrast the lesser streets were almost deserted, "and a great number of falling houses and much rubbish are to be seen every where."[15]

Educated Frenchmen joining Napoleon's fleet at Toulon in 1798 may well have expected to find Cairo a match for the Ottoman opulence of Constantinople. But the Great Porte was the center of land trade to the Orient and had been since the Middle Ages. Cairo, on the other hand, was on the road for slave caravans and Moors traveling to and from Mecca. It had no sea port, and when the Nile was low or in high flood, it was hard to reach. One of Napoleon's officers, Major Detroye, wrote:

> Once you enter Cairo, what do you find? Narrow, unpaved and dirty streets, dark houses that are falling to pieces, public buildings that look like dungeons, shops that look like stables, an atmosphere redolent of dust and garbage, blind men, half-blind men, bearded men, people dressed in rags, pressed together in the streets or squatting, smoking their pipes, like monkeys at the entrance of their cave; a few women of the people, hideous, disgusting, hiding their fleshless faces under stinking rags, and displaying their pendulous breasts through their torn gowns; yellow, skinny children covered with suppuration, devoured by flies; an unbearable stench, due to the dirt in the houses, the dust in the air, and the smell of food being fried on bad oil in the unventilated bazaars.[16]

It was through just such a scene that Boghos Bey and Belzoni rode their asses, the latter with his long legs extended to prevent them trailing on the ground. A Turkish soldier riding by on a horse, perhaps thinking they were the hated French, slashed Giovanni so severely with his stirrup that blood flowed. "The stirrups of the Turks, which are like shovels, cut very sharp," Belzoni explained, "and one of the corners, catching the calf of my leg, tore off a piece of flesh in a triangular form, two inches broad, and pretty deep."[17] The Turk slowed only long enough to shout several curses before riding off. Belzoni's audience with the Pasha was aborted. Instead, Boghos took him to the Catholic convent for the wound to be patched up, and thence back to Boulak, where he remained virtually bedridden for the best part of a month.

With nothing else to pass the time, Giovanni spent it gazing out of the broken windows at the motley of Mohammedans going indolently about somebody's business, sitting on doorsteps smoking, gaming, and expansively praying—both standing and kneeling. How Sarah passed it has gone unrecorded. We do not know whether she read books or what kinds of books they would have been if she did. But for neither her nor her husband could being "Franks" shut up in a decaying house in Boulak have had anything to commend it. Major Detroye put it like this: "No comfort, not a single convenience. Flies, mosquitoes, a thousand insects are waiting to take possession of you during the night. Bathed in sweat, exhausted, you spend the hours devoted to rest itching and breaking out in boils. You rise in the morning, unutterably sick, bleary-eyed, queasy in the stomach, with a bad taste in your mouth, your body covered with pimples, or rather ulcers."[18]

While Giovanni still lay on his mat unable to walk, chaos erupted in Cairo. The Pasha's army of Turks was in revolt in response to their commander's demand that they should learn from the French and British and adopt European drills and tactics. The troops considered the proposal an affront not only to themselves but also to Allah, and they insisted that the war-winning ways of their forebears were good enough for them. As the rebels were camped in the fields between Boulak and Cairo, and were prone to shoot people for the fun of it, the Belzonis stayed indoors. Unwisely, the wife, sister, and daughter of the Swedish consul-general did not. When they ventured out on their donkeys bound for the women's bathhouse *(hammam)* they were stopped by a soldier who, for no reason, took a pistol from his belt and shot the daughter dead. If Sarah risked a trip to the *hammam,* her husband neglected to mention it.

A second scheduled audience with Mohammed Ali took Belzoni to his palace in El-Ezbekiya Square, where he was received with encouraging civility.[19] The Pasha even inquired about the cause of his visitor's limp, although when told what had happened, he dismissed it as the kind of accident that "could not be avoided where there were troops." However, his interest in Belzoni's hydraulic proposal was more positive—although there was a snag. Mohammed Ali already had such a machine courtesy of the British government. On July 14, Turner wrote in his journal: "Mr. A, an Englishman, who has been sent out to the Pasha by the British Government, with a present of an excellent pump of 3 or 4,000 pounds sterling value. The Pasha has directed him to fix it in his gardens at Soubra."[20]

Mr. A's name was Allmark. He had arrived at Alexandria in February 1815 with his pump and the steam engine to run it, but the Pasha had been away rescuing the holy cities of Mecca and Medina from an Islamic sect known as the Wahhabis, who threatened to alienate the tribes loyal to the shrinking Ottoman Empire. Mr. Allmark's demonstration, therefore, had had to wait until Ali's victorious return in June.

Although the Wahhabis have no place in Belzoni's saga, the tribes and factions surrounding him in Egypt do. Consequently, a brief historical digression is in order. The history of Ancient Egypt ended with the death of Cleopatra in 30 BC to be followed by its Romanization, and in AD 264 by the introduction of Coptic Christianity, which included the barbarous mutilation of the ancient monuments. In AD 640, Egypt was conquered by the Arabs, who, one way and another, were still in control at the close of the eighteenth century—regardless of French and British attempts to wrest power from them. In the thirteenth century, the reigning sultan had brought to Cairo an army of slaves known as Mamelukes from whose number emerged dynasties of pashas, courtiers, and commanders who were to rule Egypt until the end of the fifteenth century. In 1515, the Turkish sultan Selin I defeated the Egyptian Mamelukes and incorporated the country into the Ottoman Empire, but left the intramural governing to the old regional beys. Over time, alliances among the Mameluke beys became more powerful than the Turkish-appointed pasha, which led to numerous petty wars, insurrections, coups, and losers' heads on poles.

After the British ousted the French from Cairo in 1801, the Ottoman Turks decided to regain their control of Egypt by destroying the Mameluke beys. Two years later, when the Turkish pasha, Mohammed Khosrov, was faced with pay demands from his Albanian troops, he used his palace artillery to disperse them until one of their officers obtained access to the overlooking citadel and used its artillery to bombard his palace. Khosrov wisely rounded up his family and fled, leaving Cairo and the country's administration torn between Turks and Albanians. The replacement pasha lasted only twenty-three days before being assassinated. Out of the resulting chaos emerged the commander of one of the Albanian regiments, who formed an alliance with the Mameluke beys and gave them back their citadel. He was Mohammed Ali, but though confirmed as viceroy of Egypt by the Turks in Constantinople in 1805, his authority was challenged by the Mamelukes, who had good reason not to trust him. He was still in power, however, when, on March 17, 1807, a British army five thousand strong

Coptic attempts to erase the old Egyptian gods from a temple wall on the island of Philae.

landed in Alexandria under General A. Mackenzie Frazer, who invited the beys to join him there to help oust Mohammed Ali. Ali countered by offering the beys numerous incentives to oppose the British—which they accepted. Battles in the Nile delta at Rosetta, Aboukir, and Alexandria left the British regulars mauled and bleeding. Two generals were among the nine hundred dead and missing when Frazer decided that enough was enough and reboarded his demoralized troops onto his waiting ships. Left behind were several hundred British heads mounted on poles in Cairo as a reminder that Europeans, for all their discipline and state-of-the-art equipment, could be defeated by the Fruit of Islam.

By the time the Belzonis arrived in Cairo eight years later, Egypt's administrators had concluded that neither the French nor the British were superior beings. Mohammed Ali's first priority, therefore, was to consolidate his position as Egypt's legally appointed pasha, and that meant controlling the often truculent and devious Mamelukes. Assassinations were an established way to success in the Moslem world, and Ali's preemptive solution was well thought out and remarkably effective. On March 1, 1811, in preparation for his campaign against the Wahhabis in Arabia, Mohammed Ali invited the beys to join him in a ceremony at the citadel honoring his son, who was to command his army. All but one of those then in Cairo accepted, and over coffee they exchanged amiable expressions of goodwill toward the Pasha and each other. With the pleasantries over, the beys and their retinues processed down the steep and narrow roadway leading to the citadel's great gate. When the first of them reached it, the gate was closed, and the Pasha's troops waiting in the flanking houses opened fire on them. A few turned back into the citadel but were shot down, while the rest were slaughtered in the trap at the gate. With more than 450 Mameluke leaders and their escorts dead, Ali gave the order to dispose of their followers throughout Egypt in an indiscriminate slaughter that today would be called ethnic cleansing. The few Mamelukes who escaped fled up the Nile into Nubia and were no longer a threat to Mohammed Ali's control of Egypt.

Apart from the revolt of the Albanian troops that occurred soon after the Belzonis' arrival, Egypt was entering an era of comparative tranquility, allowing Mohammed Ali to move his country away from its perceived medieval barbarism toward European civilization—hence the advent of Mr. Allmark and his steam-driven pump. As William Turner pointed out, Allmark was at a distinct disadvantage in that he spoke not a word of Arabic, and none of the workers assigned to his demonstration had the first idea how to operate and maintain the steam-belching monster. The predemonstration hype had led the Pasha and his courtiers to expect the pump to "inundate the whole country in an hour," and when it failed to do so, it was disdainfully abandoned. When Belzoni examined it, he concluded that "the machine might have been made to draw up more water, if the person who constructed it could have seen the place and situation in which it was to act."[21] That the Egyptians expected miracles was foremost in Belzoni's mind when it was his turn to present his own proposal to the man who had slaughtered the Mamelukes and stuck British heads on poles. Giovanni's proposition, therefore, was designed to keep Arab expectations less inflated. His machine would lift as much water with one ox as existing contraptions could with four.

Unlike his ever-warring predecessors, Mohammed Ali was a modern man eager to benefit himself and (if Allah willed it) the lot of his people. Now that he had nationalized his country's industries and commerce, the ability to improve grain productivity with Belzoni's invention would put more taxes in his coffers. There was nothing to lose by letting the large Anglo-Italian Frank show what he could do. Besides, he was an entertaining kind of foreigner, and Mohammed Ali liked to laugh at his jesters—his buffoons, as Belzoni called them. He liked to receive his supplicants while lolling among cushions on an ornate divan, and depending on whether he was stressing his Turkish allegiance or his Egyptian independence, he would wear a red fez or a white turban, either of which complemented his bushy, graying beard. Mohammed Ali was forty-six when Belzoni first met him at his palace in El-Ezbekiya Square. However, it was at his second palace at Soubra beside the Nile that Belzoni was to construct his machine, and where Mr. Allmark's steam engine remained as a mute reminder that the Pasha's favor depended on success. Nevertheless, while Giovanni was building his machine, he, Sarah, and the ever-obedient James were given a house within the palace walls and amid gardens of great beauty, altogether a vast improvement over Mr. Boghos's crumbling slum at Boulak. The Pasha's gardens had been designed and were maintained by Greek employees whose labors were overseen by one Julfur Carcaja, an old Mameluke who had survived the purge to be made governor of the Soubra palace. Giovanni got on well with him, and they often spent evenings together in his house drinking coffee and smoking their pipes. But cordial though Carcaja was, he could not be persuaded that that hydraulic engine would be of any benefit to himself or the Nileside peasants (fellaheen).

Giovanni's friendship with Carcaja was cemented when the old man fell ill and asked for a remedy for an ailment which, in reality, was no more than a cold. The nearest physician being three miles away in Cairo, it fell to Sarah to provide a homespun remedy of wine, hot water, and assorted spices. Her patient soon recovered, and so enjoyed the brew that he "continued the medicine for several days." Sarah's contribution would be of small moment were it not that it provides a rare hint at the worth of this remarkable woman. The sequel, on the other hand, says much about the state of medicinal arts in early-nineteenth-century Egypt.

Julfur Carcaja frequently expressed his gratitude by asking after the health of Mrs. Belzoni, and when Giovanni allowed that she was suffering from a pain in her side, he said he would find a cure for it. After summoning the sheik of the Soubra mosque and together studying a volume of medical knowledge, they decided on the appropriate remedy. They cut three pieces of paper into playing-card size, and on them the sheik wrote something in Arabic. Sarah was to fasten one to her forehead with a piece of string and to hang the others from her ears. The sheik next produced

Mohammed Ali Pasha, viceroy of Egypt, listening to applications and advice from European suppli- cants, ca. 1840. (From G. Ebers, Egypt, Descriptive, Historical and Pictur- esque, *1887)*

a piece of skin from a sacrificed lamb and also wrote on that. The patient was to press this to the source of the pain. Like Carcaja's cold, it eventu- ally went away—allowing him the satisfaction of having cured the physi- cian who had cured him.

Had Belzoni's hydraulic construction gone as smoothly, the course of his future life might have been very different. Instead, he found the people who were to provide wood, ironwork, and carpentry labor either stupid or stubborn. They reasoned that if the foreign machine succeeded, many would lose jobs and, therefore, a go-slow policy served them best. Besides, it equated well with their innate reluctance to overwork. Fortunately for Giovanni, Mohammed Ali Pasha did not berate him for his slowness and found his presence at the palace a useful source of European know-how. Thus, for example, when the Pasha received an electrical machine he had ordered from England and neither he nor his courtiers could assemble it, Belzoni did so and invited him to test it by sitting on the "insulating stool," which, when charged, gave him a jolt that made him jump off it. Shocking the Sovereign of all Egypt could have had unpleasant consequences, but,

John Lewis Burckhardt (Sheikh Ibrahim), traveler and scholar, from a portrait in the British Museum. (© The Trustees of the British Museum)

being in a jovial mood, he "immediately threw himself on the sofa in a fit of laughter."[22]

Although Mohammed Ali welcomed foreigners who could be useful to him, the army and the population at large did not. Consequently, as the Swedish consul's family had so tragically learned, danger lurked around any corner and behind the beard of any Albanian soldier. Riding his donkey into the narrow streets of Cairo, Belzoni encountered a heavily laden camel whose load left little passage room. As he tried to ride through, his progress was halted by an officer with a squad marching behind him. The soldier was, as Belzoni was careful to record, a *binbashi,* a junior officer who, recognizing a Frank, hit him a violent blow in the stomach. In return, Belzoni struck him across the shoulders with his whip, whereupon the *binbashi* drew his pistol and fired, the bullet singeing the hair beside Giovanni's right ear before hitting and killing one of his own soldiers. They, in turn, disarmed their officer before he could fire a second pistol, and moments later the sound of the shot and the resulting scuffle brought guards from the nearby El-Ezbekiya palace to intervene. Wrote Belzoni: "I thought my company was not wanted, so I mounted my charger, and rode off." In retrospect, he saw the incident as a warning not to give the least opportunity to men of that description, "who can murder an European with as much indifference as they would kill an insect."[23]

Belzoni had been on his way to the house of Boghos Bey, through whose good offices he was able to meet people of consequence in Cairo society, one of whom called himself Sheik Ibrahim, but whose real name was John Lewis Burckhardt. He was a Swiss born in Lausanne in November 1784, and attended the University of Leipzig before going to Cambridge University in 1806 to study Arabic. Although Belzoni lacked his academic standing, Burckhardt was to become his role model and would remain a driving force throughout Belzoni's life. But wishing to emulate someone and being able to do so were poles apart. Burckhardt was an explorer, a seeker of knowledge, but Belzoni, for all his good intentions, was fated to be a collector of desirable objects. Burckhardt had donned Arab garb, learned Arabic, and become Sheik Ibrahim before he left England. In January 1809, he had been hired by the Association for Promoting the Discovery of the Interior Parts of Africa, and his mission was to do just that. He was to begin with a two-year sojourn in Syria to absorb the manners and customs of the Islamic world and would do so in the guise of an Indian Mohammedan merchant. Not until September 1812 did Sheik Ibrahim reach Cairo, where he first met and enjoyed the hospitality of the British consul-general, Lieutenant-Colonel Ernest Missett, whose declining health was about to pave the way for his successor.[24] Between 1812 and 1816, Burckhardt made three exploratory treks into the African interior, the first reaching beyond the Third Cataract to the outskirts of Dongola, where the ousted Egyptian Mamelukes still awaited Mohammed Ali's pursuers. In short, before Belzoni reached Cairo, Sheik Ibrahim already knew the territory and what it took to be a Frank in Arab clothing.

Belzoni called his first meeting with Burckhardt a fortunate circumstance, and declared that information acquired from him was to prove "of the greatest service to me in that country" and so remembered his help with enduring gratitude.[25] In one such meeting, Belzoni met another Middle Eastern traveler who shared Burckhardt's exploratory and antiquarian interests: William John Bankes had been educated at Trinity College, Cambridge, earned his B.A. in 1808 and his M.A. in 1811, at which time he represented Truro in Parliament. His travels in Egypt and Syria may have had no greater driving force than that the more exotic Islamic world was coming to rival the classical Grand Tour as the thing that educated young men should be doing. Bankes had teamed up with another Italian, one Giovanni Finati, who, although only twenty-eight, knew Egypt well and accompanied him to Luxor and the ancient city of Thebes. There they saw the fallen head and torso of a colossal statue whom other Europeans had dubbed the Young Memnon.

"Wouldn't that look splendid in the British Museum?" thought Bankes—and Burckhardt, who previously had had the same idea, agreed with him. The problem, however, was Memnon's size and seven-ton weight, and how to get it out of the sand and shipped down the Nile. Belzoni, who had never seen either the statue or the place where it lay, confidently assured his new friends that he would be honored to undertake the job and thereby make a contribution to the British Museum.

Somebody, of course, would have to pay for it, and it is likely that both Belzoni and Burckhardt looked to Bankes. But Bankes was a collector and not a philanthropist and may have said so. True or not, Belzoni's offer went unfunded—until the next player arrived in Cairo. He was Henry Salt, the same man who Charles Dickens would claim had saved the Belzonis from poverty in Edinburgh. Fortunately for Giovanni, Salt had never heard of him, so the secret of his theatrical past was still secure. The standing of the Pasha's celebrated and oversized hydraulic engineer remained intact, awaiting only the great demonstration to earn him the applause and financial rewards that no one but Mohammed Ali could bestow.

3 } ENTER THE CONSUL-GENERAL

ON APRIL 13, 1815, at his home in England, Henry Salt read in his newspaper that Lieutenant-Colonel Ernest Missett, his Britannic Majesty's highly respected consul-general in Egypt, had resigned. Having traveled there with his patron, George Annesley, Viscount Valentia, Salt asked him to lobby Prime Minister Lord Castlereagh to secure him the job. That he did, and there being no other serious candidates, Salt was duly appointed. He had been born in Litchfield and trained as a portrait painter. In 1802, he had (as previously noted) obtained a post as secretary and draftsman for Lord Valentia to accompany him on travels through the Middle East and beyond. Just as later tourists would not be caught without their Kodak cameras to record their every step and stop, so in previous centuries no one of consequence went anywhere without his artist. It was Henry Salt's lowly role, therefore, to respond to his lordship's demands.

"Make a note of that, Henry, and while you're at it make me a sketch of that funny-looking fellow in the yellow robe." And Henry would dutifully answer: "Yes, m'Lord. Certainly, m'Lord. Any particular angle, m'Lord?" Nevertheless, four years of doing Valentia's bidding had earned Salt both a view of the world not often enjoyed by a lad from Litchfield as well as a taste for the deference due to a top dog. In the course of their travels, the draftsman and his master became friends, creating a relationship that endured after they returned to England. Valentia, like many another world traveler, was a collector, and when he was informed that he had helped Salt secure the consul-generalship, he instructed him to collect Egyptian antiquities on his behalf. He did not say who was to pay for them, but he probably knew that Salt's appointment carried a salary of £1,700 a year, thereby rendering the outlay of baksheesh to the fellaheen a matter of small concern.

Henry Salt, English consul in Cairo, 1816–27. (From J. J. Halls, The Life and Correspondence of Henry Salt, Esq., *1834)*

Henry Salt knew little or nothing about Egyptian relics, but over time his desire to please his patron developed into an obsession that was to dominate both his private and public life—as it would those of Giovanni and Sarah Belzoni.

Salt left England at the end of August 1815, but was in no hurry to take up his post in Egypt. He knew that once on his way, nobody at the Foreign Office would know where he was, and unless something politically disastrous occurred, nobody would care. He could stop in Paris to admire its architecture and to deplore his country's looting of the Louvre after the defeat of Napoleon,[1] and go on to Geneva to enjoy its "sober simplicity, solid information, and gaiety, that is delightful to contemplate."[2] Milan proved less entrancing, and Salt found the route to Venice via Padua "flat, monotonous, and uninteresting." Venice, too, scored poorly: "an uncomfortable place to reside in—everything appears to be sullied by the stagnant waters with which it is environed." Having said that, the artist in Salt prompted him to allow that the city's art collection was both fine and large. In Rome he was received by the pope, who had nice things to say about his "obligations to the English," and at Naples he took a side trip to Pompeii, which he "took some pains to examine thoroughly," and then climbed to the top of Vesuvius and peered down into its cauldron. In retrospect, however, Salt concluded that Italy was an uncomfortable country and "one to visit, not to live in." He added, "They have no fire-sides to sit round on a Christmas evening; and as to their olives, their grapes, and their macaroni, you may buy quite as good, and almost at as cheap a rate, at Mr. Allen's, or any other fruit shop in England."[3]

His Majesty's representative to Egypt had taken nigh on five months to get as far as Malta. Stranded there for want of a ship to carry him on to Alexandria, he complained about the delay and repeatedly voiced his newly acquired impatience to get to work. At an unspecified date toward the end of February 1816, Henry Salt was aboard His Majesty's ship *Woodlark* heading toward Egypt. A gratifying reception awaited him in Alexandria, his predecessor, Colonel Missett, having done all he could to make his replacement welcome. Better yet, Salt wrote, "the foreign consuls stationed here have vied in paying me every possible attention."⁴ This was a far cry from his previous arrival, pad and pencil in hand, as draftsman to Lord Valentia. To make the honey even sweeter, Salt now had his own pencil carrier in the person of Henry William Beechey, the son of the painter Sir William Beechey. In a letter to Lord Valentia, Salt wrote, "This will, for a year or two, I conceive, be very pleasant to us both," adding that "he draws well, and understands French and Italian."⁵ The young man could never have foretold that his duties would include shifting sand in prodigious quantities, discovering one of the British Museum's greatest treasures, and thereby earning himself a small niche in the annals of Egyptology.

When Henry Salt and Henry Beechey arrived at Alexandria, the Belzonis had been in Egypt for the best part of a year, during which time Giovanni seems to have been making slow progress on constructing his machine. By January 1816, it was finished and ready to earn the Pasha's approval, but Mohammed Ali was away in Alexandria, and the demonstration would have to wait for his return. There is, however, some sequential confusion: Salt stated that when he arrived the Pasha was in Cairo but planning to return to a new summer palace in Alexandria, while Belzoni said he was there and expected to return to Cairo. Nevertheless, it is at this juncture that the new consul-general meets Belzoni—probably at the house of Joussef Boghos, whom Salt called a "very gentlemanlike and agreeable man, and as much attached to the English as the interests of his master will allow."⁶ Belzoni thought no less of Boghos, and it was with him that he had enjoyed several discussions with the still incognito Sheik Ibrahim. More than once, Burckhardt repeated his wish to have the colossal bust of the Young Memnon brought down the Nile and shipped to England, and each time Belzoni reiterated his offer to undertake the task. In what may have been Giovanni's first meeting with Henry Salt, the Memnon project again came up, and once more Belzoni made his proposal, adding that he would undertake the work "without the smallest view of interest, as it was to go to the British Museum."⁷ That the museum was to be the head's destination is confirmed by a letter from Burckhardt to the African Association saying that it was to be offered "in our joint

A rare example of Henry Salt's artistic talents, his view of the south extremity of Cairo from the east. (Private collection/The Stapleton Collection/The Bridgeman Art Library International)

names," though not stating whether the offer was to be a gift or a sale.[8] It seems fair to conclude, however, that Sheik Ibrahim's mission being one of continental discovery, his motive was more altruistic than Salt's. At this early stage in his consulship, the latter was focusing on sending antiquities to grace his patron's private museum at Arley Hall in Warwickshire. By this time, however, the death of Lord Valentia's father had advanced his heir to the rank of Earl Mountnorris, thereby making him an even more valuable friend to Henry Salt.

Among other influential individuals who had supported Salt's application for the consulship was the aging and testy Sir Joseph Banks, who was not only president of the Royal Society but a trustee of the British Museum. In the latter capacity, he urged the appointee to "collect antiquities and curiosities for the British Museum," noting that as consul-general he would be in a better position to do so "than would a private and unsupported individual." According to Salt's biographer, John J. Halls, to whom he was related by marriage, Salt embraced the request "with all the natural warmth and ardour of his character, and he had hardly set his foot on the shores of Egypt, before he proceeded to carry it into execution." Salt's own correspondence, however, indicates that from the start, his collecting was on behalf of Mountnorris and his son, the new Viscount Valentia, who was collecting ancient coins.[9] The subsequent dispute over who was collecting what on behalf of whom would eventually soil the reputations of both Salt and Belzoni. But not yet. In the spring of 1816, Young Memnon still lay in the Theban sands, and Belzoni had yet to demonstrate his miracle machine.

The device worked on the same principle as a spit-turning kitchen dog wheel. Using the weight of an ox within the wheel, it could be much larger and lift more water faster than could traditional methods. "I accomplished this undertaking, not withstanding the various species of intrigue and difficulty which were incessantly thrown in my way," Belzoni declared to anyone who was prepared to listen. He was growing increasingly nervous and irritated by the Pasha's absence and by the fact that when he returned to Cairo, Mohammed Ali was in no hurry to move to his palace at Soubra. When he did, he brought with him advisors whom Belzoni scathingly termed "several connoisseurs in hydraulics."[10]

This was the moment for the engineer to don his showman's hat and extol the wonders of his invention. But remembering Mr. Allmark's failure, Belzoni claimed only that it could draw six or seven times as much water as the common machines. If he was wise, he refrained from saying (as he would in his book) that his wheel was "constructed with bad wood and bad iron, and erected by Arabian carpenters and bricklayers."[11] Nevertheless, it worked—but not up to the Pasha's expectations. He and his connoisseurs concluded that the productivity had improved only four times and not the expected six or seven. The test was unfair, Belzoni insisted. It was undertaken in competition with six ox-driven wheels of traditional design whose handlers urged their animals at such a rate that they could not have lasted an hour and even so, only managed to double their output.

While the validity of the test was still being debated, the Pasha had the single ox removed from Belzoni's wheel and replaced by fifteen men. James Curtin was one of them. For reasons that no one recorded, after a single rotation, the Arab men jumped out, leaving only James to keep walking. Although the wheel was designed with a safety catch to prevent it going into reverse, the weight of the water was too much for it. Before

Belzoni could intercede, the wheel spun backward with such velocity that it broke the catch, and James was thrown out and his thigh broken. In the ensuing pandemonium, Turkish advisors warned that the accident was a bad omen that should not be ignored, while someone more practical pointed out that Belzoni's contraption cost four times that of regular water lifters. Regardless of the fact that it was the Pasha's fault that the experiment was aborted, he declared it a failure and its creator out of a job.

Being an unemployed foreigner in Mohammed Ali's Egypt was not a condition to be relished. All Giovanni's eggs had been in his hydraulic basket, and if, as seems likely, all his theatrical equipment had been abandoned in Malta, going on to Constantinople without it was not a viable option. Nor was a return to the slums of Boulak. Being a man of action, and having learned that antiquities could be valuable, Giovanni decided to

Sarah Belzoni's view of the pyramids from the Nile's east bank.

rent a boat "at a very cheap rate" and sail up the Nile as far as the First Cataract at Aswan to see what he could find. He had counted his money and determined that in spite of the cheap rate that was as far as he could afford to go. Besides, as he noted, "having Mrs. Belzoni with me, it required some deliberation, before I could decide whether to proceed to the north or to the south." Having done so, the next step was to obtain a *firman* from Mohammed Ali that he could show to provincial beys and petty pashas who might try to deter him. It was the kind of document that, in the next century, travelers to South America on behalf of the National Geographic Society would describe as a "Dago dazzler." However, it could only be obtained from the Pasha through a foreign consul. As Belzoni was an Italian from Padua, a town then in Austrian control, an application to either would have been correct but probably unproductive. However, when asked, he had called himself a Roman, and on arrival it was to the British consul-general he applied for entry papers. Colonel Missett recorded that being a subject of the pope, Belzoni "was admitted to the privileges of a British protégé."[12] As such, it was Salt to whom Giovanni went, and in what may or may not have been a coincidence, so had Burckhardt. The latter was already aware of Belzoni's intended journey upriver that would take him past the resting place of the weighty Memnon, and had agreed with Salt that between them they would underwrite its recovery. Consequently, when Belzoni applied for his *firman,* Salt expressed delighted surprise. "This is a godsend, indeed!" he declared, and then told him what they had decided. He also gave Belzoni "a thousand piastres to excavate and buy antiquities on my [his] account,"[13] but said nothing about Memnon's destination. Belzoni, in his book, printed what he claimed were his specific instructions under the signature of Henry Salt and dated at Boulak on June 28, 1816. He was to proceed directly to the mortuary city of Thebes (opposite modern Luxor) and there:

> He will find the head referred to on the western side of the river, opposite to Carnak. In the vicinity of a village called Gornou, lying on the southern side of a ruined temple called by the natives Kossar el Dekaki.[14] To the head is still attached a portion of the shoulder . . . and will be recognized 1st, by the circumstances of its lying on its back with the face upper-most—2dly, by the face being quite perfect, and very beautiful—3dly, by its having, on one shoulder, a hole bored artificially, supposed by the French for separating the fragment of the body—and 4thly, from its being a mixed blackish and reddish granite, and covered with hieroglyphics on its shoulders. It must not be mistaken for another, lying in that neighbourhood, which is *much mutilated.*[15]

The instructions went on to require Belzoni to "keep a separate account of the expenses incurred in this undertaking, which, as well as his other expenses, will gladly be reimbursed," adding that "from the knowledge of Mr. Belzoni's character, it is confidently believed they will be as reasonable as circumstances will allow." He would later insist that nothing in his instructions said anything about Giovanni being paid for his time and labor.

Of more immediate concern was obtaining the Pasha's *firman,* without which even the most innocent of Franks could get himself killed. A contemporary fellow traveler, Edward de Montulé, outlined the process of obtaining the *firman,* which, he explained, "purports that all Beys and

Cacheffs must utmost unite in furthering your views, besides which you have a soldier completely armed to accompany you, when all that remains is to purchase presents, such as sabres, pistols, and guns of value to distribute as occasion may offer."[16] Belzoni evidently made such purchases, and being unemployed, one must assume that someone else paid for them—Henry Salt being the likely candidate. Montulé's account offered another piece of information that Belzoni neglected to provide, namely the source of the accompanying soldier, whom Belzoni identified only as his janissary. The armed protector was a Turkish soldier assigned to the expedition either by the Pasha himself or more probably by the ever-accommodating Mr. Boghos. However, the soldier's presence was not so much to ensure that the foreigners avoided an international incident by getting themselves killed, but rather to keep an eye on what they were up to. Montulé explained that once the *firman* was in hand and the kit in the boat, "it would appear that you have liberty to dig up Egypt itself"—were it not that others already had *firmans* of their own.

Having no idea what problems would present themselves when he reached the Young Memnon, Belzoni purchased a few poles and lengths of rope made from palm leaves and loaded them into his rented boat, whose crew comprised four Arab rowers, a boy with unspecified duties, and their captain *(reis)*.[17] Sarah refused to be left behind, as did the loyal but broken-legged James, and lest Belzoni's Anglo-Italian Arabic should prove more confusing than helpful, he filled out the expedition with the Turkish janissary and a Copt interpreter who claimed to have served in the French army.

Later in the nineteenth century, sailing up the Nile would become no more hazardous than yachting on the Hudson, but in 1816, dangers lurked around every uncharted bend and in every potentially hostile village. Shut out from the conversations of the crew and their *reis*, with the Copt interpreter likely to side with them, only Belzoni, the janissary, and the incapacitated James were aboard to protect Sarah from who knew what.

On June 30, still in her corseted European clothes,[18] Mrs. Belzoni sat in the stern of the boat watching the near-naked rowers bending to their oars as they pulled away from the crowded Boulak quays. If Sarah was apprehensive (as she had reason to be), for her enthusiastic husband this day was the beginning of the great adventure that would erase the memory of all those laughing Turks who had witnessed his hydraulic disaster. Following Burckhardt's lead, Belzoni had exchanged his conspicuous European

Giovanni Battista Belzoni as he saw himself while in Egypt. (Frontispiece from the 1821 edition of his Narrative*)*

clothing for loose and sensible Arab dress complete with a multicolored turban. That, coupled with his expansive black beard, would provide him an Arabian persona—at least until he opened his mouth. Out on the river amid scores of other sails, his *reis* ordered his own canvas hoisted into the brisk summer breeze. For better or worse, Project Memnon was under way.

4 } MOVING MEMNON

NO TOURIST TRAVELING the Nile does so without some preparation to enjoy what there is to see. The same must have been true of Giovanni Belzoni, whose discussions with John Burckhardt had to have instilled in him a degree of curiosity if not an avid enthusiasm for Egypt's ancient history. As the English edition of annotated illustrations from Dominique Denon's *Description de l'Égypte* was first published in English in 1816, it is highly likely that the incredibly detailed drawings of the French version had been available in Cairo eight years earlier.[1] Denon's accompanying descriptions summarized the extent of Egyptological knowledge at the close of the eighteenth century. Napoleon's cartographers had prepared a new map of the Nile from its mouth to Philae above the First Cataract at Aswan, and although the mapmakers' focus had been primarily on the delta, they had identified most of the ancient sites along the river's upper reaches. However, the majority were already well known and shown, for example, on a map in the author's collection titled *Aegyptus antiqua* and dated 1584. By 1703, the hazards of the Nile were already in the public imagination. The tavern keeper and writer Edward "Ned" Ward had likened the roar of the river under London Bridge to that heard by "the inhabitants near the Cataract of the Nile."[2] In short, the Belzonis knew what to expect and where. What neither they, nor Burckhardt, nor anyone else knew was the age of the ruins they would be visiting—although in virtually every case the writing was on the walls, often in glorious color. No one had yet been able to decipher the hieroglyphs—even though the solution was lying in a crate in the basement of the British Museum.

The 3'9"-long slab of pink and black granite that the French engineer officer Pierre Bouchard had deduced to be of more than average interest had been moved from Rosetta to the savants' headquarters in Cairo. The Greek inscription had been read even before it got there and enabled scholars at the Institut d'Egypte to tell Napoleon that the stone dated from 196 BC, and was inscribed by priests from Memphis in honor of King Ptolemy V. Egypt's new French pharaoh was sufficiently intrigued by the possibility that the stone might hold the key to ancient Egyptian history to order lithographers to be brought from Paris to make copies for circulation among favored European linguists. When Napoleon appeared to be losing his grip on Egypt, the stone (as previously noted) was moved to Alexandria and hidden in the house of the army's commander, General Jacques Menou, where the British reputedly discovered it. Another version had it aboard a departing French transport when the British diplomat William Hamilton found out and, with a handful of British soldiers, rowed out to the French ship and retrieved it.[3] Before the Rosetta Stone reached England, the French copies were already being studied in an effort to equate the Greek text with the demotic, though not yet from the latter to the hieroglyphic.[4] Although, by the time Belzoni was heading up the Nile, the translators were having some success, it would fall to him to provide a key clue, and to do so on behalf of the same William Bankes who had declined to contribute to the Memnon expedition. But that was much later.

As they sailed, rowed, towed, and poled their way upriver, the Belzonis first came to the Arab village of Ashmunein. "Here," said Giovanni, "is the first Egyptian architecture that travelers meet with on the Nile above the pyramids, and I must say that it has made a great impression on my mind." The place was the Ptolemaic ruin of Hermopolis, where still-standing columns "could not fail to inspire veneration for the people that erected such edifices."[5] In reality, to use modern language, he hadn't seen anything yet!

On July 5, the boat reached the west-bank village of Manfalut, a district capital which lies a short distance below the first set of rapids at Asyut. It was at Manfalut that Belzoni encountered Ibrahim, son of the great Mohammed Ali and Pasha of Upper Egypt, who was on his way downriver to Cairo. Traveling with him was someone whose name Belzoni knew but perhaps had never met. The forty-year-old Bernardino Drovetti had been a colonel in Napoleon's Egyptian campaign of 1798, and subsequently France's consul-general in Cairo. He was also a confidant of Mohammed Ali, hence his traveling association with the Pasha of Upper Egypt. Born at Barbania in the Piedmont, Drovetti had taken French nationality and

The Rosetta Stone (196 BC). Taken from the French by the British in 1801, it is now in the British Museum. The text is inscribed in hieroglyphics, demotic Egyptian, and Greek. (© The Trustees of the British Museum)

consequently was no friend to the English or anyone carrying British papers.[6] Furthermore, he was an avid collector of antiquities and was well established among the beys and fellaheen along the Nile. Drovetti was the competition, and in political standing he had the edge on the newly arrived Henry Salt. Belzoni was at pains to note that in truth Drovetti was only "the ex-consul-general of the late government of France," having been ousted when Napoleon's government was dissolved. The reality, however, was that he was still France's man in Egypt, and until the arrival of Belzoni, he had no rivals in the collecting field. Word had already reached Drovetti that Salt's man was on his way to corral the Young Memnon—

Bernardino Drovetti, French consul in Egypt from 1802 to 1814, and again from 1821 to 1829. (Engraving from Atti della Reale Academia della Scienze di Torino, *1935)*

knowledge that enabled the Frenchman to give the failed hydraulic engineer a bit of helpful advice. "The Arabs at Thebes won't work for you," he said. "I've had occasion to try them."[7]

Bernardino Drovetti sported a provocatively twirled moustache of the style worn by villains in Victorian melodramas, a growth that extended to his muttonchop whiskers, which, coupled with his heavy eyebrows, gave him a suitably menacing appearance. He, nevertheless, smiled benevolently on Belzoni and, in an apparently sincere gesture of goodwill, told him that he was welcome to take the lid of a sarcophagus recently discovered at Thebes, but which Drovetti's Arab workers had been unable to extract from its tomb. "So if you can take it out, you're welcome to it," he said—probably with a wry smile.

Belzoni thanked him and, back on his boat, proceeded upriver to Asyut, where he was to present his credentials to the regional governor, known as the Deftardár Bey—who was not at home. While waiting for him to return, Giovanni met Ibrahim Pasha's physician, a Mr. Sotto, who had been recommended as a traveler's facilitator. He also offered advice:

"The bust was a mass of stone not worth the carriage."

"There were no boats to be had."

"Permission to hire workmen would be hard to secure."

"Do not meddle in this business. You will meet with many disagreeable things, and have many obstacles to encounter."[8]

Mr. Sotto had been pleasant and polite, but devoid of encouragement. The same could be said of the Deftardár Bey, who did provide instructions to the cacheff of Erment,[9] the province that included the ruins of Thebes and the bust of the Young Memnon.[10] It had taken six days to gain an audience with the bey, during which time Belzoni explored Asyut, the capital of Upper Egypt. He found it a bustling place and the principal trading station for caravans from Darfur, selling "Negroes,"[11] feathers, elephants' tusks (Belzoni called them teeth), and gum. Ibrahim Pasha, as regional viceroy, had the right to be the first to select from the caravans and to name his own price. Only then could the merchants begin to trade. Not surprisingly, Ibrahim Pasha was not well liked—as Giovanni learned through his interpreter. A minor culprit brought to trial at the viceroy's court was asked a few questions before being found guilty and sentenced to be tied to the mouth of a cannon, which "was then fired off, loaded with a ball, so that the body was scattered about in pieces at a considerable distance." No less unpleasant had been the fate of two Arabs who had been provoked into killing a soldier and were "fastened to a pole, like two rabbits on a spit, and roasted alive at a slow fire." Belzoni noted that this barbaric man would be heir to the government of Egypt upon the death of Mohammed Ali.[12]

The brutality of both the Egyptian Turks and what remained of the Mameluke fellaheen was to be a constant concern both to Giovanni and to his long-suffering wife. Rarely does she intrude into his narrative, and then only in an afterthought. "Mrs. Belzoni," he wrote, "had by this time accustomed herself to travel, and was equally indifferent with myself about accommodations."[13] Her opinions, suggestions, or advice never made it into his recorded deliberations; nor do we know whether she accompanied him on his treks into the villages or was privy to all he was learning about living and surviving in Arab Egypt. Did he, one wonders, tell her about the young black slaves brought into Asyut from Darfur and converted into eunuchs for sale to merchants from Cairo to Mecca?

"As soon as the operation is performed," Belzoni wrote, "the boys are buried in the ground, all but the head and shoulders; and many, who are not of strong constitutions, die with the excruciating pain. It is calculated," he added, "that the operation, during its performance or afterwards, proves fatal to two out of three."[14]

On July 15, Belzoni stopped the boat to visit the fathers at a Coptic monastery, who in turn took him to the local governor, who told him that there were many antiquities in his town: "But you can't have them; they are all enchanted by the devil." The governor then told Belzoni that about six miles into the mountains beyond the Nile Valley there was a large gold ring stuck into the rock: "But you can't get it out." His soldiers had fired several cannon shots to try to blow it loose. When they failed, a man eating a cucumber threw the rind at it, whereupon the ring fell to the ground. "It must have been fixed there by enchantment so that nothing but the rind of a cucumber could make it fall," explained the governor. Belzoni did not discover what had happened to the ring after it fell or whether it had sprung back when no cucumber was around. "What sort of a country must that be," he asked, "which allows itself to be ruled by a man of so elevated a mind!"[15]

Still fifty miles downriver from Thebes, the next stop was at Dendera and the great temple to the goddess Hathor, which Belzoni called by its Greek name of Tentyra. Still one of the most complete of the pharaonic temples, it stands two miles back from the river and required the Belzonis to rent asses to get there. In modern times, a bus is better. Even late in the twentieth century, *Nagel's Encyclopedia Guide to Egypt* recommended that any other method be taken only by visitors "familiar with the language and customs of the country."[16] But for the Belzonis, who could claim neither, donkeys it had to be. Once there, Giovanni was so struck by the magnificence of the architecture that he seated himself "on the ground, and for a considerable time was lost in admiration." His book devoted three pages to a description of the temple and displayed considerable knowledge of its layout, asserting, "I should have no scruple in saying, that it is of much later date than many others." But as he had yet to see the "many others," we have to remember that he was writing three years later, and that his details were the product of subsequent visits, as were some of his educated opinions. Thus, when citing Denon as having called the Dendera temple the "sanctuary of the arts and sciences," it is highly unlikely that Belzoni was toting a copy of the *Description de l'Égypte* on this,

Entrance to the great temple dedicated to the goddess Hathor at Dendera (view from the north). Rebuilt in the Ptolemaic and Roman Periods.

The zodiac on the ceiling of a Dendera roof chapel. The drawing was made by Denon, but in publishing it, he drew the attention of looters. The zodiac is now in the Louvre, having been replaced in the temple by a plaster copy.

his first journey up the Nile. Nevertheless, he was right about the date. Although there had been a temple at Dendera as early as the Fourth Dynasty (ca. 2613–2494 BC), what Belzoni was admiring was not begun until the reign of Nectanebo I (380–342 BC), and continued to be worked on by the Romans into the second century AD. Unable to read the hieroglyphics, Belzoni could not have known that at the southwest exterior corner in low relief stand the figures of Cleopatra and her son Caesarion.[17] Nevertheless, he did see in a small shrine at the roof level a ceiling depicting the zodiac for which Dendera is famed and which Denon thought sublime and described as the sanctuary of the arts and sciences. Belzoni referred to it as "the famous zodiac," but said nothing about cutting it out of the roof. Nevertheless, Henry Salt would cast his eye on it, but was to be beaten to the trove by a Frenchman, Jean Baptiste Lelorrain, who in 1820 used gunpowder to help free the stone blocks and then shipped them to France, where he sold them to the king for 150,000 francs. There was big money to be made in Egypt by anyone who could export the heavy stuff, but Belzoni would persistently argue that, as a neo-British subject, his only desire was to enrich the collections of the British Museum. Although Sir Joseph Banks had asked Salt to do so, there is no evidence that Belzoni had ever visited the museum, and so one may suppose that he acquired his zeal from Burckhardt or from Henry Salt, who (as I have noted) was more focused on supplying his patron, Lord Mountnorris.

On July 22, like every tourist in a *dahabilah,* or cruise boat, from then until now, the Belzonis began their visit to Thebes by landing at the modern town of Luxor, which then was, and still is, built on the ancient city's urban ruins. In 1816, the great temples of Luxor and Karnak dwarfed the ramshackle Arab town—as they did Giovanni's memory of Dendera. His first reaction was no different from that of the modern tourist: "It is absolutely impossible to imagine the scene displayed, without seeing it. The most sublime ideas, that can be formed from the most magnificent specimens of our present architecture would give a very incorrect picture of these ruins; for such is the difference, not only in magnitude, but in form, proportion, and construction, that even the pencil can convey but a faint idea of the whole."[18] Elsewhere I have put the same enthusiasm a little differently: I tell students that they cannot put man's architectural accomplishments in true perspective until they have stood in the shadow of the columns that support the great hypostyle hall at Karnak.

But Belzoni was not there to be an awed tourist. He had work to do, and it was on the other side, the *west* side, of the river. The pharaonic city of Thebes was divided by the Nile, the temples and secular buildings on the east bank being largely the record of the living, while those on the west were devoted to the memories of the great and lesser dead. In the period of the Middle Kingdom (ca. 2133–1991 BC), Egypt's capital had moved from Memphis to Thebes and was dedicated to Amon-Rë, the greatest of the gods. By the seventh century BC, however, the political center had gravitated back to the north, and Thebes had lost its importance. Thebes was twice plundered by the Assyrians, and an earthquake in 27 BC toppled much of what was left—including, perhaps, the Young Memnon.

The temple of Amon at Karnak (view from the west), looking from the Great Court toward the hypostyle hall.

The Colossi of Memnon on the Nile's west bank, guardians of the lost mortuary temple of Amenophis III at Thebes.

The name Memnon was coined by the Greeks to identify the king whose enormous statues are all that is left of the mortuary temple of Amenophis III. The statues stood sixty feet high in the arable floodplain of the river, and Belzoni had to pass them on his way to the temple then called the Memnonium and which had nothing to do with the twin co-lossi.[19] The temple would later be identified as that of the most famous of the Egyptian New Kingdom pharaohs, Ramesses II (1304–1237 BC). In its ruins lay (and still lies) an enormous statue of the king whom Bel-zoni identified as Memnon, then added "or Sesostris, or Osymandias, or Phamenoph, or perhaps some other king of Egypt; for such are the vari-ous opinions of its origin, and so many names have been given to it, that at last it has no name at all."[20] His frustration at being unable to read the writing on the walls is one still shared by most tourists who wish to do more than marvel.

The "old" Memnon had been lying on its back since the earthquake of 27 BC, and since it is big but no longer beautiful, no one has been inspired to move it. Fortunately for Belzoni, the Young Memnon would prove more manageable. He found it "with its face upwards, and apparently smiling at me, at the thought of being taken to England." He added that his expectations

One of a pair of colossal figures of Ramesses II that stood at the approach to the second court in his mortuary temple known as the Ramesseum (view from the south).

Belzoni's impression of the forecourt of the temple of Amon at Karnak, seen from the top of the first pylon. Beyond are the ruined and collapsed columns of the hypostyle hall.

were "exceeded by its beauty, but not by its size." When he had lobbied to be Henry Salt's moving man, Giovanni had no idea of the scale of the problem. He had simply needed a job. Whether or not he could succeed in it was something to be worried about later. The time to worry had arrived. Even if he was too occupied to consider the price of failure, Sarah surely was not. Adding Young Memnon to his hydraulic disaster would again leave her husband unemployed and penniless in an alien land.

The Ramesseum lies beyond the Nile's floodplain at the foot of the western mountain scarp, thus a two-mile trek back and forth from boat to work site. Consequently, Belzoni built his base camp inside the temple ruin, constructing a hut from the fallen stones "in which we were handsomely lodged."[21] He did not describe the architecture of the handsome lodging, but at least Sarah could be assured that she would not be rained on. The average temperature at Luxor at the end of July is 104° F. Along with Sarah, the camp (if not the hut) was shared with the Copt interpreter and a Greek carpenter who had been hired at Asyut. The boat's rowers and their *reis* were no longer part of the team and probably were discharged as soon as Belzoni realized that a much bigger barge was needed to float the prize. There was no way that three men could even begin to move the statue, and neither the interpreter nor the carpenter had been hired for such heavy lifting. A gang of at least eighty local Arabs would be needed for the job. Furthermore, there was no ready source of materials to augment the eighteen poles and vine ropes that Belzoni had brought from Boulak. And time was short. In a month the river would be rising again to flood the valley up to the entrance of the Ramesseum, making it impossible to move the statue to the river's deep-water edge until the following year. Now was the moment to find the cacheff of Erment and show him the copy of Salt's *firman* from Mohammed Ali as well as that supplied by the Deftardár Bey at Asyut. It would be up to the cacheff to supply the labor—and preferably without delay.

The cacheff received his visitor with smiling politeness, which Belzoni noted "was peculiar to the Turks, even when they do not mean in the slightest degree to comply with your wishes," and over coffee promised that he would do all he could to help. But there was a problem. "At the present season," he explained, "the men are all occupied. It would be better to wait until after the inundation of the Nile."

Belzoni answered that waiting was not an option. Besides, he said, "I have seen a great many Arabs about the villages, who appeared perfectly

The Ramesseum's second pylon, looking toward the great hypostyle hall (view from the south).

idle, and who would be glad to gain something by being employed." The cacheff sadly shook his head. "You are mistaken, for they would sooner starve than undertake a task so arduous as yours; since to remove that stone, they must be helped by Mahomet, or they will never stir it by the thickness of a thumb." Belzoni was sure that someone had gotten to the cacheff before him. "And besides," the cacheff went on, "we are just beginning the fasting of Ramadan. I cannot spare any men because they are working in the fields for the Pasha, whose work cannot be interrupted."[22]

In that case, Belzoni told him, he would go out and find men for himself and hire them in accordance with his *firman* from the Great Pasha. The threat worked. The cacheff said he would see what he could do to get his brother to round up a gang that would be on the site ready to work on the very next morning.

No one showed up; not on that day, not the next day, nor the next. Belzoni was desperate. A camel ride to Erment[23] found the cacheff busy designing a tomb for a Mohammedan saint, but he allowed himself to be interrupted to join Belzoni in smoking a pipe and drinking coffee. As for providing labor, that was still a problem.

"Allow me to present you with some good raw coffee and a bag of gunpowder." Belzoni saw that he had the man's attention, and went on to tell him that if he would cooperate there would be valuable gifts for him, but if not, there would be none. Again the cacheff promised help, but this time he gave Belzoni a written order to the mayor, or *caimakan,* of the village of Gournou, which lies adjacent to the Ramesseum.[24] Gournou was not a place receptive to infidels. Its houses were of mud brick built over ancient tombs, which provided the inhabitants with cool sleeping quarters and a source of portable antiquities that could be sold to collectors. It turned out that the *caimakan* was in business with an Alexandria relic dealer and wanted nothing to do with any foreign competition. But on receiving the cacheff's order, he reluctantly agreed to furnish a crew to start the next day. No one appeared.

To add to Belzoni's frustration, in talking to assorted idle Arabs he learned that they would be glad to earn the thirty paras he offered but dared not do so without the blessing of the cacheff or the *caimakan.* Finally, on July 27, they sent a handful of men, and once the idlers in Gournou learned that they had been allowed to assist the infidel, they clamored to join the force. Project Memnon was finally off the ground— albeit only metaphorically.

5 } THE DEVIL MADE THEM DO IT

WITH THE HELP OF LEVERS, rollers, and a cart built by the carpenter, the process of moving Young Memnon was, in Belzoni's words, "very simple." He added that "work of no other description could be executed by these people as their utmost sagacity reaches only to pulling a rope, or sitting on the extremity of a lever as a counterpoise." Although Belzoni's enthusiasm for Gournou's labor force was minimal, the statue, once hoisted onto four wooden rollers, began to move. The pullers and pushers were amazed, but rather than congratulate themselves on their achievement, "it was the devil," they said, "that did it." Belzoni, on the other hand, called it engineering and dispatched an Arab courier to Cairo with the good news that "the bust had begun its journey towards England."[1] Meanwhile, a rumor was spreading that if the infidel was paying to have an old stone moved, it had to be filled with gold and should not be allowed to be taken away. How Belzoni scotched that has gone unrecorded; of more concern was the realization that his long and arduous days in the broiling sun had been too much for him. The air, he said, was inflamed, and even at night the wind continued extremely hot, and in the Ramesseum the stones of the family's handsome lodging became so hot that no one dared touch them.

The next morning, in spite of a turgid stomach, Giovanni kept his crew at work, and by the day's end he had the colossus fifty yards out of the Ramesseum—though breaking the bases of two columns in doing so. No doubt he concluded that with shattered stones strewn everywhere, two more could do no harm. But even if Belzoni had needed to demolish half the temple, his single-minded devotion to the task at hand would have allowed him to justify it. That evening, however, his stomach ailment was

Belzoni's watercolor drawing of Young Memnon being removed from the Ramesseum. This was one of six lithographs separately published in 1822. (© The Royal Geographical Society, London/The Bridgeman Art Library International)

worse, and he described himself as "very poorly." Traveling on the Nile in a boat was one thing, but toiling in the sun directing a body of men whom he called no better than beasts was proving to be quite another. Monday, July 29, found Belzoni unable to work or even to stand. Keeping house in the Ramesseum to avoid the journey to the river, he decided, had been a bad idea, and so he sent a camel loaded with the family's beds, kitchen pottery, and supplies back to the boat. Being a man who, under normal circumstances, possessed a sense of humor, he would have been amused and amazed to know that sixty years later a popular guidebook would relate that "boat life on the Nile is the most enjoyable of all restoratives for the sick, and for lovers of all that is luxurious in travel, of all that is glorious in memory, of the grand, the beautiful, the picturesque, and the strange, Egyptian travel is the perfection of life."[2] The guidebook said nothing about heat stroke, and at the day's end Belzoni felt no better. Nevertheless, after a night afloat he was able to return to work, and he was satisfied that before sundown on Tuesday he had successfully moved the bust 150 yards closer to the Nile. That success came to naught on Wednesday, when the platform's rollers sank into the sand and necessitated building a new road that added another 300 yards to the journey.

The illness known to later tourists as "Pharaoh's revenge" was not Belzoni's alone. James Curtin, who still had not fully recovered from his broken bone, also went down with it. It may have been Sarah who urged her husband to send the young man back to Cairo. She, on the other hand, had taken the heat surprisingly well "and enjoyed tolerable health all the time." Belzoni added that she was spending much of her time with the Gournou women in the cool of the tombs under their houses. Although Giovanni was eager to work all day, his crew was not. They had the good sense to rest from twelve to two, and watching Belzoni still out in the sun, they may have knowingly muttered about mad dogs and Englishmen.

The next three days brought renewed and accelerated progress, but at sundown on the third, the bust had reached a low area in the plain which Belzoni feared would be the first to flood. Nevertheless, at dusk on August 5 he was confident that the next morning's work would get Memnon and his vehicle out of danger. He was shocked, therefore, to find that his work crew had vanished. The carpenter explained that the *caimakan* of Gournou had given orders that his men should no longer work for the Christian dog. When Belzoni tried to track him down, he was told that the *caimakan* had gone to Luxor. But with the rising river close to a level that would begin to inundate the valley, destroy the platform, and sink the colossus into the mud, something had to be done and done quickly.

Belzoni found the man in Luxor and tried to reason with him, but got only "saucy answers" and a flood of insults. When the arrogant *caimakan* dared to push him, the exasperated Belzoni pushed back. The Turk drew his sword but quickly wished he hadn't, as the one-time "Patagonian Sampson" used his size and strength to disarm him. Humbled and frightened, the man pursued Belzoni back to his boat, claiming that he was only following orders given him by his master, the cacheff of Erment. He also admitted that his antiquities dealer friend in Alexandria, though a Christian, was as anxious as the cacheff to prevent Young Memnon from being taken away and that Belzoni's achievement had been carefully monitored. The cacheff intended to let him get as far as the low plain and leave the rising river to do the rest.

Back aboard his boat, Belzoni ordered its *reis* to head upstream to Erment. That eight-mile stretch of the Nile was beset with shifting and uncharted sandbars which, without a favorable wind, made progress frustratingly slow. It was sunset when he finally arrived and found the cacheff in the midst of hosting a Ramadan dinner for his officials and assorted Arab travelers. It was no time to do anything but smile as Belzoni was invited to share in the feast. To have refused would have been an unforgivable and an unforgettable insult. "At the very moment they order your throat to be cut," Belzoni noted, "they will not fail to salute you, apparently, with the utmost cordiality."[3] Eventually, he found the moment to express his concerns but received only the explanation that all available men were working in the fields to harvest before the river flooded over them. But if Belzoni would wait until next year, he would have all the men he wanted. Having heard all this before, Giovanni replied that he would return immediately to Luxor and hire men who were not in the cacheff's jurisdiction. As he got up to leave, the cacheff commented on the fine pistols that Belzoni carried in his belt. "They are at your service," Giovanni quickly replied.

"We shall be friends," the smiling cacheff answered, patting Belzoni on the knee. And they were, to the extent that he got his work permit and was back at Gournou by dawn. On the morning of August 12, the Young Memnon reached the riverbank and needed only a barge large enough to send it on its way to Alexandria. Since there were none at Luxor not already assigned to the Pasha, Belzoni sent a big-boat request to Salt in Cairo and then turned his attention to Bernardino Drovetti's magnanimous gift of the sarcophagus lid.

Two Arabs who said they knew where it was agreed to lead Belzoni to it, and he and his Greek interpreter followed them, candles in their hands, into a small tunnel in the side of the scarp behind Gournou. To enter they had to remove most of their clothes and in places had to slide, as Giovanni said, like a crocodile, to get through. Eventually the tunnel opened into a chamber from which several other passages exited, all of them dead-ending. "I had no doubt but these recesses were burial places as we continually walked over skulls and other bones."[4] It would be observations such as this that would damn Belzoni in the eyes of future armchair archaeologists; but in truth he had made no claims to be an archaeologist. If old hands like Drovetti and Burckhardt had no qualms about such potentially damaging explorations, why should Belzoni? Besides, he was only doing his job.

The labyrinth in which Belzoni found himself had tunnels too small to drag or to house a large sarcophagus. Something was wrong—and the candles were burning low. He sent the interpreter and one of the Arabs ahead down one of the larger tunnels while he remained in the chamber with the second guide. "Have you ever been here before?" Giovanni asked.

"Never," replied the Arab.

"But you do know how to get us out of here?"

He didn't, and sat staring, as Belzoni put it, "like an idiot." Eventually, after several false starts, they caught up with the interpreter, whose Arab companion had fallen into one of the pits dug by the original tomb builders to discourage robbers. After rescuing the injured guide, Belzoni came to the stone sarcophagus and found that it had been brought into the burial chamber through a much larger tunnel whose mouth had only recently been blocked up. Belzoni figured that the tunnel-crawling experience had been a setup to make him think that the lid was more inaccessible than it was, and that he would have to pay the Arabs well who would bring it out. Although the sarcophagus was barely a hundred yards in from the entrance, extracting its lid would call for a good deal of hard labor to clear the tunnel's rubble. Belzoni, therefore, put his hired hands to work and left them to it. When he returned three days later, the lid was still in the tomb and the workers had gone. When Belzoni's new friend, the cacheff of Erment, learned that Gournou fellahs were clearing the tomb's entrance, he had them arrested and thrown in jail. A further appeal to him showed that the gift of the pistols had run its course, gift-bearing agents of Drovetti having just arrived at Erment. The sarcophagus and its lid had been sold to the ex-French consul, the cacheff explained, and no one else could have it.

But was this the same burial whose lid Drovetti had given to Belzoni, and did the cacheff bestow it on Drovetti before or after Giovanni was told he could have it? Due in part to Belzoni's confusion with dates, previous writers have grappled with the problem and have often got it wrong, mistaking Drovetti's lid for another from an already well-known tomb—that of Ramesses III (1198–1166 BC). It was this lid that Belzoni claimed for himself and eventually donated to the Fitzwilliam Museum in Cambridge.

Readers have been tempted to suppose that the labyrinthine tomb through which Belzoni had been crawling was that of a king. But royal tombs were not so constructed, and this one was not in the Valley of

Edward de Montulé's drawing of the entrance to a royal tomb in the Valley of Kings. It is believed to be that of Ramesses III. (From Montulé's Travels in Egypt, *1821)*

Kings but in the scarp behind Gournou and one among the many found and robbed by the villagers. The Egyptologist Dylan Bickerstaffe has recently reexamined the evidence and concluded that the Drovetti lid is not at Cambridge but in the British Museum and came from the sarcophagus of Setau, an important official in the court of Ramesses II.[5] It was long-identified in the museum as No. 78 and "Found by Drovetti and given to

Salt." More enlightened labeling now allows that the lid was "Removed from the tomb by Belzoni in 1817."

The Cambridge lid was found by Belzoni in the burial chamber of the "Harpers' Tomb," so named because the Scottish explorer Edward Bruce visited it in 1769 and found harpists in the wall decoration of one of the secondary chambers.[6] Thirty years later, the tomb was ransacked by Napoleon's soldiers and savants, who were thought to have pried open the sarcophagus, dumping the broken lid facedown on the muddy floor. It remained there until Belzoni turned it over and recognized it as something worth taking home—but not, it seems, needing to be mentioned to Henry Salt. Several years later, Salt's employee, Greek interpreter Giovanni D'Athanasi, would extract the sarcophagus and add it to his master's second collection, which he sold to the French. Whether Salt knew that Belzoni had taken the top is unrecorded; nevertheless, the bottom wound up in Paris at the Louvre, where it remains.

The tomb of Ramesses III is in the center of the Valley of Kings, and although it is one of the longest and deepest of the royal tombs, it did not require Giovanni to "creep on the ground, like crocodiles" to explore it.[7] The French traveler Edward de Montulé was there in 1819 and recalled Denon's description, adding that after being open for twenty years and exposed to the air and humidity, "the colours are much obliterated, parts of the walls have given way, and the smoke of flambeaus and lamps have blackened the ceiling; and it is inhabited only by bats."[8] Montulé's drawing titled the *Entrance of One of the Royal Tombs at Thebes* is almost certainly that of Ramesses III and clearly was not one whose entrance presented a problem—even to one as tall as Belzoni.

Later in his narrative, Giovanni described taking visitors into "The Harpists' Tomb," saying that he considered it the best, and, unlike Montulé, he considered it in an "excellent state of preservation." When his guests reached the burial chamber, he showed them "an enormous sarcophagus, of one single piece of granite, measuring ten feet long, five wide, six high and six inches thick, covered with hieroglyphs inside and out. This," he added," is one of the largest sarcophagi remaining in perfection at this day."[9] He did not mention its lid.

To be fair to Belzoni, it is possible that he had not yet recognized the value of the inverted lid and that neither he nor the cacheff of Erment believed that they were discussing anything but the ownership of Drovetti's gift. Giovanni knew that the cacheff was in Drovetti's pocket and that

Granite lid from the sarcophagus of Ramesses III given by Belzoni to the Fitz-william Museum in 1823. The king is shown in the guise of Osiris attended by the goddesses Nephthys and Isis. (The Fitzwilliam Museum)

there was nothing to be gained by prolonging the discussion. Ensuring the safe shipment of Young Memnon was all that mattered. He, therefore, beat a courteous retreat, posted guards to protect the colossus, and set out to explore upstream while waiting for a heavy-duty barge to be sent from Cairo.

Knowing that the locals of Luxor were as mercenary as they were lazy, one wonders why Belzoni risked leaving the great prize in their hands. What was his motivation?

Many others had been at least as far south as the First Cataract at Aswan; Belzoni could not, therefore, have imagined that he would be venturing where no European had gone before. Curiosity, then? He had an inquiring mind, of that there can be no doubt. But he was also a mercenary man, and so was unlikely to embark on anything that lacked the prospect of an advantageous end product. In short, he was looking for portable plunder, though whether on his own account, Henry Salt's, or the British Museum's, is left unstated.

With James having gone back to Cairo, and the carpenter discharged (after completing his contribution to Project Memnon), besides the *reis* and his crew there remained only Sarah, the interpreter, and the janissary guard to continue the voyage.[10] Several minor pauses along the way brought them to Edfu, whose temple to the god Horus is the most complete of all those surviving from Ancient Egypt. Once again, Belzoni was in marveling mode. He called the ruins superior to Dendera "in point of preservation, and is superior in magnitude." However, the Arabs treated them with no more respect than any other ruin. The *pronaos* (sacred precinct), he wrote, was "completely encumbered with Arab huts. The portico is also magnificent; unfortunately above three-fourths of it covered with rubbish."[11] He added that the fellahs had built part of their village on the roof, but to those who had to live there, doing so made a great deal of sense. The biting flies and mosquitoes spent most of their time a few feet above the ground and never ascended to the wind-blown heights of the temple roofs.

Belzoni found a small shrine standing apart from the main temple, with an avenue of partially exposed sphinxes leading to it. On digging out several of them, he found that they all had a lion's body and a female head "as large as life." They had to be worth money. "There are vast heaps of ruins all round these temples," he added, "and many relics of antiquity may be buried there."[12] Continuing up the Nile, the Belzoni expedition

The author at Edfu taking a close look at the falcon god Horus. This well-preserved temple is of late date, not having been completed until 57 BC.

A discarded temple shrine known to guides as the "holly of hollies" lying amid debris left by time and Elephantine Island's earlier excavators.

came to an abrupt halt at the town of Aswan, where the river broke up into the series of partially submerged rocks and rapids of the First Cataract. To go any farther would require renting a new boat and a new crew. The required negotiations with the aga of Aswan being delayed while he celebrated the last two days of Ramadan, Belzoni took a ferry to the midstream island of Elephantine, where the old town of Aswan had once stood and where Knum, the god of the cataract, had his temple. Local Arabs told him that the temple was dedicated to the serpent Knuphis[13] and that a great treasure was hidden on the island and watched over by a man-eating snake. The snake was of prodigious size, emerged only at night, and had a light on its head which blinded anyone who looked at it. The treasure had never been found, and the illuminating serpent guarded it still; so said Belzoni's informant. Giovanni's interest, however, was not in overpowering the mythical snake, but in identifying any very real antiquities that could be shipped down the Nile. But the pickings proved poor. He found only a granite statue of Osiris "about double the size of life. . . . But it was so mutilated that it did not appear worth taking away."[14] Still on the island today, and almost certainly seen by Belzoni, is a granite temple shrine that guides describe as the "holly of hollies." Being both heavy and undecorated, no one has been inclined to take it home, though trenches allegedly dug by twentieth-century German archaeologists had been left open.[15]

After two days of negotiating, arguing, and finally threatening, Belzoni got his boat, and at a rate cheaper than it had been offered at the outset, an outcome he thought highly satisfactory. It is clear that Giovanni was a good and persistent negotiator and that he enjoyed the give-and-take of it—at least until he ran out of patience. On the morning of August 27, the boat reached the island of Philae, and, standing in the stern before the sun rose, Belzoni watched the growing light as it revealed the great temple of Isis. Later visitors would call it the "Pearl of the Nile," and Belzoni, not knowing what to expect, declared that the ruins "surpassed every thing that imagination could anticipate." But awe did not make him lose sight of his purpose.

"I observed several blocks of stone," he wrote, "with hieroglyphics on them in great perfection, that might be taken away, and an obelisk of granite about twenty-two feet in length, and two in breadth. I thought this might also easily be removed, as it lies in a good situation, and not far from the water-side."[16] Again, modern archaeologists shudder at Belzoni's

The temple of Isis on the island of Philae in the process of being dismantled so as to be saved from the rising waters of Lake Nasser (view from the south across the outer colonnade to the first pylon and the rear cofferdam).

Philistine approach to one of the world's great historic sites. However, he was seeing the mute stones of a dead culture that neither Mamelukes, Copts, nor Turks considered anything more than building materials. The Philae temple builders of the Twenty-sixth Dynasty (664–525 BC) had not been the ancestors of any but the Copts, whose religious monuments were considered unworthy of Arab veneration. Besides, Mohammed Ali Pasha had no interest in ancient rocks beyond such use as he could make of them in providing *firmans* to allow eccentric foreigners to ship them home. The idea that the ancient, rubbish-filled places could become moneymaking tourist attractions was a concept still several decades up the road. Historic-site preservation was an equally distant philosophy that was not yet in the minds of men better educated and more attuned to art appreciation than the barber's son from Padua—who had Drovetti and the hated French close behind him competing for the best loot. In truth, however, and apparently unbeknownst to Giovanni, Drovetti was ahead of him, having already seen the obelisk and claimed it as his own.

In England in the same year, perhaps moved by a report of Belzoni's activities in the *Quarterly Review,* the poet Percy Bysshe Shelley was inspired to write about an Egypt he had never seen and a king whose name was invented by the Roman historian Diodorus Siculus. Nevertheless, like many another Egyptian myth, Ozymandias lives on:

> I met a traveller from an antique land
> Who said: Two vast and trunkless legs of stone
> Stand in the desert. Near them, on the sand,
> Half sunk, a shattered visage lies, whose frown,
> And wrinkled lip, and sneer of cold command,
> Tell that its sculptor well those passions read,
> Which yet survive, stamped on these lifeless things,
> The hand that mocked them, and the heart that fed,
> And on the pedestal these words appear:
> "My name is Ozymandias, King of Kings:
> Look upon my works, ye Mighty, and despair!"

Giovanni Belzoni did not despair, but nor did he attempt to move the largest of the colossal figures of Ramesses II, whose shattered visage still lies faceup in the sand and ruins of the Ramesseum. Shifting Young Memnon was challenge enough.

6 } STAFF PROBLEMS AT ABU SIMBEL

THE FIRST CATARACT at Aswan marked the southern extremity of Mohammed Ali's cultural domain. Beyond it stretched Nubia, into which the last of the Mamelukes had retreated, slaughtering and terrifying the villagers living along the river as they headed down to Dongola in the Sudan. For thousands of years, Nubia had been a battleground for invading armies of Egyptians, Persians, Greeks, Romans, and Arabs, all in search of slaves, ivory, and the fruits of tropical Africa. The French were the most recent intruders. On reaching Aswan, Napoleon's army had given up its pursuit of the Mamelukes, and in the years immediately preceding Belzoni's expedition, the Nubian tribes had been content to fight each other. Nevertheless, Belzoni must have known that he was putting Sarah at risk by taking her into a potentially hostile region. On the first day out after leaving Philae, possibility became reality.

The boat had moored at an unidentified east-bank village while the *reis*, his crewmen, and the janissary went ashore to buy food supplies. Only Belzoni, Sarah, and the interpreter were still aboard when a group of near-naked Nubians approached the boat and indicated that they wanted to see what was there. As the supplies were covered with mats and Belzoni was not about to invite them to do so, they stood arguing among themselves, then retreated into the village. The interpreter had no idea what they had been discussing as the Nubians did not speak Arabic. A few minutes later, they returned along with others who were approaching by boat, all armed with spears and crocodile-skin shields. With his crew still absent and possibly killed, Belzoni opened a case of loaded pistols, gave one to Sarah, another to the interpreter, and took two for himself. He was well aware that since the guns were only single-shot flintlocks and slow to reload, their first four shots would almost certainly be their last. A spear carrier who appeared to be the tribal leader stepped up to the moored boat, but stopped when Belzoni confronted him. "I pointed a pistol at him, making signs," he wrote, "that if he did not retire, I would shoot at him." Although his followers urged him on, the Nubian hesitated, eyeing the pistol, and then retreated to consult with his warriors. They were still conferring when the *reis* and the sailors returned from the village to defuse the confrontation. The *reis,* who was able to understand the Nubians' dialect, explained that the men did not mean to attack the Belzonis; they only wanted their boat to enable them to assault another village on the other side of the river. A relieved Giovanni summed it up like this: "Whatever might have been their intention, whether to attack us, or to fight others, neither would have been a pleasant adventure to us."[1] To be on the safe side, however, his *reis* quickly pulled away from the shore and moored in midriver.

The next day, August 29, the expedition reached the village of El Kalabsha and its temple dedicated to the Nubian god Mandulis, much of it built in the reign of the Roman emperor Augustus.[2] After exploring it, Belzoni emerged to be confronted by more spear-and-shield-carrying tribesmen, who by their gestures demanded money. He refused to be threatened but said that he would give them gifts if they would bring him antiquities. "This they did," he wrote, "and I bought several tombstones with Greek inscriptions."

Belzoni had rented the boat at Aswan, the contract being to go as far as the Second Cataract, beyond which no boat could pass. But although the goal was to see the cataract, his discussions with Burckhardt had suggested a more pertinent prize. In the side of a hill set back from the Nile's west bank were two temples, one of them of gigantic size but almost completely buried in sand. Burckhardt had been as far as the Second Cataract three years earlier and had been the first modern European to see the temples near the village then called Ebsambal, better known today as Abu Simbel. The smaller of the two was located a little more than a hundred yards to the north but hidden from the great temple by a stream of windblown sand that swept down between them. The lesser temple was dedicated to Nefertari, the wife of Ramesses II, and to the cow-headed sky goddess Hathor, both of whom stood at the entrance. First Burckhardt and then Belzoni found it free of sand but full of garbage.[3] Burckhardt had explained that it "serves as a place of refuge to the inhabitants of

Belzoni's view of the Abu Simbel temples as he found them before his excavations began.

Ballyane, and the neighbouring Arabs, against a Moggrebyn tribe of Bedouins, who regularly, every year, make incursions into these parts."[4] There was no knowing how long the larger southern temple had been buried, but Burckhardt speculated that "could the sand be cleared away, a vast temple would be discovered." This was the prospect that excited Belzoni. But when he saw the magnitude of the accumulation, his usual optimism deserted him. Judging by the size of the statue whose head alone was visible, there had to be at least thirty-five feet of sand over the entrance. Tunneling into it would, as Belzoni put it, be like making a hole in the water. A small army of local labor would therefore be needed to haul the sand away, a labor force that he would have to try to recruit from the local cacheff.

The ruler of the Abu Simbel district was Hassan Cacheff,[5] who declined to meet the strangers, and so it was his son Daoud Cacheff with whom Belzoni would have to deal. He found him sitting in a grove of palm trees surrounded by his deputies, most of them near-naked but armed with swords and spears. Daoud appeared to be a man of about fifty, attired in a pale blue gown and wearing a white rag on his head as a turban. He was seated on a ragged mat with his sword and gun beside him. Standing nearby was a younger brother who, said Belzoni, treated him very roughly. It would not be the last time, for Khalil Cacheff would prove to be far harder to deal with than would Daoud. But at this first encounter, Daoud, being the senior cacheff, had the authority to help or not as he chose. In Giovanni's opinion, this ragged assembly of indolent warriors was not an encouraging group and one he would later discover had nothing better to do with their lives than to extort revenue from the villages under their control. "The life of a man here is not considered of so much worth as that of a cat among us," Belzoni wrote. "If he has not what he wants, he takes it wherever he can find it; if refused, he uses force; if resisted, the opponent is murdered."[6] Nevertheless, these were the people to whom Belzoni had to explain that he wanted permission to enter the buried temple.

It was clear from their reaction that the deputies thought he was insane. When Daoud asked him why he wanted to do anything so useless, he tried to explain that he came in search of ancient stones. Giovanni knew that his response sounded lame, but he was unprepared for the cacheff's response. He replied that a few months earlier another man had come from Cairo in search of treasure and had taken away a great deal of gold in his boat. "What have you to do with stones," Daoud demanded, "were it not that you are able to procure gold from them?"[7]

The question made sense, but Belzoni's answer probably did not. "The stones I wish to take away are broken pieces belonging to the old Pharaoh people; and by these pieces we are in hope of learning whether our ancestors came from that country." The explanation was at some distance from the truth, but when followed by offers of handsome gifts, Daoud seemed to be ready to humor the large foreigner. However, offers of money in payment for labor received an unexpected response.

"What money do you mean? What can we do with it? We cannot buy anything here or at Dongola." Belzoni showed him a piastre, which was passed around among the growing gathering of tribesmen. One asked who would give him anything for so small a piece of metal? He was convinced, he said, that "no one will give six grains of dhoura for so small a bit of iron." To demonstrate the value of money, Giovanni sent one of the cacheff's men to his boat instructing him to exchange the piastre for dhoura[8]—which he did and returned with the grain wrapped in a rag. Daoud Cacheff professed to be impressed and agreed that he could provide workers, but at four piastres a day.[9]

"Not four," Belzoni told him, "two piastres a day."

"Four."

"No, not four. Two per man, per day." After prolonged haggling, Daoud agreed on two, but then admitted that he had known about money all along. A few months earlier, that other stranger had offered him three hundred piastres if his men would open the temple. No one, he said, was prepared to work for bits of metal. Belzoni may or may not have pointed out that the bits of metal were not iron but an alloy of copper and silver. It was more likely, however, that he was recovering from the surprising news that he was not the first foreigner to try to buy his way into the great temple of Abu Simbel. It could not have been Burckhardt or he would have said so. Later, Giovanni learned his name. It was the magnanimous coffin-lid donor, Bernardino Drovetti.

On his first voyage to the Second Cataract in 1816, Drovetti had been accompanied by a pair of Belzoni's future adversaries, Frédéric Cailliaud, a mineralogist from Nantes who was supposed to be searching for emerald mines on behalf of Mohammed Ali, and Jean-Jacques Rifaud, a sculptor and avid digger from Marseilles renowned for carving his name on the antiquities he discovered. The greedy trio stopped at Abu Simbel on their way up and, as Belzoni had learned, made a deal with Hassan Cacheff, paying him three hundred piastres in advance to have the temple entrance uncovered by the time he returned. When Drovetti did so, nothing had been accomplished—too much work, they said—and so Hassan gave the money back. Before the disappointed Drovetti left, Cailliaud would claim to "have succeeded in forcing his way into the temple."[10] As there was still about fifty feet of sand to be moved before the way in could be reached, this seems to have been Cailliaud's canard unknown to Belzoni, Burckhardt, or anyone else.

Winning the support of Daoud and his men was a necessary first step, but no work could begin without the permission of his father, whose residence was at the village of Eschke, another day and a half upriver. It was also halfway to the Second Cataract, which remained Belzoni's ultimate destination. Consequently, calling on Hassan Cacheff could wait until the return voyage.

Immediately north of the cataract lay the sprawling town of Wadi

Halfa, which for centuries had been the trading gateway between the Sudan and Egypt. Belzoni had learned that its inhabitants had a reputation as robbers and were the terror of neighboring villages. At one of them, nevertheless, Belzoni was able to rent donkeys, and thus mounted, his expedition made its first visit to the cataract. How Sarah fared riding astride or sidesaddle on a donkey went unrecorded, but long before she rode to the cataract, she had become inured to every hardship and inconvenience. If it is true that she began her adulthood as a circus rope dancer, it follows that taking risks was an accepted facet of her character. Although her husband never allowed concern for her well-being to get in the way of his plans, there were times when he did express concern for her safety. One of those moments was when he unwisely tried to pole and row his rented boat up into the foot of the cataract and struck a rock.

"The shock was terrible," he remembered, "and I must confess, having Mrs. Belzoni aboard, I felt no small degree of alarm, as I thought the boat was split in two. For my own part," he went on, "perhaps I might have

Bernardino Drovetti with his accomplices at Karnak. The fez-wearing European may be Jean-Jacques Rifaud. (An engraving from the Comte de Forbin's Voyage dans le Levant, *1819; private collection/The Stapleton Collection/The Bridgeman Art Library International)*

swam on shore; but Mrs. Belzoni was no small charge to me on this occasion. However, it pleased God, and to my astonishment, there was no harm done."[11]

At Wadi Halfa and elsewhere, it had become Sarah's role to calm and befriend the nervous Nubian women while Giovanni dealt with the men. On departing their moorings below Wadi Halfa, he bestowed baksheesh on those who had been helpful, while Sarah gave the women gifts of glass-bead necklaces "with which they were wonderfully pleased: though, as it is their custom to take all, and give nothing, they did not even return us thanks for what they received; but took their presents, laughed, and ran away immediately."[12] Sarah would later publish her own account of her observations concerning Nubian and Egyptian women, and in her opening paragraph she would note that "as it was my lot to ascend the Nile, I contrived to see the various modes of living among these half wild people."[13] Later in the century, other women would be following in her quasi-anthropological footsteps, but none outshone her pioneering contribution to African feminist history.

There were more wild women demanding beads when Belzoni, returning downstream, stopped to meet Hassan Cacheff. While Sarah did her best not to enrage anyone, he put his case to the old man. His initial response was the same as his son's: It simply couldn't be done.

"But suppose it could," Belzoni persisted.

Hassan laughed. "If you find the temple full of gold, half of it is to be mine."

"Agreed," said Belzoni. "But if it is only full of stones, they are all my property."

Hassan had no trouble with that. He had no use for old stones, he said. He also said that he knew where the temple's entrance was located. The round ball on the large head protruding from the sand concealed it. Remove it, and the entrance is open. More useful, however, was Hassan's letter of permission addressed to his son at Abu Simbel.

The next day, September 16, the Belzonis were back at Daoud's village to present him with his father's letter. In theory, sand shifting could now begin—were it not for another, familiar problem. "I found these people complete savages," wrote an exasperated Belzoni, "and entirely unacquainted with any kind of labour." Not only was work something that did not appeal to them, but as we have seen, money was something for which they claimed to have no use.

Abu Simbel. The figure of the falcon-headed Rë-Harakhti is flanked by four giant statues of the seated Ramesses II, all carved out of the natural pink sandstone. Viewed after reconstruction to escape the rising water of Lake Nasser.

Giovanni had had enough, and said so. Thus confronted with the loss of Frankish gifts, Daoud Cacheff had a talk with his men, and secured an agreement that they would work—at half the wages Giovanni had previously proposed. But when he accepted, the spokesman for the men insisted that they should provide whatever number they chose. Thirty would be more than sufficient, Belzoni replied.

"A hundred, no less," answered the spokesman. Knowing that he could not afford to pay so large a crew, Belzoni again told him to forget it. But after more haggling, both sides agreed to settle for forty. They would be on-site before the sun rose the next morning. Giovanni returned to his boat "heartily wishing he had done with these people." Needless to say, the sun came up without them. When asked why, Daoud explained that someone had seen a marauding Bedouin out in the desert and so all the village was on alert for a possible attack. Further diplomacy brought a handful of men to work, and in the course of the next two days more joined them. On September 21, however, so many turned up that Belzoni had to tell them that he did not have sufficient money to pay them all, but he would divide what he had among them. The men thought that a reasonable solution and in consequence he had the services of eighty men for the price of forty. In the course of the morning, two of them broke away from their gang and went down to the Belzoni boat intending to rob it. Only Sarah and one local girl were on board and could be expected to offer little resistance—or so they assumed. However, underestimating the resourcefulness of a woman has always been a mistake, but rarely more so than in confronting a pipe-smoking Sarah Belzoni. When the men saw that she was armed with a pistol and seemed likely to use it, they fled up the hill with Sarah in pursuit. Fortunately for everyone, she lost them in a gaggle of their compatriots. Belzoni put it like this: "It was impossible to find them out; for they were all like so many lumps of chocolate seated on the sand, and not to be distinguished the one from the other."[14]

On September 22, in spite of considerable progress in shifting the sand and exposing more of the door-flanking colossi, Belzoni realized that much more time and money would be needed if the opening was to be completed. He thought it ironic that the piastres that the Nubian villagers had dismissed as useless bits of iron were now in such demand that he could not meet it. Not only was Belzoni short of money, he was also becoming alarmingly low on his European food supplies. More than once Daoud Cacheff had invited himself to dinner on the boat and then brought several hungry courtiers to keep him company. On one such visit, he saw Giovanni drinking a cup of red liquor that he had poured from a bottle, and so wanted to try it. With only a few bottles left aboard, the request was honored with reluctance and the silent hope that the cacheff would not find it to his taste. But he did, and within three days the Belzonis' wine cellar was empty. Giovanni blamed the janissary for having revealed its existence: "Instead of assisting me in my dealings with these people, I found he was the first to suggest to them what they never would have thought of."[15] In short, Belzoni was deep in an alien land with no one he could rely on but Sarah and perhaps his Greek interpreter—whose linguistic talents did not extend to Nubian dialects. Lingering any longer could put their lives at risk. Consequently, he informed Daoud Cacheff that he had to return to Cairo and would be back in three or four months to complete the temple clearance. Before leaving, he made Daoud vow not to let anyone else continue where he had left off; but Belzoni had no expectations that the promise would be kept once another Frank arrived with pockets ajingle with pieces of metal.

Two hours after setting sail for Aswan, a Turkish soldier on a dromedary appeared on the east bank, shouting in Arabic for the boat to stop. Not knowing who he was or what he wanted, Giovanni thought it best to ignore him. But the soldier kept pace with their descent and at a point where the river narrowed and forced the boat close to the shore, the soldier fired a warning pistol. He shouted that he had letters to Belzoni from the bey of Esna. Written in Arabic by individuals whose names were unknown to him, they demanded that he cease any projects he had launched in Nubia and return immediately to Cairo. Belzoni was sure the letters were fakes, but although the soldier had left his mount and sailed to Aswan on the boat, he would not or could not say who had hired him to deliver them. Nevertheless, their message was clear; someone was going to considerable lengths to drive Giovanni out of the antiquities business.

7 } A PRESENT FROM PHILAE

ON HIS RETURN, Belzoni again stopped at Philae and more carefully examined the obelisk he had spotted on his way upriver. Bigger than Young Memnon, it could look splendid in the forecourt of the British Museum. Twenty-two feet long and two wide at the base made it heavy but not unmanageable if a large enough boat could be obtained to carry it off. However, it would have to wait until the next season when the river level was right. In the meantime, he pointed the obelisk out to the aga of Aswan and told him that he had taken possession of it in the name of His Britannic Majesty's consul-general in Cairo.[1] He also dispensed four dollars to hire a guard to watch over it. Belzoni would later confess that he could not guess that the Philae obelisk was destined to cause him more trouble than anything else he was to achieve in Egypt, and very nearly cost him his life.

The obelisk was not the only treasure that caught Giovanni's attention. A fallen wall panel depicting the god Osiris receiving offerings from priests and women was a highly desirable trophy and likely to fetch a worthy sum in the antiquities market. But when put together, it was fourteen feet long and twelve tall, and consisted of twelve pieces each approximately three feet square and two feet thick. To make their weight manageable, Belzoni's solution was to pay the aga of Aswan a hundred piastres to have each stone trimmed down to a six-inch thickness, and to ship them to Luxor on the first available boat.

But there were no available boats, not even one to get the Belzonis back to Thebes—or so they were led to believe. The aga was apologetic, but if there were no boats, there was nothing he could do about it. However, there was, he said, a man who wished to speak with Giovanni on a very private matter. Would he be interested in buying a large diamond?

Belzoni knew little about diamonds, but he did know that they could be very desirable, particularly when cheaply bought. Yes, he said, he would like to examine the diamond. The aga explained that the stone had been found some years ago and had been preserved in the finder's family. He now being dead, the present owner wished to sell it. The latter proved to be an old man who carried his treasure in a small wooden box in a pocket on his belt. In the box were several pieces of paper, one inside another, each of which he carefully unfolded, finally handing the gem to Giovanni, who, by this time, had reached the required level of anticipation. The old man sighed, the aga smiled, and Belzoni hesitated before telling them that he was holding the glass stopper from a common cruet bottle. His words, he said, "affected their minds like the unhappy tidings of some great misfortune."[2] Whether they knew what they had and hoped the Frank did not, or whether they really believed that the stopper was a diamond was never revealed. But it became certain that the aga was doing everything he could to part Belzoni from his money.

The lack of boats had been a ploy to keep the golden goose from leaving. Not until Belzoni stated that he planned to rent two camels for Sarah and himself and continue on land to Esna did the aga reveal that a boat could be had, albeit at a high price. It turned out to be his.

The returning Belzoni expedition finally left Aswan on the morning of September 30 after further haggling with the aga and acceding to his demand for oil, vinegar, and several empty bottles—presumably those whose contents had greased the wheels of cooperation from Daoud Cacheff at Abu Simbel. Two days later, the boat was at Esna, and on October 4 it reached Luxor. But the expected boat to transport Young Memnon had not arrived from Cairo. A frustrated Belzoni was about to send a courier to Salt with a renewed request when a large boat arrived carrying two Frenchmen, Messrs. Jean-Jacques Rifaud and Frédéric Cailliaud, the same pair who had been with Drovetti at Abu Simbel eighteen months earlier. Belzoni's pyramid-visiting friend William Turner had traveled with Cailliaud and called him "a diminutive effeminate fop" whose conversation was not without interest.[3] His opinion of Young Memnon, however, did not endear him to Belzoni. Cailliaud scoffed that the only reason Napoleon's soldiers had not taken it was because they thought it worthless. When the Frenchmen's guide and dragoman learned that Belzoni had gathered a large collection of portable relics aboard his boat, he warned that if he continued he would have his throat cut "by order of two personages," one

Ram-headed sphinxes beside the road that linked the temples of Karnak to those of Luxor, seen in the approach to Karnak's first pylon.

of them unidentified, but the other the cacheff of Erment. Shortly thereafter Belzoni heard the Frenchmen telling villagers at Gournou that if they sold any antiquities to the English, they could expect to be beaten by the cacheff. Messrs. Rifaud and Cailliaud evidently had been primed to thwart Belzoni when and wherever they could, but as he did not plan to stay any longer than was necessary to ship Young Memnon, their machinations were of small concern.

A packet from Henry Salt in Cairo had replenished Giovanni's fund of money, and having found lodging for Sarah in Luxor, he set about hiring a gang of men to dig for him amid the ruins of Karnak. He had chosen a location undisturbed by Bonaparte's diggers, but not far from the series of sphinxes they had found and lost when the British invaders took possession of them. Several days of digging yielded eighteen lion-headed figures, plus a white statue of great beauty that Belzoni determined (or was told) represented the Ptolemaic deity Jupiter Ammon. Later, the French director-general of museums, the Compte de Forbin, would claim that Belzoni's discoveries were not really his, the figures having been found by the French army and reburied when it was forced to retreat without them. Had that been so, Belzoni was sure that Drovetti would have known where they were and would have already shipped them to Alexandria.

While the sphinxes were still being excavated, Belzoni found that he needed more cash and so returned to Esna to borrow it from a Greek moneylender. Once back at Karnak, he expected to find the sphinxes already transferred to a Luxor quay ready for shipment. Instead, they were still where Belzoni had left them, a regional cacheff having issued a written order that nothing was to be carried away by the English. In the meantime, Calil Bey, a senior official in Mohammed Ali's government, arrived at Luxor. Calil was an Albanian who had advantageously married the Pasha's sister and was governor of Upper Egypt from Esna to Aswan. Being a man of a wider world, he encouraged European travelers and was already known to Belzoni. Calil Bey's arrival brought instant changes of heart among hitherto hostile local officials. Although Belzoni had seen the cacheff's restraining order, the man now claimed that he knew nothing about it and would be glad to give the Englishman whatever permission he wanted.

Giovanni's principal concern remained to seal the deal with the owner of the boat that had brought the Frenchmen to Luxor. Having taken them on to Aswan, it was now back, but rather than being ready to receive Young Memnon, it was laden with dates that the owner said could not be off-loaded. Furthermore, said the boat owner, the previously signed contract meant nothing as the boat could not bear the weight of the colossus. On their way to Aswan, Drovetti's friends had been sowing seeds. Even if the boat did not break up, they warned, when it reached Cairo its owner would never get paid.

Eventually, after much more squatting, pipe smoking, and coffee drinking, thanks to the intervention of Calil Bey, the boat was rented and its dates off-loaded. It remained only to move Memnon to the riverbank and into the center of the boat without sinking it. It was now November 15, and the river had receded about a hundred feet, leaving the statue on a bank fifteen feet above the boat's gunwale. With four palm-wood poles, Belzoni created a bridge across which the sculpture could be drawn over its rollers with a squad of men pulling and others easing off behind. Progress was slow, but had it been otherwise, the huge piece of granite would have propelled itself across the boat and down into the river. If that should happen, Giovanni feared, "my return to Europe would not be very welcome, particularly to the antiquaries."[4] But it didn't. Without the help of any modern equipment, Giovanni Belzoni accomplished an engineering feat worthy of the Ancient Egyptian temple builders.

The Belzonis had arrived at Luxor on November 8. After noting that Sarah was deposited in an Arab house, Giovanni's narrative had nothing more to say about her through the following forty days. One is left to suppose that she was happily housed and making her own amusement while her husband toiled. But not so. Her own account allows a glimpse of the real Sarah that never intrudes into Giovanni's story of hardships faced and overcome.

"This was the first time I had ever been left alone with the Arabs without an interpreter or an European," she wrote, adding, with only "about twenty Arab words in my mouth." The lodging Belzoni had secured for her was on the top of the house and proved to have no roof and was used for sun-drying dates. It had an oven in a corner, a fireplace of three bricks for a pot to stand on, but no chimney, and a water jar. Furthermore, Sarah had to share her quarters with the women of the house: one old, four daughters, and the wife of the owner. In words that for the first time allow her true feelings to echo down the years, she wrote: "I never in my life felt so isolated and miserable." Roofless and exposed to the burning sun, she developed a violent fever and then ophthalmia, which, after twenty days, left her virtually blind. "I cannot describe the agony I felt on that occasion: I thought I had lost my sight for ever," she wrote. "The last stage of the disorder was truly dreadful; the eyelids lost their power; I could not lift them up." With no medication to help her, she washed her eyes with water but was told by the women that this was the worst thing she could do. They, instead, boiled garlic and let the steam dampen her eyes. At first she had no faith in the cure, but at the end of forty miserable days Sarah's sight began to return. "By this time," she explained, "Mr. B. had got the colossal head on board."[5] Where, one might ask, had Mr. B. been through the forty days of his wife's torment? It is true that he did mention her ophthalmia but only in the context of his own, which he said was so severe that he could barely see. However, while Sarah languished in her roofless penthouse, Giovanni was off pursuing his researches amid the tombs of Gournou and digging for treasures at Karnak.

After loading Young Memnon, Belzoni's ophthalmia either continued or returned, and throughout the first twelve days of his triumphant return to Cairo he shut himself in the boat's cabin unable to open his eyes. If Sarah administered the steamed garlic treatment, neither she nor he had occasion to mention it. On arriving at Boulak on December 15, Belzoni learned that Salt was away in Alexandria, having left instructions with secretary Beechey. With the exception of the Memnon, all the antiquities were to be taken ashore and lodged in the consulate. Belzoni thought this odd, and probably said so to Beechey. "I could not conceive the reason of this distinction, as I thought that all the articles I collected were to go to the British Museum."[6] But as Salt was paying the piper, Belzoni did as he was asked. On January, 3, 1817, Young Memnon left Boulak and arrived at Rosetta on January 10, thence to Alexandria for shipment, where a hundred British seamen with proper tackle had little difficulty lifting it ashore.

Giovanni was justifiably proud of his achievement and on January 2, 1818, wrote a long letter to a friend in Paris with a view to its being published in French journals and left no doubt that it was he, Belzoni, who alone had fulfilled this Herculean task: "I have succeeded in embarking on the Nile the upper part of the famous statue of Memnon. This grand wreck, which had lain for so many centuries amidst the ruins of the palace destroyed by Cambyses, is now, on its way to the British Museum. . . . I succeeded in effecting it without the aid of any machine, by the sole power of some Arabs, however ill qualified these people now sunk into the indolence of savage life, may be for such rude labours."[7]

Belzoni had been effusively congratulated by Burckhardt when he reached Cairo. One must assume that in Alexandria, Consul-General Salt was equally delighted, although Giovanni commented only that "I will not mention the kind reception of the consul-general," thereby leaving room for any number of interpretations. However, Salt's biographer, John J. Halls, was at pains to note that the consul professed admiration for Belzoni's achievement while adding that Giovanni was a "strangely jealous individual."[8]

Although it is likely that Belzoni did not see Henry Salt until he reached Alexandria, Salt had to have had news of the arriving treasures in letters and memos from secretary Beechey. On December 28, in a letter to Lord Mountnorris, Salt wrote that he had been very successful in assembling a collection of antiquities, adding, "I shall in the spring have to send you a cargo of such things as I believe you have not before seen." The reason that he neglected to describe them is simple enough: They were in Cairo and he was still in Alexandria. Continuing in the same letter, Salt declared, "I am so bit with the prospect of what may still be done in Upper Egypt, as to feel unable to abstain from forming a collection myself," albeit promising that should he die or part with it, his lordship should have first refusal of it. Nothing in the letter said anything about a prior commitment to the British Museum, though he did say that he had suggested that Drovetti should sell his collection to the museum. By any standard, this was a curious proposal as it was well known that Drovetti was collecting for France and was a virulent rival of the British. Salt told Mountnorris that he had had access to the collection that included "a great variety of curious articles, and some of extraordinary value,"[9] that could be worth three or four thousand pounds. It is apparent that in Salt's mind collecting and selling were on a par with collecting and learning.

Unfortunately, only one side of the Salt–Mountnorris correspondence survives, but in one letter, his lordship evidently asked for a mummy and received this in return:[10] "As to sending a mummy entire, it is almost impossible, owing to the objections made by the captains of the ships to carry them. There are some at Alexandria that have waited four years. If I can get a good head, you may depend on having it."[11] Salt may have found that shipping crocodiles was more easily accomplished. In an 1817 letter to Sir Francis Darwin, Salt wrote that he had secured a large crocodile at Thebes, a noble specimen "stuffed and ready prepared, when it was attacked by the vultures" who tore it apart.[12] Lord Mountnorris evidently fared better. The Donor's Book of the Bristol Institution notes that in 1827 his lordship gave it a mummified crocodile, which remained in the Bristol City Museum until 1959, when it was ordered destroyed, it being "in very poor condition & of little interest & occupying too much room."[13]

Belzoni had no interest in mummies. He had floundered and crawled among too many in the tunnels of Gournou to see them as more than heaps of worthless rags and bones. It was portable Egyptian art that excited him, and he believed that he could find it behind the buried façade at Abu Simbel. On telling Salt what he had in mind, he was delighted when the consul agreed to underwrite a second expedition. Nothing was written regarding the possible results of opening the temple. Belzoni asked only that if he were successful, Salt should provide him with a letter of recommendation to the Society of Antiquaries of London. Giovanni explained that as he had no other ambition "than to serve the nation at large," he "intended to make certain proposals to the members of that honourable society."[14] Although the nature of those proposals went unstated, Salt agreed to write the letter. It cost him nothing but a promise. Nevertheless, he did warn Belzoni not to expect too much from the gentlemen of the society.

A fanciful mid-nineteenth-century engraving of a mummy pit being robbed by a Gournou woman.

As Giovanni saw it, he was the instigator of the return to Abu Simbel, but Salt thought otherwise. On learning that the opening was achievable and that Drovetti was employing a half dozen agents in Upper Egypt and Nubia, Salt wrote, "I succeeded in engaging Mr. Belzoni to stay another year." It was important, Salt explained, to strike "while the iron was hot (to use a vulgar phrase), all the world having begun to look for antiques."[15]

While Belzoni had been away on his first journey into Nubia, a new player had entered the field. He was another quasi-Englishman with the same first names: Giovanni Battista Caviglia. Born in Genoa in 1770, he owned a Mediterranean trading ship based at Malta and on the strength of that connection claimed to be a British subject, and like Belzoni used this to enjoy the protection and patronage of the British consul-general. Salt had employed him to explore (or reexplore) the interior of the Great Pyramid and to clear the sand from the paws of the Giza Sphinx. It was not surprising, therefore, to hear Salt proposing that the two Giovanni Battistas should work as a team. Belzoni declined. He wanted, he said, to make his own discoveries, independent of anyone.

What Salt expected Caviglia to achieve in the Great Pyramid is uncertain. The pyramid had been open for several hundred years, and local Arabs earned piastres by showing foreign visitors like Turner and Belzoni through its passages and chambers. The first known Englishman (later to be a temporary American) entered it and made drawings of the interior in 1611. He was George Sandys, who in 1621 became secretary to the Virginia colony at Jamestown.[16] More accurately measured drawings were made in 1638 by another Englishman, the mathematician John Greaves, who went to Giza specifically for the purpose of measuring the pyramids. His *Pyramidographia, or a Description of the Pyramids in Aegypt* would be published eight years later and remains a pioneering classic on the subject.

Few archaeologists want to pick up a project previously dug and milked by someone else. For Belzoni, therefore, the prospect of being first into the temple at Abu Simbel was far more appealing. Consequently, after returning to Cairo with Salt, he began preparations for the second expedition, and while there again sought the advice of Burckhardt (alias Sheik Ibrahim), whom he considered his mentor. He was, said Giovanni, "the most candid, disinterested, and sincere being I have ever met with: totally free from that invidious and selfish disposition, which is so often found in travellers." Belzoni called him a "true explorer" who made no parade of his knowledge.[17] The respect was mutual, prompting Burckhardt to insist to Salt that between them they should give Belzoni a monetary gift in recognition of his Memnon accomplishment, half of it from Burckhardt and half from Salt. Though not squarely stated, the implication was that there would have been no gift had it not been for Sheik Ibrahim's prompting. Even at this early stage in the Belzoni–Salt relationship, one senses that the latter saw Giovanni not as a compatriot, but as an able but mercurial employee who needed to be watched. To that end, Salt instructed a surprised Henry Beechey to accompany Belzoni on the Abu Simbel adventure.

Had Salt proposed sending Caviglia as Belzoni's traveling and digging companion, the sound of Giovanni's objection would have been heard all the way to Rosetta, but Beechey was not seen as a threat or a stealer of thunder. Indeed, it is possible that Belzoni did not detect any ulterior motive in Salt's decision. "Nothing could suit me better," wrote Giovanni, "than to have a companion in a young gentleman, with the prospect of whose society, from what I had seen of him, I had much reason to be pleased."[18] His only caveat related to the young gentleman's ability to forsake the comfort of a well-appointed house in favor of "a rough uneasy boat." But if Mrs. Belzoni could do it, so could Beechey. This time, however, Giovanni chose to leave Sarah behind in Cairo to be looked after by the family of the embassy's chief secretary. She was not pleased, and undoubtedly said so. Not easily thwarted, five months later Sarah would catch up with her less than overjoyed husband at Philae.

8 } MESSING WITH MUMMIES

NOTHING IN EGYPT was more useful than mats, and Beechey used them to advantage in closing in the open sides of the boat's stern cabin and covering the supplies of foodstuffs, bottles of wine, jars of freshwater, guns, and other gifts for beys, cacheffs, and agas. Covered, too, was the lifting tackle to move the Philae obelisk—this a side trip that seems to have passed unmentioned in the planning with Consul Salt. Nevertheless, it had been discussed with Burckhardt, who, in a letter of February 20, 1817, wrote that "If Mr. Belzoni had had a flat bottomed boat at his command, he is confident that he should have been able to float down one of the small obelisks of Philae."[1]

Thanks to Belzoni's experience and his friend Burckhardt's wise counsel, this expedition was much better outfitted than the first. In addition to the *reis* and his Arab crew, the boat's company comprised a Greek servant (perhaps the Greek interpreter of the previous trip), a janissary provided by Mohammed Ali Pasha, and a cook who one supposes assumed duties previously handled by Sarah. Frugality was not among the cook's talents, however, and provisions expected to last six months were depleted in one. Consequently, the untested Henry Beechey found his diet abruptly converted to living off the land. The Pasha's janissary proved to be useless and "did scarcely any thing except treat the Christian dogs with insolence,"[2] and so was fired.

Expedition Abu Simbel left Boulak on the same day that Burckhardt wrote his letter praising Belzoni as being "as enterprising as he is intelligent, high minded, and disinterested."[3] It was, however, a slow start; a contrary wind allowed such little progress that in four days the boat was still in sight of the pyramids. In one of the early stops for leg stretching,

Giovanni took Beechey and the crew to visit a Bedouin camp. After Giovanni told the sheik that they were travelers in pursuit of antiquities, the Bedouin leader directed them to the next village, where he had seen a large statue half-buried in the sand. The following day, therefore, the wind having dropped completely away, Belzoni landed again and went in search of the potential treasure. The villagers took him to a shapeless lump of rock and explained that it had once been a camel, but God had turned it to stone. Before the transformation, the smaller stones scattered around it had been watermelons and part of the camel's load. Belzoni thanked his guides for their very reasonable explanation—and returned to his boat.

That evening the expedition reached the village of Meimond, where an Arab feast was in progress. Drawn to it by the sound of tambourines, singing, and hand clapping, Belzoni found a gathering of about thirty men and two dagger-wielding women. The women would rush at the men with their daggers and then retreat, only to do it again and again. "This," said Belzoni, "is a sort of Bedouin dance, and is the most decent of all I ever saw in Egypt."[4] What he meant by *decent* was not immediately clear, but became so when he continued. "No sooner was it ended, than, in order I suppose to please us, they immediately began another, in the fashion of the country, which fully compensated for the extraordinary modesty of the first."[5] Giovanni declared it more disgusting than entertaining, and again retreated to the boat. After spending a year among Arabs and now being without his wife, one wonders whether modesty and prudery were inherent in his character or were a pose for the benefit of the tenderfoot Henry Beechey.

March 5 brought Belzoni to the town of El Minya,[6] where it was necessary to get a new *firman* from governor Hamet Bey, who claimed control of all the boats on the river and called himself Admiral of the Nile. Two bottles of rum were all that were needed to secure the permit, but less encouraging was the news that two Copts dressed like Europeans were in town. Identified as agents of Bernardino Drovetti, they reportedly were hastening to Thebes in what Belzoni described as a "forced march." But why the hurry? The answer, Belzoni deduced, could only be that Drovetti wanted his men to out-distance Henry Salt's expedition and buy up all the antiquities unearthed by the Arabs in the previous season. More alarming to Belzoni, however, was the prospect of the Copts reaching his dig at Karnak ahead of him and claiming it for their own.

Drovetti's men were traveling on land and could be expected to assume

Belzoni's rendering of an Arab dance, with the women brandishing knives.

that Belzoni would be going more slowly by boat. Giovanni well knew that its progress was reliant on the caprices of the wind and his *reis*'s skill in avoiding sandbanks, and so decided to beat his competition at its own game. Beechey would stay on the boat and proceed upstream at a disarmingly leisurely pace. Its mat-walled cabin would prevent watchers from knowing who else was aboard—and specifically from recognizing that Belzoni was not. He, meanwhile, rented a horse for himself and an ass for his Greek servant, and together, just before midnight on March 6, they started their hell-for-leather, 266-mile desert dash to Luxor and Karnak. It took five days, during which time they stopped at Christian monasteries for brief rests, food, and to change mounts. "Any one who has been in the country," Belzoni reminded his readers, "may form some idea of the inconveniences a person must undergo, travelling through a tract entirely destitute of the necessaries of life."[7]

Giovanni and his servant did enjoy the satisfaction of reaching Luxor ahead of Drovetti's two Copts—but not soon enough to avoid being thwarted by an old acquaintance, Hamed, the Deftardár Bey of Asyut, who had decided that if the Franks valued antiquities, he, too, would become a collector. Shortly before Belzoni's return to Thebes, Hamed had visited the Karnak ruins and been told where the Englishman had been digging for sphinxes. He thereupon took possession of the excavation, put his physician in charge of the dig, and went on his way. The doctor was a Piedmontese named Moroki and a compatriot of Drovetti—though he claimed that he was working solely for the bey. True or not, Belzoni was forced to stand idly by as the doctor's men unearthed several sphinxes, only four of which, he was pleased to note, were in a condition to be worth taking.

If there had been any doubt about Dr. Moroki's allegiance, it was quickly erased. Before closing down his excavation and returning to Asyut as the bey had ordered, he crossed to Gournou and forbade (yet again) the inhabitants to sell anything to the English. However, a visit by Belzoni to Erment and its cacheff overrode the doctor's ban, enabling a crew of tomb hunters to be hired to work for him in the hills of Gournou while he returned to Karnak to pay more Arabs to dig in front of the great temple's second gateway. Situated behind piles of rubble and fallen columns, the gate pylon was flanked by the usual colossal statues seemingly too vast even for Belzoni to cart away. But having cleared the sand from around the base of one of them, he found that it was seated on a chair from which the upper body could be separated. He did so and wrote that he planned to add the chair as soon as Beechey arrived with hauling equipment. Having embarked on that act of infamy, Belzoni was moved to express his unbridled admiration for all he was seeing. "I seemed alone in the midst of all that is most sacred in the world. . . . [T]hese altogether had such an effect upon my soul, so as to separate me in imagination from the rest of mortals, exalt me on high over all, and to cause me to forget entirely the trifles and follies of life."[8] In the two centuries that have followed Belzoni's spiritual revelation, countless tourists have been similarly inspired by the wonders of Karnak—mercifully without a *firman* to tear it apart. Not so Drovetti's agents, who arrived soon after Belzoni and set to work to haul away the sphinxes unearthed by Dr. Moroki and theoretically the property of the Deftardár Bey.

Giovanni knew that he could not successfully challenge the agents, and so moved his operation to the west bank, where the cacheff had ordered the residents of Gournou to cooperate. Unlike the more distant inhabitants of Nubia, these Arabs had no trouble recognizing the value of money.

Regrettably, Belzoni was short of it. Before his overland race to Karnak, he had wisely left his cash on the boat with Beechey, whose cruise upriver was proving more leisurely than anticipated. Renting a small boat and going back to find his colleague was Belzoni's next imperative.

He found Beechey three days away at Kena, a town at the head of the only road to the Red Sea. The reason for Beechey's apparent dalliance has gone unrecorded. All that mattered was that Belzoni now had the money to keep the Gournou Arabs at work on his behalf. In his usual uncharitable opinion, he considered them "a wretched set of people . . . superior to any other Arabs in cunning and deceit, and the most independent of any in Egypt."[9] No one had been able to tame these people who lived in the caves and tunnels of Gournou—not the French, not the Mamelukes, and not Mohammed Ali's new regional governors. They had been "hunted like wild beasts by every successive government" without any lasting success. It might be said that they lived like rabbits in a warren were it not that rabbit warrens are interconnected. The Gournou burial tunnels went deep into the mountainside, but most led only to the burial chamber and its often untidily strewn mummies. Belzoni recalled the horror he felt at his first sight of them: "The blackness of the wall, the faint light given by the candles or torches for want of air, the different objects that surrounded me, seeming to converse with each other, and the Arabs with the candles or torches in their hands, naked and covered with dust, themselves resembling living mummies, absolutely formed a scene that cannot be described."[10] Yet having said that, he went on to do so in one of the most dramatic passages in the annals of archaeological history. To paraphrase it would be to destroy its "you are there" sense of immediacy:

In such a situation I found myself several times, and often returned exhausted and fainting, till at last I became inured to it, and indifferent to what I suffered, except for the dust, which never failed to choke my throat and nose; and though fortunately, I am destitute of the sense of smelling,[11] I could taste that the mummies were rather unpleasant to swallow. After the exertion of entering into such a place, through a passage of fifty, a hundred, three hundred or perhaps six hundred yards, nearly overcome, I sought a resting place, found one, and contrived to sit; but when my weight bore on the body of an Egyptian, it crushed like a band-box. I naturally had recourse to my hands to sustain my weight, but they found no better support; so that I sunk altogether among the broken mummies, with a crash of bones, rags, and wooden cases, which raised such a dust as kept me motionless for a quarter of an hour, waiting till it subsided again. I could not remove from the place, however, without increasing it, and every step I took I crushed a mummy in some part or other.[12]

That description, and others like it, have led to Belzoni being condemned by modern archaeologists as their profession's most dastardly plunderer—overlooking, of course, that in 1817 there was no archaeological profession. Nevertheless, Giovanni's description of his adventures in the Gournou tunnels was sufficiently engrossing for the French tourist Edward de Montulé to include it in an appendix to his own book of his travels in Egypt.[13]

Belzoni's enduringly graphic image of crashing coffins and crumbling corpses belies the truth that at the same time he was studying the styles of the mummies and their embalming processes to a degree unparalleled since Herodotus had described them in the fifth century BC.[14] "I plainly saw the various degrees and customs of the diverse classes, from the peasant to the king," Giovanni wrote, before going on to describe them. While doing so he apologized for contradicting his "old guide Herodotus; for on this point and many others, he was not well informed by the Egyptians."[15]

Lest one is tempted to assume that ancient Egyptian tombs were filled with riches akin to those Howard Carter would find with Tutankhamen, it is important to realize that thousands, perhaps hundreds of thousands of Theban citizens went to their resting places with little more than the linen that wrapped them. Belzoni had discovered that "Few or no papyri are to be found among the lower order, and if any occur they are only small pieces stuck upon the breast with a little gum or asphaltum."[16] "The purpose of my researches," he blandly explained, "was to rob the Egyptians of their papyri; of which I found a few hidden in their breasts, under their arms, in the space above the knees, or on the legs, and covered by the numerous folds of cloth that envelop the mummy."[17] Though extremely fragile, papyri contained hieroglyphic and demotic inscriptions much prized by European collectors. Nevertheless, wresting them intact from their long-dead owners and then getting them out into the sunlight was no mean feat, Giovanni Belzoni being a very large man working in very small tunnels.

Although the entrances to the lesser tombs had long been homes to

Mummified hands purchased in London in 1954. Those right and center may be from the same woman.

Gournou's inhabitants and their livestock, deeper into the scarp hundreds of mummies remained unmolested in their chambers and pits. Hundreds, perhaps thousands more had been broken up and ground down into medicinal powder to be incorporated into the elixirs of European apothecaries, a use discovered by an Arab doctor in the twelfth century AD. In 1587, another visiting Englishman shipped home six hundred pounds of dried mummy flesh.[18] The medicinal practice was still widespread in the seventeenth and eighteenth centuries, and as recently as the 1980s mummy dust was said to be available at forty dollars per ounce in a New York pharmacy serving those engaging in occult practices.[19] Perhaps because unscrupulous robbers were prone to substituting low-grade dust for real mummy grindings, intact hands, feet, and even heads were exported to be pulverized by the buyer.[20]

The tomb robbers of old had been searching for pharaohs' gold and had no notion that sheets of papyrus had any value. Indeed, they did not—until the arrival of the French army in 1798 and the subsequent eruption of Egyptomania that was to engulf the salons and museums of Europe. Stimulated by "researchers" like Drovetti and Belzoni, the local Arab men organized themselves into teams or companies to extract and market papyri. An old man from one such group, while trying to make a secret deal with Giovanni, showed him, along with papyri, "a brazen vessel, one of the finest and most perfect pieces of Egyptian antiquity I have ever seen of the kind," he exclaimed. "It was covered with engraved hieroglyphics, very finely executed."[21] Belzoni added that he supposed it to be a sacred vessel used by the Egyptians. He and Beechey were still admiring it when the old man produced another exactly like it. Were that scene being played out a hundred years later, one would be mindful that the increasing scarcity of treasures had turned the Gournou men from finding to faking. In reality, however, these were cast-bronze *situlae* (holy-water containers) akin to one in the Drovetti Collection in the Turin Museum.[22]

Delighted with his Gournou purchases, Giovanni turned again to his new dig at Karnak, where he was finding yet another line of sphinxes. Under one of them lay a rusted iron sickle, which he deduced had been buried long before Egypt was invaded by the Persians, offering proof, therefore, that iron was smelted there as early as 525 BC. Subsequent Egyptologists have disputed this assumption, and,even Belzoni was not sure that he was right. Why, he asked, if the Egyptians had agricultural tools of iron, did they not have comparable weapons?

While Belzoni was busy supervising his crew at Karnak to prevent the workers from stealing what they found, Beechey was busy in the nearby Luxor temple setting up a base apartment in one of its chambers and furnishing it with the ever-useful Arab mats.[23] Sleeping on the moored boat and cooled by the Nile breeze would have been preferable—were it not overrun with rats. When attempts to oust them failed, Beechey and the crew unloaded all the provisions and then sank the boat. The men were happy to see the critters swimming for their lives and disappearing under the Luxor jetties. With the boat refloated, the supplies reembarked, and the vermin problem solved, it pleased nobody to see the rats all cheerfully returning and, as Belzoni remarked, "no doubt grateful to us for having

The court of Amenophis II in the temple complex at Luxor (view from the south). The temple is dedicated to the god Amon, who there took the ithyphallic form of the god Min.

given them a fresh appetite and a good bathing."[24] Beechey's apartment in the Luxor temple, though hot and dusty, was deemed infinitely preferable to battling the boat's rodent squatters.

Through much of April, Belzoni's digging and buying went on uninterrupted. As most of his chosen sites were the product of guesswork, some proved productive and others not. In the vicinity of Gournou, he was digging "at the end of an avenue where sphinxes must have stood" leading to a ramped causeway and the ruins of a temple which did not greatly excite him.[25] More interesting was a "granite door nine feet high by five wide, and one and a half thick." He added that it was "covered with hieroglyphics and figures neatly cut. . . . It had been painted, and was buried entirely under ground."[26] This time the fellahs' labor had paid off.

On the other side of the river at Karnak, Beechey was supervising another of Belzoni's site selections, namely "a spot of ground at the foot of a heap of earth, where part of a large colossus projected out."[27] This proved to be one of Beechey's great archaeological moments. Lying faceup in the sand was a granite head larger than that of Young Memnon, complete save for its beard, one ear, and part of the chin. Belzoni considered it beautiful workmanship, and being broken from its shoulders, the ten-foot-tall head

The partially reconstructed mortuary temple and tomb of Queen Hatshepsut (1503–1482 BC), rising in two tiers against the face of the Libyan mountains at Deir El-Bahri (view from the east).

Belzoni's rendering of the giant head and arm attributed to Amenophis III, found by Beechey in the temple of Mut at Karnak. The face had been retooled to mirror that of Ramesses II. The painting suggests that although the arm belonged to the torso, the head did not.

was considerably more portable—even though it took eight days to haul it a mile to Luxor.[28] He also retrieved an arm which he believed came from the same figure, and to be sure that nobody else carried it off, he carved his name deep into the granite—where modern tourists to the British Museum wonder at the meaning of that *ancient* word.

The spring of 1817 had been good to Belzoni. Along with the head and arm, he at last had Drovetti's "take it if you can" coffin lid at quayside, plus an altar from Karnak and four large, lion-headed statues of the goddess Sekhmet. Those, plus an impressive assortment of small stuff from pottery to mummified animals and birds, gave him a potential boatload of treasures larger than that of his first Theban voyage. Then Giovanni's luck ran out. Before he could load and set out down the river, trouble came up it. Hamed, the Deftardár Bey, arrived from Asyut, his mind already poisoned by Drovetti's gift-giving agents, who had hurried to meet him. They complained that they were unable to buy a single antiquity, Belzoni having bought them all. Hamed Bey then issued orders to all the local cacheffs and sheiks instructing them that they should sell no more and let their men work no more for the English.

Basalt figures of the lion-headed goddess Sekhmet, several of which were recovered by Belzoni. (© The Trustees of the British Museum)

The next morning Belzoni went in search of "the mighty potentate," whom he found seated on a divan and surrounded by cacheffs and assorted retainers. The bey received him coolly and said that he had heard complaints from the Arab workers that the English had drawn their swords and threatened to cut off their heads. "Nonsense!" snapped Belzoni.

It soon became apparent that in spite of being deputy ruler of all Upper Egypt, Hamed knew very little about the area. He asked for directions to Gournou and ordered horses to get him there. Belzoni rode with him, trying without success to talk him out of his embargo. On arrival at the ruined temple of Ramesses III at Medinet Habu,[29] the bey summoned the terrified sheik, who he had been told favored the English.

"Find me a mummy that has not been opened," the bey ordered.

"I will do what I can," the sheik replied. "But it will take time."

"Dig under your feet. Find it now!"

The old man tried to explain that mummies were not found in the temples but in the tunnels of Gournou. Fortunately, one of the attending cacheffs agreed that this was so.

"Then you have an hour to find it," growled the bey as he ordered the shaken sheik away. Probably to Belzoni's surprise, when the potentate's party moved on to Gournou, the mummy was awaiting him. On seeing it, Hamed Bey shouted that he was sure the casing had been opened and ordered the sheik to be stretched on the ground and the soles of his feet beaten with rods. This punishment, the *bastinado*, if taken to extremes could result in the death of the victim, and the bey was in no mood to re-

lent. Giovanni knew that the unfortunate man was being punished for being his friend, but there was nothing he could say to halt it. His interpreter
tried to intercede on behalf of the English consul-general, but to no avail.
To the rod wielder, Hamed demanded, "Go on, go on, and hard." By this
time, wrote the horrified Belzoni, "the poor fellow was like the mummy
that lay by his side, deprived of sense and feeling."[30] Hamed then had the
mummy cut open. On finding nothing wrapped in it, he ordered that
unless he was brought another that was intact he would have the sheik
thrown into the river. Belzoni then told the bey that he intended to write
to Cairo to inform the Pasha how his Deftardár was violating the *firman.*
If the threat did not put the fear of Allah into him, it seemed to produce
a change of heart. Hamed Bey told Giovanni's interpreter that he would
send an order the next morning authorizing the Gournou men to resume
working for the English. Twenty men could work for eight days. Shortly
thereafter another order came from the bey telling the Gournouese that
they were to sell neither to the English nor the French, and that they were
to have three pristine mummies ready for him on his return. He specifically stated that the finders were to be the same men who had been working for the English.

The *bastinadoed* sheik, who was still unable to walk, was terrified lest
he could expect more of the same. However, when the great man returned
on May 3, he seemed to have forgotten about the three mummies and
instead spent his time at Luxor examining Belzoni's quayside collection,
and then, "like a being bewildered, ran here and there among the ruins,
to seek for antiquities, without knowing where he went."[31] In the midst of
this curious activity, Belzoni managed to talk him into agreeing to provide
an order to the people of Gournou allowing them to sell their discoveries to the English and another order to the upriver cacheffs at Aswan and
elsewhere under his authority to provide protection to Belzoni and his
people as they continued south toward Abu Simbel. By the time the bey
departed, Belzoni had his *firman.* Equally encouraging was the news that
Drovetti's men were packing up and returning to Cairo.

Belzoni now had Thebes to himself and was free to dig at Karnak as
and where he pleased. But getting back on track at Gournou was less easily achieved. Its people were still in shock at the brutal treatment of their
sheik, and were reluctant to take Belzoni's word that he and they now had
the blessing of the bey. As only one of them could read, and the document

was in Arabic and in a hand that Giovanni could not decipher, he called a general meeting of the villagers and their leaders to hear the *firman* read to them by the only literate sheik.

While the silent and expectant audience waited to hear the great man's words, the sheik began to read them to himself to be sure that he had them correctly. Stopping halfway through, he turned to Belzoni with a look of surprise. "You wish me to read this aloud?"

"Indeed. Just as it's written."

And so he did:

"It is the will and pleasure of Hamed, the Deftardár Bey and present ruler of Upper Egypt, that no Sheiks, Fellahs, or other persons, shall from this moment sell any article of antiquity to the English party, or work for them; on the contrary, it is hereby ordered, that everything that may be found shall be sold to the party of Mr. Drovetti; and whoever disobeys this order will incur the displeasure of the Bey."[32]

A few years later, actors in Victorian melodramas would have cried, "Foiled again!"

9 } RETURN TO ABU SIMBEL

BELZONI HAD LOST the game but he was not about to cede the match. With the Luxor and Gournou Arabs unable to dig but not openly hostile, and the bey and his Turkish cohorts gone, a leisurely departure upriver seemed to be the most reasonable plan. To that end, he assembled everything he had bought or found, built a mud-brick wall around it, covered the piles with dirt, and hired a guard to watch over them until he and Henry Beechey returned from Abu Simbel. A letter to Consul Salt in Cairo had explained what had happened and asked him for more money to cover the expense of continuing the voyage. Remembering that before the expedition had set out, the Abu Simbel goal had been at the center of planning discussions with both Salt and Burckhardt, Belzoni's next comment is hard to explain. "We would proceed to open the temple of Abu Simbel," he wrote, "a project that was deemed nearly imaginary, a castle in the air, as no one supposed any temple really existed there." Deemed by whom? Burckhardt had been there, so had Drovetti, and so had William Bankes, all three known to Henry Salt. One might conclude, therefore, that the words were not in the letter, but hyperbole later added by Belzoni for the amazement of his English readers.

While waiting for an answer, Belzoni would have an unexpected opportunity to become a pioneering tour guide. Two Coptic Christian priests at whose monastery he had enjoyed hospitality now sought to have the favor returned. They had come to see the ruins. Giovanni saw them as a sounding board for all he had been learning and a chance to enthuse over the wonders of the temples and tombs. We may assume that Beechey had long since tired of his leader's effusions and welcomed the new audience. As Belzoni explained it: "To me it was in general a source of pleasure to show these things to strangers, to hear their remarks, and to observe their astonishment, and satisfaction, after coming so far to view what cannot be seen any where else." That sentiment has been echoed down the years by countless tour guides, but so has his next sentence: "At the same time no vexation can be greater to a lover of antiquity than when he witnesses indifference even to what is most striking, which is often the case." The two holy fathers had lived for ten years at their monastery a mere three days' ride from Thebes, yet had not previously been moved to visit these wonders of the world. They turned out to have as much interest in the antiquities as did the asses that brought them, and only became animated when they saw the name of a friend scrawled in charcoal on one of the hieroglyph-covered walls. That discovery led them to look for the names of others they might have known. Belzoni complained that not only was he disappointed at his guests' lack of taste, but he was provoked by their indifference.[1] However, he did not profess any dismay at the existence of the Christians' disfiguring graffiti, nor at the deliberate damage wrought by the early Copts during their pre-Arab dominance of Egypt. Although his inscribing of the statuary he intended to take away could be explained (if not condoned) as a necessary identification to protect it from Drovetti, his penchant for engraving his name on immovable objects was inexcusable—at least in modern eyes. Thus on a column in the Ramesseum we find "BELZONI" writ large, and under it, albeit with less depth and grandeur, the name "SALT." The antiquity hunters' desecration of the monuments began a fashion for intellectual butchery from which few if any buildings and tombs would escape, the names and addresses of one family of tourists sometimes defacing those of their predecessors.[2]

The day that the holy fathers failed to live up to Belzoni's expectations was the beginning of the *camseen* winds.[3] Giovanni's description of such winds provides a dramatic meteorological moment. Blowing four or five days at a time, the wind is

> so very strong that it raises the sand to a great height, forming a general cloud, so thick it is impossible to keep the eyes open. . . . It forces the sand into the houses through every cranny, and fills every thing with it. The caravans cannot continue in the deserts; the boats cannot continue their voyages, and travellers are obliged to eat sand in spite of their teeth. The whole is like a chaos. Often a quantity of sand and small stones ascends to a great height, and forms a column sixty or

Belzoni's name carved deep into one of the pillars of the Ramesseum. Neither Hetley nor E. G. Geddes has been identified. Below "Belzoni" is the name "Salt," less boldly cut but embellished with an encircling groove. It seems improbable that both names were cut at the same time. It is more likely that Salt later found his employee's graffito and refused to be upstaged.

seventy feet in diameter, and so thick, that were it steady on one spot, it would appear a solid mass. This not only revolves within its circumference, but runs in a circular direction over a great space of ground, sometimes maintaining itself in motion for half an hour, and where it falls it accumulates a small hill of sand. God help the poor traveller who is caught under it![4]

In short, a desert tornado. That description, though interesting in its record of a natural phenomenon, also says much about Belzoni's objectivity and concern for detail, as well as offering a glimpse of his wry sense of humor. This, coupled with perseverance, had to have been the cornerstone of his ability to withstand and overcome the seemingly endless difficulties and obstructions that were strewn in his path.

On May 23, the Abu Simbel expedition left Luxor and headed upriver to Aswan without lingering at the historic sites along the way. Belzoni had seen them all before, and he assured Beechey that they would explore them in detail on their return. However, after passing the cataract at Aswan, they did stop at Philae, whose "ruins [are] truly magnificent, particularly at some distance."[5] Belzoni's estimate of the abutting temples' evolution is on a par with Thomas Jefferson's sequencing of an Indian mound at his Shadwell birthplace in Virginia,[6] both men independently looking at the past with the logic born of common sense—the basis on which all archaeological reasoning rests. Referring to the second temple, Belzoni noted that it had to be of more modern construction employing materials salvaged from an older structure. He noted specifically that in one of the columns opposite the gate in the portico, he found a hieroglyphically inscribed stone inverted and evidently reused.

The Philae island had been subject to flooding and the entrance to the temples was deep in mud (see p. 80). In the Christian era, one had been converted into a chapel and the sculptured walls coated with obscuring mud which in turn was incised with Coptic symbols. The outer walls had been further damaged in 1799 by bullet strikes when the island was fiercely defended by its Nubian inhabitants after the French army reached Aswan in its pursuit of the Mamelukes. Denon, who accompanied the troops, wrote that the Nubians, "naked, and with large swords, long pikes, muskets, and bucklers, and stationed on the top of the rock declared war against us."[7] Anyone but the French would have said that the natives were only defending their island. Before they were driven off it, rather than surrender to the invaders, the women drowned their babies and infants in the Nile. The French, however, were proud of their achievement in taking control of Egypt from Aswan to the sea and carved on the temple pylon an inscription that began "République Françoise An 6, Le 13 Messidor. Une Armée Françoise commandée par Bonaparte est descendue à Alexandrie." The claim was dated "An 7 de la République, de Jes. Chr. 1799."[8]

With Philae secured, Denon and his savants drew a detailed plan of the temples and made several drawings, while noting that the island was "almost entirely covered with the most superb edifices of different ages."[9] Belzoni agreed, calling them "the most superb group of ruins I ever beheld together in so small a space of ground."[10] He proceeded to make a wax model of the entry pylon but had trouble getting it to stay in shape, the temperature being 124° F in the shade. He added that it could have been hotter, as the mercury had reached the top of the tube.

The obelisk on which Giovanni had rested a covetous eye and hired a guard to watch over was still there, though the guard apparently was not. He noted that on one face of it a Greek inscription had been "discovered by an English traveller, Mr. Banks, who, not having time to dig it out, left it."[11] He was referring to the same William Bankes (with an "e") who had traveled the Nile in 1815 and whom Burckhardt had tried to interest in financing the removal of Young Memnon.[12] Bankes may well have intended to haul the obelisk away from Philae, but until Belzoni provided the necessary skill, he would have been unable to do so. Along with the tempting obelisk, Belzoni's twelve-foot wall panel, which he had trimmed down to a six-inch thickness, was still on the island, but the finely chiseled figures that made it so desirable had been deliberately defaced, rendering it worthless.

We are not told what Henry Beechey and the rest of the team were doing while Belzoni was pursuing his acquisitive researches, but they doubtless were relieved when a courier arrived with Salt's reply. It had taken him eighteen days of hard riding. The letter came with money and an agreement that Project Abu Simbel should continue. As previously noted, the level of both information and agreement between Salt and Belzoni is cloudy at best. According to the latter, Salt "entertained strong doubts of the existence of a temple there," and in the letter wrote that he thought no entrance would be found and that, instead, "it would turn out to be like some of the mausoleums round the pyramids."[13] In spite of Salt's apparent inconsistency, the project was still on track, and on June 16 the group was ready to leave on the second leg of the journey, taking with them two unexpected and unlikely helpers.

They were British navy captains: the Honorable Charles Leonard Irby and James Mangles, aged twenty-nine and thirty-two, both having retired from the sea due to ill-health which they hoped would be improved by a trip on the Nile. It was. Mangles lived to be eighty-one and Irby to fifty-six after marrying his friend's sister in 1825. Together they brought a welcome sense of fun to an otherwise rather stolid enterprise. June 4 being George III's birthday, the captains proposed a celebration. An old British flag that just happened to be aboard the boat was hoisted atop the main temple's entrance pylon, and at noon, all the expedition's five firearms discharged a twenty-one-gun salute—and overheated. As Belzoni observed, the natives could not understand why the English wasted so much gunpowder without killing anyone. The jolly celebration continued through the evening, unintentionally heralding the arrival of another traveler.

On June 5, Sarah Belzoni caught up with her happy husband, expecting to join him in opening the Abu Simbel temple. To her dismay, he told her that he only had one boat and so had no room for her; furthermore, he could not afford to rent another. That he did have space for his new chums, Irby and Mangles, cannot have escaped Sarah. She insisted that she could shift sand with the best of them, but to no avail. On June 16, Operation Abu Simbel set sail with a crew of eight (five men and three boys),[14] Captains Irby and Mangles, Henry Beechey, two servants, and Mahomet, a janissary supplied by Consul Salt and whose real name was Giovanni Finati.[15] Aged thirty and a native of Ferrara, Finati had been a soldier in the army of Mohammed Ali. He spoke Arabic, French, some English, as well as his native Italian, and he had previously traveled the Nile as janissary and friend to William Bankes. His current assignment had been to catch up with Beechey at Thebes, but on finding Beechey gone, Finati continued to Esna, the largest town between Luxor and Aswan. There he met up with Beechey's Greek interpreter, Giovanni D'Athanasi, and went on with him to Philae.[16] D'Athanasi, known as Yanni, had worked first for Consul-General Misset and on his retirement became a servant to, and excavator for, Henry Salt. Captain Irby did not think much of either D'Athanasi or Finati. He considered Yanni an unreliable interpreter and thought the janissary a coward "showing how little use these fellows are to protect travellers."[17] Although it was not yet an issue, Belzoni's assistants were all Salt's men, paid by him and loyal to him rather than to their oddball leader. Beechey would later say that he found Belzoni difficult to work with, being of "so suspicious and dissatisfied a disposition, that it was in some respects difficult to keep on any terms with him."[18] Burckhardt, one remembers, saw him quite differently: "as enterprising as he is intelligent, high-minded, and disinterested."[19]

Left behind on the roof of the Philae temple were Sarah and the Irish James Curtin, who had accompanied her from Cairo. On the day after their arrival, James added his own embellishment to the Philae architecture by inscribing a framed graffito reading "June 6, 1817 H. J. Curtin, Native of Limerick, Ireland," thereby identifying his place of birth—information recorded nowhere else.[20]

Remaining with James and Sarah was a quantity of baggage sent from Cairo to provide Beechey with what were considered the necessities of civilized life, including silver spoons and forks, which Sarah dismissed as "such unnecessary things."[21] Needed, however, was housing, which she and James constructed from mud bricks. Before he left, Belzoni had hired guards to protect them. Sarah, in turn, kept loaded pistols to defend herself from her protectors. But there was little protection on the rooftop from the searing sun and the overstretched thermometer.

On the river under a cooling breeze and free from insects, Giovanni's boat made a relatively uneventful run to the village of Abu Simbel, marred only by Belzoni being bitten while bathing. Irby explained that it was their practice to bathe each evening and again in the morning before continuing upstream. At one such evening stop, Giovanni was bitten on the foot, "which caused him to cry out somewhat loudly for assistance." The next morning he again swam in the river and was again bitten on the same foot, this time drawing blood and "taking a piece out of the toe." Belzoni said that he felt something twisting round his leg, and although that sounds like a water snake, Irby recorded that they all agreed that the attacker must have been a water lizard.[22] Although no lasting damage was done to Giovanni's toe, what makes the event noteworthy is that his *Narrative* said nothing about it, perhaps because his response to the bites had been somewhat less than heroic.

On reaching Abu Simbel, Belzoni expected to present himself to the cacheffs Daoud and his less obliging brother Khalil. But both were away. Because the two captains had planned to reach the Second Cataract, Belzoni agreed to take them there before starting work on the Abu Simbel sand. At Wadi Halfa, however, the boat's crew demanded money from their passengers, and when Giovanni declined, the men went ashore and refused to reboard. The crew, all eight from one family, evidently had cohorts among the Wadi Halfa inhabitants, who menacingly joined them at the river's edge. "Pay up or sail the boat yourself," they shouted. They knew, and Belzoni knew, that even with two British navy captains aboard, there was no way that they could navigate the shoals and sandbars at the foot of the cataract. But Giovanni decided to call their bluff and said he would do just that, then began to strike the sail, this being the first step in letting the river carry the boat down in its current. He had scarcely begun before one of the crew came to parley. Belzoni replied that they could have baksheesh once they had taken the boat out into midstream, but not before. The stand-off had wasted a day, but proved to be of no account as the Abu Simbel cacheff brothers had not yet returned.

Four days later, a lone messenger on a camel arrived at Abu Simbel— not with a permit but with a question. Was Belzoni the same man who had been there last year and wanted to open the temple? On learning that he was, the courier mounted his camel and rode off. Three more days of waiting finally brought results. Daoud and Khalil arrived and set up house in a pair of rush-built huts on one of the river's many sandbanks, and it was there that the English supplicants had to go. Belzoni presented Daoud with a gun, powder and ball shot, a shawl, tobacco, and a bar of soap, diplomatic generosity that turned out to have been a politically poor idea—and an enraged Khalil loudly said so. Because it had been

Daoud who had provided both permission and labor in the previous year, Giovanni assumed that gifts to him would again pave the way. This time, however, Khalil insisted that he was every bit as important a potentate as his brother and that the gifts to one and not the other were an insult of stratospheric proportions. An offer of one of the team's five guns was refused, and when Daoud invited his visitors to dine with him, Khalil retired to his hut in a sustained huff. Sometime later, when Belzoni and the captains went to try to make peace with him, he proved more tractable, having sent them a message demanding a gun and its powder and shot. Irby recalled that "we immediately gave him ours, which, though good for nothing, was, nevertheless, the best-looking one we had."[23] Work could begin in the morning, and thirty men would be there to do it.

Well, not exactly. Eventually a handful arrived and began to dig. Very sensibly, Belzoni decided not to shovel straight in toward the doorway for fear that the flanking sand mountains would fall in on him. Instead, he focused on reducing the slope of the scarps on either side while leaving the pile in front of the door until last. The cacheffs and their diggers were as eager as Belzoni to open the entrance and became volubly frustrated when three days were spent shifting sand that seemed to be getting them nowhere. Belzoni then offered what today would be called a "turn key" contract. He would pay the cacheffs three hundred piastres to open the entrance—no matter how long it took. That seemed like a fair bargain, and prompted Khalil to increase the crew to eighty men. Giovanni paid the money, half at the outset and the rest on the third day, and on that basis work went on. However, on that third day the crew discovered that the work was more tiring than they expected, and remembering that Ramadan would begin on the following morning, they quit en masse. Wrote an exasperated Belzoni, "they left us with our temple, the sand, and the treasure, and contented themselves with keeping the three hundred piastres."[24]

Although the first day of Ramadan was set aside for fasting and devotions, the holy writ allowed men to return to work thereafter, although they were obliged to fast until the evening. Belzoni's hopes that his eighty unenthusiastic helpers would return on the following day were not realized. Their leaders, cacheffs Daoud and Khalil, had also decamped, leaving no one to whom complaints could be made. An old English adage advises that if one wants a job done properly, one should do it oneself. There is no knowing whether Belzoni from Padua was aware of that advice, but he certainly came to that conclusion. Henceforth the sand shifting would be done by himself, Beechey, the captains Irby and Mangles, Yanni the interpreter, and the janissary Finati, plus the boat crew who either had abandoned their hijacking plans or been paid off. In all, the Abu Simbel team counted fourteen able bodies who every day rose before dawn and toiled until the sun got up. Villagers from the east side of the river watched with amazement as these strange white men (one much bigger than the others) shoveled sand. Eventually some of the watchers came across and offered their services, which at first were gladly accepted. Unfortunately, it soon became apparent that the east Nile people were at war with those of westerly Abu Simbel and got into disruptive fights with them that were, at best, unhelpful. For the safety of the continuing operation, therefore, they had to be sent home.

Several days later, a boat was seen approaching from the east filled with well-armed men who obviously intended to make their presence felt. No one knew who they were, and a local Abu Simbel sand-shifter named Musmar who claimed to know everything about everybody assured Belzoni that no matter who was in the boat, none would dare come near him as he was afraid of no one. The team had previously listened to his tales of defying the raiding Bedouins and found his presence reassuring. But when the boatload of strangers came close to the Abu Simbel shore, Musmar fled and was never seen again.

It turned out that the strangers were less bellicose than their weapons suggested. Led by an old man and his son, they were the cacheffs of the east-bank village of Ibrim several miles downriver. They were also at war with Daoud and Khalil, a detail that made them even more welcome. Belzoni apologized for not having gifts to give them as he had none left. The old man replied that he had not come for gifts but hoped that when Belzoni returned to Cairo he would put in a good word to Mohammed Ali on their behalf. Giovanni assured him that he had no reason not to do so, and with the usual formalities the meeting ended.

Belzoni had learned that when dealing with Arabs nothing was quite as it sounded or seemed, and the cacheff of Ibrim was no exception. On leaving the Englishmen, he and his followers went away to view the second, smaller temple, accompanied by the interpreter Yanni, to whom the cacheff imparted some unexpected information. It was the Ibrim people who were masters of this stretch of the river and not the Abu Simbel cacheffs. If the latter killed one man, they would kill two. They could stop the

The Abu Simbel temple of Queen Nefertari, consort of Ramesses II.

The rock-hewn temple at Abu Simbel built to glorify Ramesses II, its sanctuary dedicated to the patron gods of Egypt's principal cities: Thebes, Heliopolis, and Memphis. Queen Nefertari is visible beside the legs of her husband (view from the east).

sand-shifting operation or they could permit it to continue. The option was theirs alone. Knowing that the English had given Daoud and Khalil guns and soap, they, being the superior tribe, should be given as much or more. If Belzoni failed to comply he could expect dire consequences. Once again, therefore, trouble with the natives threatened to unhorse Project Abu Simbel.

More feather-smoothing was needed, and the unfortunate Yanni was charged with carrying messages back and forth. When the cacheffs insisted that Belzoni had no business interfering with the temple without written permission, the interpreter took him the Pasha's *firman.* The old man was not impressed. He said he could not understand a word of it. In any case, it was not addressed to him and therefore worthless. The bottom line was simple to read: No presents, no permit. And Belzoni had no presents to give.

While the English team debated its sparse options, Ibrim's senior cacheff made the next move, unexpectedly ordering his men back into their boat and heading upstream toward the Abu Simbel village. There being no point in standing idle awaiting their return, Belzoni and his sand-movers went back to work on their late-afternoon shift, expecting that at any moment the Ibrim men would return. But none came—nor did they the next day. Inquiries at the village yielded the surprising news that the boat had left in the night.

Digging continued unmolested through the rest of the month, each day revealing a little more of the great temple's façade. The doorway proved to be where Belzoni and Burckhardt had expected it to be, namely directly below a standing figure of the falcon-headed and sun disc–wearing god Rë-Harakhti.[25] On the evening of July 31, the sand fell away from the top of a cavity beyond which there was only darkness. Salt's prophecy that there was no doorway and no temple behind the façade was wrong.

No one knew how long the sand had sealed the entrance; it could have been thousands of years. Speculation that the temple might still contain its portable furniture or even African gold locked in its storerooms was a mouthwatering but unlikely possibility. When the last pharaonic guard quit his post, villagers would have stripped its furnishings for firewood, and any gold would have gone with the guard. Nevertheless, the black cavity was itself exciting enough, and the temptation to enlarge it must have been hard to resist. But Giovanni Battista Belzoni was a patient and cautious man who reasoned that the air inside might be dangerously foul:

"Let's give it time to clear. The temple had been waiting since who knew when. One more night of silence would do it no harm." So they waited.

When at dawn on the morning of Monday, August 1, 1817, the team was ready to expose the rest of the doorway, Belzoni discovered that his eight-man boat crew was conspicuously absent.

10 } THE GREAT DISCOVERY

AFTER THE WADI HALFA shakedown attempt, Belzoni's boat crew appeared to have learned its lesson, and the *reis*'s cooperation through the July of digging had given the appearance of acquiescence. In reality, the lesson they had learned was that if at first you don't succeed, try again. And so they had. The men were persuaded by the Abu Simbel cacheffs that if the Englishmen seemed to be succeeding in opening the temple, the crew should do everything in their power to deter them. Consequently, the boat's *reis* first refused to work, and when that failed, he threatened to take the boat and leave Belzoni stranded. Before dawn on revelation morning, Yanni had been sent to rouse the crew, who normally slept aboard. He found them awake and noisily cursing their employers as Christian dogs who had paid them only two piastres a day when they were worth four, overlooking, perhaps, that their *reis* only paid them seven a month. When Yanni returned with the crew's demands, Belzoni went down to the boat, ignored the mixed pleading and cursing, and instead busied himself removing all his weapons and ammunition, and with the janissary's help brought them up to the base camp. It is, however, odd that the usually cautious Belzoni and the navy captains would leave their weapons on the boat and potentially in the grasp of their unreliable crew. Nevertheless, the unspoken message was clear: With success within reach, no threats would delay the great denouement.

There is no doubt that Belzoni wanted to be the first in—as would any archaeologist at any time. He cannot have been amused, therefore, to find that his moment had been muted by the janissary Finati (alias Mahomet), who had managed to squeeze through the hole while everyone else was still enlarging it. Not surprisingly, this coup is recorded by Finati, as well as by Irby, but not by Belzoni.

BELZONI

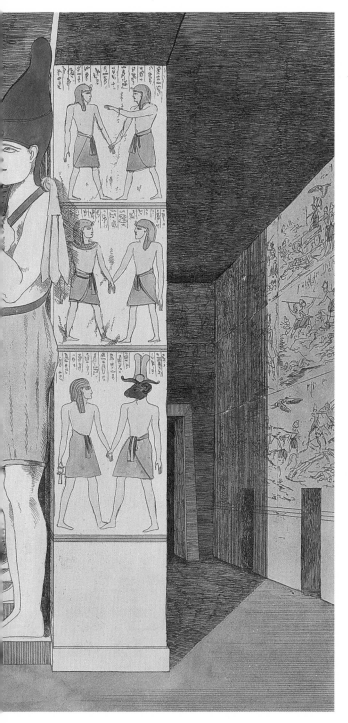

The hypostyle hall at Abu Simbel as Belzoni first saw it. Possibly drawn later from sketches made at its opening in 1817.

The opening was still being expanded when the boat crew clambered up the slope dressed in the formality of their turbans and gowns and armed with an assortment of weapons that included pikes, swords, daggers, and, as Irby described them, "two old rusty pistols which would be more likely to kill the person who fired, than him who was fired at."[1] But Belzoni was not to be intimidated, even though the *reis* ranted and threw sand in the air—which, Irby noted, stuck to his perspiring face. When, however, it became evident that these theatrics were getting him nowhere, the *reis* agreed that to leave now would mean no payment for the crew's labors and no baksheesh when the temple was opened. On the other hand, staying another day or two would win them both. Consequently, they happily stripped off their finery, and laughing and shouting "tyep, tyep" (meaning good, good!), they set joyfully to work. The crisis had been averted, but Belzoni and the captains had not forgotten what one of the crewmen had told the cook, who told Yanni, who told Irby: the crew could very easily murder Belzoni and all his people. There being neither law nor justice in Nubia, after committing the crime they could fly to the mountains where no one would pursue them. They were not the poor people the English took them for, the sailor added, and the fact that his brethren had kept the French at bay for four years proved it.[2] Belzoni knew all this to be true and breathed a sigh of relief at having again dodged the Arabs' bullet.

With the hole sufficiently enlarged, and with candles in their hands, Giovanni, Beechey, and the gallant captains made their formal entry into what proved to be a vast chamber (the hypostyle hall, or *speos*), its rock-hewn ceiling supported by four pairs of square columns fronted by thirty-foot standing figures of Ramesses II, those on the left wearing the crown of Upper Egypt, and their companions on the right (north) wearing also the crown of Lower Egypt. Later scholars would interpret these as representing both the ancient unification of the country and the supremacy of Upper Egypt. Extending 207 feet into the cliff, the temple was constructed to commemorate the thirtieth year of Ramesses's reign in 1254 BC; but that, too, waited to be recognized until the Rosetta Stone yielded its secrets.[3]

Because the weeks of sand clearance had always started at or before dawn, Belzoni must have noticed that the first rays of the rising sun shone directly on the temple's façade, highlighting the hawk-headed god and its sun-disk crown. Egyptology still being in its infancy, he may not have understood that the temple was dedicated to Re, the sun god, or that it was oriented so that dawn's first rays would shaft through to the holy sanctuary and bring alive whatever figures might inhabit it. But so it proved; extending as it did 105 feet into the stygian darkness to illuminate not one god but the four patron deities of Egypt's principal cities: Amon-Rë of Thebes, Rë-Harakhti of Heliopolis, and Ptah of Memphis, and the fourth the divinization of Pharaoh Ramesses himself.[4] Unable to read the writing on the walls, Belzoni had to be content to measure and describe—which he did with commendable accuracy considering that once the sun moved, the temple's interior returned to the darkness of night.[5] If his own drawing of the interior is to be believed, he illuminated it with burning torches whose smoke would have added to the claustrophobic atmosphere as he took his measurements and made his sketches. However, we know from Irby's account that the explorers carried only candles rather than the flambeaux shown in Belzoni's picture. An obvious explanation may be that he added his figure later and substituted the burning torch to justify a picture that could not be so brightly lit with candles. Evidence that the drawing does record the first entry is provided by the presence of freestanding sculptures which both Giovanni and Irby reported hauling away to their boat.

Although Belzoni had the satisfaction of having succeeded in opening one of Ancient Egypt's largest temples and having been the first expedition leader to set foot in its interior, the shortage of portable loot was a disappointment. According to Irby, they "brought down to the boat some statues of calcareous stone" that included two sphinxes with lions' bodies and hawks' heads, a monkey, and a kneeling female figure with an altar having a ram's head on it.[6] The drawing shows another figure broken and lying on its back in the middle of the hall. However, nobody recalled asking what had become of the rest of it or why any of the sculptures were where they were found. One might have expected that moving the statuary would have prompted some discussion about the condition of the floor and whether it retained footprints of the last to leave.[7] But only Finati thought to record that it "was covered over with a very black and fine dust, which, observing its resemblance to the remains of decayed lintels in most of the doorways, was conjectured to be pulverized wood."[8]

Regardless of its date, Belzoni's drawing of the entry hall is certainly dramatic and captures the grandeur of the columns, but when colored it lost the sense of revelation that all who enter the temple must experience. The effect is not helped by Giovanni having drawn the king's loincloths as

Etched by A. Aglio, after a Drawing by G. Belzoni.

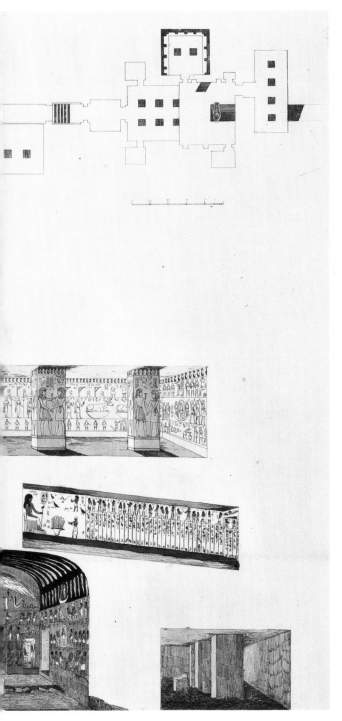

Belzoni's sectional view of the interior of Seti I's tomb showing the sarcophagus still in situ in the vaulted burial chamber.

pairs of blue bloomers more suited to Victorian ladies of modest means (see p. 128). He admitted that his renderings left something to be desired, writing that "the heat was so great in the interior of the temple that it scarcely permitted us to take any drawings, as the perspiration from our hands soon rendered the paper quite wet. Accordingly," he added, "we left this operation to succeeding travellers" who would visit after the interior had had time to cool down.[9] Beechey's drawings fared no better. While attempting to sketch in the sanctuary, he "spoiled his drawing book . . . the perspiration having entirely soaked through it."[10]

Just as Napoleon's army had left its calling card at Philae so, in 654 BC, Greek mercenaries had ensured that they would be remembered at Abu Simbel. Carved into the left leg of the doorway-flanking colossus an inscription began: "When King Psammeticus came to Elephantine, the companions of Psammeticus, son of Theokles wrote this."[11] But even then the temple was nearly six hundred years old and probably as empty as Belzoni found it.

Their job done, on August 4, 1817, the Abu Simbel team began its return voyage, but was halted at a west-bank village when Daoud Cacheff sent word that he wished to come aboard. Having done so, he invited Belzoni and the captains ashore to enjoy his hospitality. Not knowing what to expect, they went with some hesitation. The possibility of being knifed or poisoned on behalf of Drovetti on the one hand, or paving the way for better relations if, and when, Giovanni returned on the other, had to be carefully weighed. But Belzoni, ever the optimist, chose the latter. Nevertheless, he reminded Daoud that he had not been well treated by the Abu Simbel villagers, and that in the final days of digging the fellahs had been barred from providing any food. Daoud Cacheff quickly answered that he knew nothing about it. However, on recognizing a man standing beside him as one of the Abu Simbel irritants, Belzoni wisely chose not to press the matter. Consequently, the meeting remained politely cordial, and at its end Daoud's wife gave Belzoni a gift for Sarah of a goat, two small baskets, and a palm-leaf carpet. Giovanni, in return, gave her two pairs of Turkish boots and a couple of small mirrors.[12] If he thought that this was the successful conclusion of his jousting with the cacheffs of Abu Simbel, he was forgetting the fraternal jealousy of brother Khalil.

Word carried on the Nile as swiftly as its waters flowed, and by the time Belzoni's boat reached the regional capital at Derr, Khalil Cacheff was waiting to offer his congratulations. Giovanni observed that he did his best to "avoid meeting such a sincere friend," but having been sent gifts of aqua vita and a lamb, courtesy took precedence. Once again he risked speaking his mind and complained that he and his people had been forced to exist on boiled dhoura after the villagers refused to sell them any food. Like his brother, Khalil expressed ignorance and regret while knowing all the while that Belzoni knew very well that it was he who had given the villagers' their orders. Like Giovanni, Khalil Cacheff was looking ahead to the Englishmen's next gift-bearing visit, and so bid them a safe journey amid much smiling, bowing, and the sorrow of parting. "It was plain to be seen," wrote Belzoni, "that it was all forced politeness."[13] Nevertheless, feigned politeness was better than none, and the returning expedition continued downriver without incident save for a brief skirmish at the Nubian temple of El Kalabsha. There, the locals demanded baksheesh before allowing Belzoni to land.[14] Finati threatened them with his gun—which they resented, and they in turn, seized it from him. Retrieving it led to a chase and what Belzoni called a scuffle, prompting his decision to forego the visit to El Kalabsha.[15]

On or about August 11, the boat reached the island of Philae. Sarah had been left on the sweltering roof of its temple for fifty-six frustrating days, but neither she nor her husband wrote anything about their reunion—perhaps because the words that passed between them were best left unrecorded. In retrospect, however, she did say this: "I was informed by some one who was there, that the boatmen, as well as the servants of Mr. Salt [Yanni and Finati], who accompanied Mr. Beechey, had as much merit in assisting in the concern as the other gentlemen, but they were not English. Had I been there, I should have helped to remove the sand as well as them, as far as my strength would have allowed me on such occasion, and claimed as much merit."

Although bitterly disappointed, Sarah was fiercely supportive of Giovanni's achievement, and became enraged when he was denied the credit. "Truth must be sacrificed by some travellers, because they are absolutely afraid of speaking, for fear of gaining the ill will of some of their colleagues. Such," she added, "is liberality and love of truth at the present day."[16] When, eventually, they returned to England she still hoped that one day she could go back to enter the temple at Abu Simbel. Although she would never do so, that deep-felt desire had a remarkable afterlife.

By the 1860s, Egypt had become a haven for consumptives, one of whom was Lady Lucie Duff Gordon, who was living alone in a mud-brick

Above: *Graffiti in the El Kab tomb of Pahari, a palace official of the Twenty-eighth Dynasty. In the center are the names of Captains Mangles and Irby and the date "Aug: 15 1817." Here and elsewhere they enclosed their names within a box. Perhaps showing a reluctance to deface a face, they omitted the lower-right corner. Below: More graffiti at El Kab in the tomb of Pahari. This and adjacent tombs possess murals of great cultural interest but have been subjected to more vandalism than those in the Theban necropolis. Belzoni's name is in the center with the date 1817. He was preceded by a someone in 1804 whose name is now defaced.*

house at Luxor. One of her friends was an ancient Arab named Ismain whom she knew as "great-grandfather," and who had been a guide for Belzoni. She called him a splendid old man "who always thought I was Mme. Belzoni and wanted to take me up to Abu Simbel to meet my husband."[17] Ismain died on January 14, 1867, three years before Sarah's own death.

Belzoni's only recorded comment regarding his wife's forced isolation at Philae was terse and project-focused: "Mrs. Belzoni went to Aswan by land, and we resolved to pass the cataract in the boat in which we came." Although the boat had been rented at Aswan for the southward journey and should have been returned to the aga, keeping it made sense now that the heavy sculptures were on board and the river in sufficient flood to make the cataract navigable. Not wishing to see his boat smashed to pieces, the aga naturally demurred, and Belzoni, just as naturally, made light of it. "The barbarians made objections and took some advantage," he recalled, "but they will do any thing for money."[18]

Once again Belzoni had guessed correctly. The boat made it through the rapids with barely a scratch and carried the Abu Simbel expedition safely back to Luxor. Sarah returned to her rented apartment on the roof of the Luxor temple, while Belzoni and Beechey again took up residence in their temple chamber. The gallant captains returned to Cairo, pausing on their way to visit the tombs of El Kab and to carve their names and the date "Aug: 15, 1817" on a still fairly pristine fresco.[19] They invariably carved a box around their names to ensure that posterity would know that they were together. In this instance, however, one suspects that vandalism had its limits, the box being incomplete due, it would seem, to the captains' reluctance to deface a face. Belzoni, too, left his calling card, though he was not the first to do so. A largely obliterated someone was there in 1804.

Meanwhile, at Luxor, Beechey busied himself drawing whatever inspired him. Belzoni had intended to go back to Gournou to continue searching for mummies until he found that two of Drovetti's deputies were already there. They were not "of the same cast [*sic*]" as the indigenous Copts who had preceded them, he noted, and evidently were less easily hoodwinked or challenged. Both were Piedmontese, one a *renegado* from Napoleon's army and the other a refugee from the Piedmont when its government was overthrown. They had been relatively successful in their digging, and Belzoni elected to leave them to it. Instead, he moved his operation to the valley known to the Arabs as Biban el-Maluk, to tourists as the Valley of Kings, and to Egyptologists as the Royal Necropolis of Thebes. Here were interred the bodies of kings of the Eighteenth to Twentieth Dynasties (ca. 1567–1085 BC). The historian Strabo knew of forty tombs that had already been robbed, and today the number stands at sixty-two, one of the most spectacular having been destined to bear the name of Giovanni Belzoni.

Before beginning work, Belzoni returned to his old friend the cacheff of Erment, only to find that he had fallen foul of the Deftardár Bey and had been ousted. In consequence, authority had shifted to the east bank at the village of Ghoust, where the cacheff was sufficiently impressed by the Pasha's *firman* to release a handful of fellahs, who began digging on October 6. Three days later, they had exposed the first new tomb which, disappointingly, had never been finished or occupied. Another proved more productive—once he got past "a well built wall of stones of various sizes." To breach it, Belzoni used a pole and another length of palm tree to construct a battering ram, which he used to pound the wall until it collapsed. Like later excavators who used explosives to advance their efforts, Giovanni has been condemned as the man who opened tombs with a battering ram. In truth, however, his approach did no harm and was no more reprehensible than modern archaeologists using heavy equipment to remove barren soil. In 1817, there were no archaeological purists looking over his shoulder. All that mattered was finding something exciting. How he got there was unimportant.

Here was a tomb that had not been opened by Arab robbers and held promise of riches beyond price. A staircase led down to a corridor at the entrance to which lay four mummies in painted wooden coffins. Farther down the corridor lay four more, each set in a recess four inches into the floor. The walls were well painted but unfinished and marked in the red ochre used by the stonemasons to plan further work. Labeled today as tomb No. 25, the identities of the eight occupants are unknown, but their presence is thought to have been a reuse of a repository originally intended for someone more exalted. Although Belzoni took the mummies apart while searching for objets d'art, he undoubtedly kept the painted coffins; what became of them, however, is anyone's guess. As for the untold riches, there were none.

On the morning of October 11, 1817, Belzoni again found himself burdened with the kind of chore that is the bane and lot of every archaeologist. He had to serve as tour guide for three gentlemen wished on him by Henry Salt, who was still in Cairo. He had taken the VIPs around and through the usual places when he received word that a new tomb discovered by his workmen on the previous day was now open for inspection. Decades later it would be identified as that of Ramesses I of the Nineteenth Dynasty (ca. 1320–1318 BC); but as so often happened, the king was gone—removed by priests who had shifted him to a site safe from robbers. In his stead, his granite sarcophagus contained two unidentified mummies. Although forty redeposited royal mummies would be found together in 1881, Ramesses I was not among them. Nevertheless, there remained enough artifacts in the tomb to impress the visitors. In a corner of the burial chamber was standing a figure more than six feet tall and carved from sycamore wood brought from Lebanon. In a side chamber, Belzoni found another just like it, though not as well preserved. These are thought to be the king's spiritual doubles *(ka)* and usually were identified by a pair of upraised arms attached to the figure's head.[20] More portable were "a number of little images of wood, well carved, representing symbolical figures."[21]

The next day Belzoni took his three visitors to visit a mummy pit that he had excavated six months earlier. In his *Narrative,* he describes its wall decoration as including two harpists, one of whose instruments had nine strings, the other fourteen.[22] One might think it remarkable that Belzoni, having visited Bruce's tomb, omitted to mention its harp players, which, in spite of Montulé's description of the tomb's deteriorated condition, were still well enough preserved to be drawn by the Egyptologist John Gardner Wilkinson at some time in the 1820s.[23] In truth, Belzoni said very little about the tomb that contained one of the two finest sarcophagi that he, or anyone else, ever purloined and shipped to Europe.

On October 16, with the English tourists out of the way, Belzoni returned to his excavations. He called it a fortunate day, "one of the best perhaps of my life," quickly adding, "I do not mean to say that fortune has made me rich, for I do not consider all rich men fortunate; but she has given me that satisfaction, that extreme pleasure, which wealth cannot purchase; the pleasure of discovering, what has long been sought in vain, and of presenting the world with a new and perfect monument of Egyptian antiquity."[24]

The Valley of Kings is surely one of the earth's most inhospitable places—as perhaps millions of tourists have since discovered. It can be foot-scorchingly hot, can be swept by wind-blown dust, and lacks so much as a single tree or shrub to contrast with the endless screes and piles of rocks, few of them left unturned by generations of disappointed looters. Nevertheless, it was there, not fifteen yards from his previous "discovery," that Belzoni was to reveal the rock-filled entrance that was to ensure his immortality.

The site had previously been ignored because it lay in the path of rainwater that occasionally flooded down from the mountain behind it. Local wisdom had it that no tomb builder would choose so vulnerable a location. But Belzoni thought otherwise. The opening lay eighteen feet below the surface and led to a thirty-two-foot-long, elaborately decorated corridor, beyond which was a flight of stairs.[25] At its bottom, Belzoni found a doorway that opened into another corridor more than thirty-seven feet long whose decoration was even more spectacular than the first (see p. 132). Lit only by his burning torch, the life-sized figures of the Egyptian gods seemed to crowd around, while the spread-winged god Horus with its falcon's head swooped down on him from the painted blackness of the ceiling. Was it possible, Giovanni asked himself, that a few feet farther might bring him to the pharaoh's gold? Not today. Ahead lay a trap designed to prevent intruders from finding out. A pit thirteen feet wide and thirty deep served not only to discourage visitors but to catch rainwater running down from the mountain. A piece of rope left by the last to leave hung down the near side but crumbled to dust when Belzoni touched it. Another with a piece of wood attached dangled from the far side, presumably left by an ancient but unauthorized visitor. Beyond the pit, Giovanni's torch revealed a two-foot hole in a plastered wall. But the gulf had yet to be bridged, so whatever might lie behind would keep its secrets for one more day.

11 } ENDURING ACHIEVEMENTS

THE HOLE IN THE WALL could have only one interpretation: Somebody had been there first. But it had been sufficiently long ago for the dangling rope to have rotted away. Also on the plus side was the small size of the hole. Nothing big could have been hauled through it. These were all factors Belzoni had in mind as he retreated up the steps and out into the sunlight. Tomorrow he would find wood to straddle the pit and gather the tools needed to enlarge the hole in the wall. Had he lived a hundred years later (specifically until 1922), he would have known that the hole through his tomb's blocking wall would be paralleled by another of almost the same size that allowed robbers access into the tomb of the relatively unimportant boy king Tutankhamen—but from whom they stole virtually nothing.

By that yardstick, once across the pit and through the opening, Belzoni could expect to find wealth beyond his imagining—thrones sheathed in gold and decorated with lapis lazuli, rubies and emeralds, beds and couches adorned with lion and cow heads in gold, dismantled chariots, boxes and chests filled with gems and bead-encrusted fabrics, alabaster jars of many sizes, model boats to sail the king into the afterlife, games to amuse him, and figures both life-sized and in miniature to attend him, and everywhere the glint of sheet gold. Salt would be ecstatic, Lord Mountnorris would be overjoyed, and the British Museum and the Society of Antiquaries would receive Giovanni as the hero who trumped the French. The public acclaim might even prompt Prime Minister Castlereagh to propose a knighthood. The prospects were golden.

Meanwhile, in Cairo, unaware of the news about to break in Thebes, Consul-General Salt was preparing to accompany a group of distinguished tourists upriver to Luxor. Distributed through three large boats, they were the Irish peer Somerset Lowry-Corry, second Earl of Belmore, his wife, children, assorted relatives, several servants, his chaplain, and his physician. Salt had no doubt that Giovanni would have unearthed more relics to amaze the Belmores and enhance his own reputation.

After constructing a crude bridge sufficient to carry his weight, Giovanni squeezed through the robbers' hole and held his torch aloft, revealing another highly decorated passage which continued into the darkness beyond his smoking light. No glint of gold shone back at him, but it would make sense that the treasures would be stashed in the immediate vicinity of the mummy. But one passage and one chamber after another contained nothing but an echo. Nevertheless, the new tomb proved to be even more spectacularly decorated than its entry passages suggested. Extending 330 feet into the mountain, one corridor or set of stairs led to another painted chamber until the king's burial place was reached. In it stood his sarcophagus, which Belzoni described as "not having its equal in the world." Nine feet long and 3'7" wide, he determined it to have been made from "the finest oriental alabaster" carved inside and out with several hundred figures associated with the king's funeral rites and procession. When lit from inside, the sarcophagus became glowingly transparent. Belzoni admitted that he lacked the words to create "an adequate idea of this beautiful and valuable piece of antiquity." Unfortunately, however, it, too, was empty.

Although life-sized figures of the dead man adorned the chamber and corridor walls along with cartouches bearing his name, Belzoni had no way of knowing who he was. But even as Belzoni was opening his tomb, Jean François Champollion was successfully working to relate the Rosetta Stone's demotic signs to Coptic and thence to the hieroglyphic. Simultaneously, an English physician, Thomas Young, had been intrigued by a papyrus bought in Luxor in 1814 by the traveler Sir William Boughton and tried to interpret its hieroglyphics by means of the Rosetta Stone's texts. Young was among the first to guess that the cartouches enclosed royal names, and correctly identified those of Tuthmosis and Ptolemy.[1] In 1818, however, neither Young nor Champollion had deciphered the name Seti.

Seti I—father of Ramesses II, the most flamboyant of all the New Kingdom monarchs—had a fourteen-year reign from 1318 to 1304 BC.[2] A military officer before becoming king, Seti had a reign marked by successful warfare against the Hittites in Syria and the first Battle of Kadesh. His temple at Abydos dedicated to the god Osiris, Lord of the Underworld, is one of the best preserved of the great Egyptian monuments, and his history is spelled out on its walls in low relief. More importantly, Seti's interest in his country's history prompted the inclusion of the cartouches for seventy-six of his predecessors. It is surprising, therefore, that he was entombed in the Theban Valley of Kings rather than at Abydos, where the great god Osiris was believed to have been buried. A smaller building behind Seti's temple was long thought to be its location, but when excavated proved to be an unfinished cenotaph for Seti himself. None of this was known to Belzoni, who was struggling to figure out how and when someone had hauled the king out of his coffin and pushed him through the two-foot hole in the wall. And what had happened to all the chests, beds, chariots, canopies, and thrones that had been with him? If the robbers had stripped the gold and jewels from them while rifling the tomb, where were all the broken pieces that were not worth taking?

Thanks to Champollion, Seti's name was deciphered long before the mystery of his removal was solved. The first clue was unearthed in the 1850s. A papyrus dating from ca. 1126 BC recorded the confession of a tomb robber brought before the mayor of Eastern Thebes: "We opened their coffins and the cloth in which they were wrapped and found the

One of the most historically important walls surviving from Ancient Egypt. In a small sanctuary at the rear of the temple of Horus at Abydos are the cartouches of seventy-six of Seti I's predecessors. This enormous and delicately executed chronology is known to Egyptologists worldwide as the Abydos King List.

Belzoni's rendering of a panel in the tomb of Seti I showing the king being presented by the falcon-headed Horus to Osiris, god of the underworld, and to Hathor, mother and queen of the gods.

noble mummy of the king, equipped like a warrior. There were many sacred eye amulets and ornaments of gold at his neck, and a mask of gold upon him." The unidentified thief also admitted that he and his cohorts went on to rob his queen: "The Royal Wife [was] similarly adorned and we took all that we found on her, too. We set fire to the wrappings."[3] In the succeeding years, more robbers were brought to trial, but the looting went on. To save their charges from desecration, priests took to moving the royal mummies from one tomb to another, though leaving behind the nonessential tomb furniture. It seemed likely, therefore, that Seti had either been saved by the priests or burned by the robbers.

The information to solve the mystery proved to be a secret held by the Gournou family of Abd-el-Rasoul[4] who, in 1871, found another tomb north of Deir el-Bahari. For ten years they had made their living selling relics from royal mummies to wealthy visitors—as well as to a British consular agent in Luxor who eventually secured a monopoly of the loot. The trade became so obvious that in April 1881, the Abd-el-Rasoul brothers, Ahmed and Mohammed, were arrested and tortured to make them reveal the source of the treasures. Although their inducements included beatings and a hot iron pot placed on their heads, they remained silent and were released. Shortly afterward, however, the brothers fell out, and in July, Mohammed agreed to confess. The German archaeologist Emil Brugsch, working for the Antiquities Organization in Cairo, was sent to Gournou to inspect the site. It turned out to be the Eighteenth Dynasty tomb of Queen Inhapy into which had been stacked the coffins and mummies of thirty-two kings, among them that of Seti I, who was not in particularly good condition, his head having been broken off and reattached in the process of rewrapping by the priests.[5]

Belzoni found the broken lid of Seti's sarcophagus "before the first entrance," making it difficult to reconstruct the sequence that led to the king's removal. Who broke the lid and what was the point of removing the fragments? Had the priests been the first rescuers into the tomb, they surely would have carefully removed the lid and left it where it lay. If the robbers got there first, perhaps they robbed the body of its gold and left it in its coffin for the priests to find. Then again, who made the hole through the wall that sealed the passage beyond the protective pit? If it was the priests who broke in, why not make the hole much larger, the future survival of the tomb being unimportant?

Regardless of these yet-to-be-answered questions, the reality was that

Belzoni found no treasure of the caliber that the world associates with Tutankhamen. However, in one chamber Giovanni did find a mummified bull and numerous small wooden figures wrapped in linen and coated with resin. Elsewhere, he came upon "figures of fine earth baked, coloured blue, and strongly varnished." In small rooms flanking the burial chamber were "some wooden statues standing erect, four feet high, with a circular hole inside, as if to contain a roll of papyrus which no doubt they did." So who took them? In the Twentieth Dynasty, when the robbery is assumed to have taken place, papyri had no market value, and none accompanied Seti when he was found in the crowded tomb at Deir el-Bahari. Whatever the explanation, Belzoni's portable pickings were meager. Nevertheless, Seti's tomb did contain one more surprise. His empty and lidless sarcophagus lay in a rock-filled recess in the floor, and when it and the rocks were removed, the opening led to a flight of steps leading down to a wall that sealed the entrance to a small tunnel. With the wall breached, Belzoni followed the passage three hundred feet into the mountain until he found it choked with vast quantities of bat dung. He could go no farther without digging through it, a task he declined—due in part to the instability of the roof. As this tunnel could not have been accessed after the wall was built and the sarcophagus deposited, one might argue that it had to exit somewhere in the mountain where it had remained open long enough for the bats to come and go. But why?

One possible explanation has been that the enormous quantity of rock that had to be removed to create the tomb was dragged through the tunnel and dumped where it would not draw attention to the king's burial place.[6] However, the Egyptologist Dr. Stuart Tyson Smith has pointed out that, by the Nineteenth Dynasty, burials were no longer carried out in secrecy.[7] A later report stated that the shaft had been explored for another two hundred feet and that "gates appear to have been placed at intervals down the length of the tunnel."[8] Belzoni mentioned no gates, but recent exploration directed by Dr. Zahi Hawass found such a doorway, and written beside it in hieratic script was the message, "Move the door jamb and make the passage wider." The clearance eventually reached a flight of fifty-two descending steps at the bottom of which the tunnel abruptly ended.[9] Dr. Hawass had believed that it would lead him to a secret chamber— a hidden tomb within the tomb. Dr. Tyson Smith disagreed and conjectured that the tunnel was a corridor leading to a chamber at the level of the valley's groundwater and the cave of the god Sokar through whose

Alessandro Ricci's drawing of a corridor ceiling panel in the tomb of Seti I. The spread-winged vulture holds signs for truth and eternity. Below are left- and right-facing cartouches of Seti and Osiris.

domain the dead king would enter the afterlife. That statement gets us much deeper into ancient Egyptian religion than most readers will want to delve. Suffice it to say that Sokar was a god of the underworld through whose domain the risen god Osiris had to travel on his celestial boat, rowed on the primordial waters of Nun, one of the gods of the Creation. Nun was also responsible for having brought order to the chaos that preceded it. What matters here, however, is Nun's association with water and Seti's need to follow Osiris through it.

Alessandro Ricci's drawing of a panel in the tomb of Seti I. In the center are the dual cartouches of the king flanked by the goddess Maat, deity of morality and justice. The unfinished upper panel is flanked by the royal cartouches.

At Seti's Abydos temple a groundwater-filled chamber and tunnel complex represented the ceremonial burial place of Osiris. As this Osirian ceremony was practiced in the Abydos temple while Seti lived, it is reasonable to deduce that it was also to be performed at his death, albeit at a water level far below that at Abydos.

Unfortunately, none of this explains Belzoni's bats. The presumption had been that they entered through the tunnel's exit, but if it had no exit, how did they get in? Dr. Hawass reported no such bat-dung barrier, nor did his predecessor, Sheik Ali Abd-el-Rasoul of Gourno, who in

1960 obtained a *firman* from the Egyptian Antiquities Service to solve the mystery.[10] If Ali's name sounds familiar, it should be. He was an offspring of the Abd-el-Rasoul family who, in 1881, had found the Deir el-Bahari cache of kings and handsomely profited from it. Ali believed that Belzoni's empty sarcophagus was only a ploy to confuse robbers, and that the real burial place lay at the end of the tunnel. He and forty of his relatives excavated it for another 150 feet until lack of money forced them to quit. Nevertheless, Ali's theory had some substance, at least to the extent that Belzoni had found the tomb bereft of burial treasures—which might have been carried down the tunnel with the king. Like the tunnel itself, that likelihood was small, descending as it did at an angle of up to 47°.

Even if true, Ali's explanation failed to include Belzoni's bats. As the pit under the sarcophagus was filled with rocks and the tunnel entrance sealed, that approach was undeniably bat-proof. Much as one would like to take Giovanni at his word, it is hard to ignore the possibility that there were no bats and that he invented that unpleasant accumulation to tell his readers why he quit digging. He had found the sarcophagus, and that was payoff enough.

Ever since Belzoni found the hole in the entrance wall, it has been assumed that the tomb had been looted. But the clearance was too clean and the hole too small. I suggest that priests who removed Seti intended to place him in another tomb and so took all the ritually associated objects with him. They would also have taken the sarcophagus if someone had not dropped the lid on its way out, but with the lid broken, the casket was abandoned. Such a theory also explains the salvaging of the ritual-related papyri from the wooden figures.

Once the news got out that the big Englishman had found a new tomb, rumors abounded, not the least of them being that it was not Belzoni who found the tomb but one of the Gournou fellahs who sold him the information. There was no more truth in that rumor than that the real burial place was not in the sarcophagus but at the other end of the tunnel beneath it. Most attractive of all the rumors, however, was that a vast treasure had been discovered in the tomb. It was one that prompted one of Belzoni's Arab laborers to claim that he had seen a column of Turkish horsemen heading into the valley. This one turned out to be true. Hamad, the aga of Kena[11] and ruler of the eastern half of Thebes, had heard the rumors and was coming to inspect the treasures. He stopped short of the tomb's entrance and fired several guns, which made Belzoni think he was

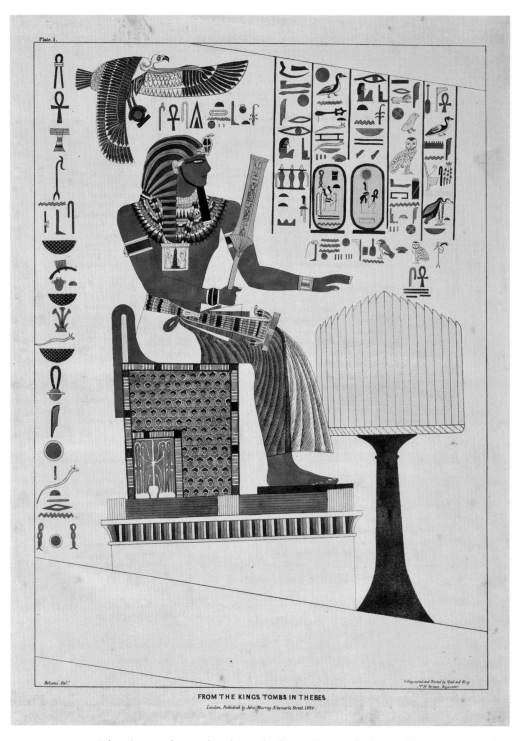

FROM THE KINGS TOMBS IN THEBES

London. Published by John Murray Albemarle Street. 1820.

Belzoni's copy of a panel in the tomb of Seti I showing the king holding a scepter and seated in front of an offering table piled with bread.

under attack. Hamad had no jurisdiction over the western half of Thebes, but Giovanni ruefully supposed that "in the case of treasure being discovered, the first that hears of it seizes it as a matter of privilege."[12] Reluctantly, he led the aga into the tomb followed by his Turkish retinue, none of whom showed the slightest interest in the murals; instead "his numerous followers were like hounds, searching in every hole and corner."

"Where," demanded Hamad, "have you put the treasure?"

"What treasure?"

"The treasure you found in this place."

"There is no treasure."

The aga laughed. "I have been told by a person to whom I can give great credit that you have found in this place a large golden cock filled with diamonds and pearls. I must see it," he insisted. "Where is it?"

Eventually, Hamad realized that if there was a treasure, it certainly was no longer in the tomb. On his way out, Belzoni asked him what he thought of the wonderfully painted figures that he could see on the walls all around him. Affording them barely a glance, he replied, "This would be a good place for a harem, as the women would have something to look at." With that, the disgruntled aga and his soldiers mounted their horses and galloped away.

Several days later, Lord Belmore's boats reached Kena, and it was there that Henry Salt learned of the great discovery. Consequently, when the Belmore boats reached Luxor and decanted their tourist load, Belzoni's tomb headed their list of things to see. They were all suitably impressed by the extent of the murals and dazzled by their state of preservation, prompting Salt to write to Lord Mountnorris on January 18, 1818: "I have the pleasure to announce to you that, under my auspices, a brilliant discovery has been made of a new king's tomb, exquisitely painted, and with the colours as fresh as on the day it was completed; it throws everything else," he added, "as far as colour goes, completely into the background"—which was where Salt left Belzoni. In the same letter, Salt revealed that "In the new tomb I have found a sarcophagus of white alabaster, covered with hieroglyphics: the sarcophagus itself entire, and enough of the cover to make out its shape."[13] He would not, he said, rest easy, until he had it safe in Cairo, another project that required the skills of the still uncredited Giovanni Belzoni. In another letter written from the "Kings' Tombs" to an unidentified Mr. B, Salt again claimed to have been the discoverer, noting that "I have completed six drawings already, *coloured* in the tomb by candlelight."[14]

In the same self-serving letter to Lord Mountnorris, Salt wrote that he had assembled a collection of statuary, "thirty papyrus and an innumerable list of smaller things," adding, "I shall be able to spare you many fine articles, and the rest I think, if the idea is approved, of offering to the British Museum." That could be read as a proposed gift were it not that he added, "all I wish is, to be reimbursed for my expenses," explaining that the funds he had inherited from his father's death were now running low.[15] Belzoni was also feeling the piastre pinch. "My purse was now pretty well exhausted," he wrote. The money he had received from Salt and Burckhardt as a reward for shipping Young Memnon was gone. Worse was the news brought by the Belmore boats. On October 15, 1817, two days before the flotilla left Boulak, Sheik Ibrahim (John Lewis Burckhardt) had died in Cairo after a ten-day struggle with dysentery. Salt wrote, "It has been a great shock to me, for he was almost the only *conversable* friend I had in Cairo."[16] For Belzoni, the loss was infinitely greater. Burckhardt had not only been his teacher but also an ally who saw him as an equal and not as an employee to be exploited.

Lord Belmore became so enthused over all that had already been found that he resolved to top it with new discoveries of his own and prevailed on Belzoni to show him likely spots in which to start digging. Salt, who had no experience of tomb hunting, had to stand aside while Belzoni became his lordship's man of the hour. Perhaps irritated by being upstaged, Salt did his best to behave as His Britannic Majesty's host and in doing so allowed his ego to balloon. He described Belzoni as his employee and made free use of the personal pronoun. Listening to all this, grieving over the loss of Burckhardt, and being constantly conscious of his desire to succeed, Giovanni developed a bitterness toward Henry Salt that soon burst into an open confrontation.

A few days after the Belmores had continued on their way to the cataracts, and while Salt was giving instructions on extracting the sarcophagus and shipping it to Cairo, Belzoni exploded. He was not, he said, Henry Salt's hired hand, not now and never had been! Nor was he in the business for personal gain. His sole intent was to enrich the collections of the British Museum. "I positively deny," Giovanni later declared, that he was ever employed by Salt in any shape whatever.[17]

Years later, when John Halls was working on Salt's biography, a letter from Henry Beechey put the encounter in a very different light. "Belzoni (poor fellow! he had many good points about him,) was often in the habit

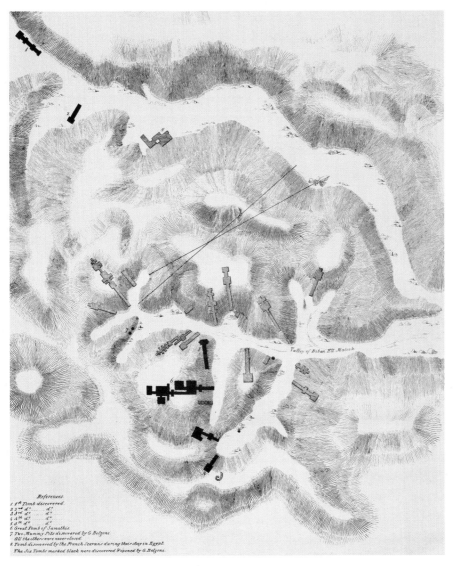

Belzoni's map of the Valley of Kings showing the known tombs and highlighting those that he opened.

of using very violent language, and *frequently* declared that he was not employed by Mr. Salt, though it would have puzzled him very much to prove the assertion. . . . There never was a man better treated, *in every respect*, by another than Belzoni was by our poor friend [Salt], though he never would allow it. . . . In fact he was, on some points, more than half mad, and this was certainly one of them."[18] Numerous instances are on record that Salt was generous in his praise and allowed that it was indeed

Belzoni who found the tomb and its sarcophagus. Furthermore, Salt had volunteered to pay him an allowance of a thousand piastres a month—which happened to be twice the salary earned by Mohammed Ali's physicians. But at that moment in 1817, Belzoni was suffering from what modern medics might call clinical depression. Consequently, what passed between these two men were "repeated and very unpleasant altercations . . . in which he [Belzoni] unfolded pretensions to which I [Salt] told him I could never accede."[19] Shortly thereafter, Belzoni set sail for Cairo carrying a boatload of antiquities most of which he agreed belonged to Salt. While there, he was to assemble the necessary equipment to bring out the sarcophagus. In addition, however, he said he had personal business to transact in Cairo, but neglected to say what it was.

Even before the Belmore party's arrival, Belzoni had in mind to construct a life-sized reproduction of his tomb that could be exhibited in London. After his spat with Salt, he was even more determined to do so. To that end, therefore, he was anxious not to linger unduly in Cairo. He would return as quickly to Thebes as the Nile would permit and, once there, set to work to make wax casts of all his tomb's figures and draw all its hieroglyphs. But Belzoni's mercurial disposition, coupled with his antagonism toward anyone who denied him his due, could turn firmly laid plans to mud overnight.

The treasure boat reached Boulak on December 23, where Belzoni supervised the unloading of the antiquities into the consulate and then took up residence there himself. Sarah had returned with her husband, but unfortunately she has left no record of her feelings regarding the grand reproduction plan or his growing animosity toward the consul. We know only that she planned to leave Giovanni to his waxworks and make a pilgrimage to the Holy Land, taking James Curtin with her. When Belzoni finished his copying, he would join her in Jerusalem.[20]

The unloading of Belzoni's boat at Boulak had drawn the attention of another newly arrived person of prominence, namely Louis Nicolas Philippe Auguste Le Compte de Forbin, director-general of French museums, who was making his first visit to Egypt on behalf of the Louvre. Belzoni did not like him and called him "the celebrated and veracious Count de Forbin."[21] Nevertheless, when the count called at the consulate asking to view the newly found treasures, Giovanni was obliged to let him do so. Among the sculptures Belzoni had brought from Thebes were some that he had kept for himself and intended to send as gifts to his hometown of

Padua. Although not actually identified as such, these were almost certainly Sekhmet figures from Karnak. Forbin offered to buy them. Belzoni knew that there were plenty more where those came from and so "consented to gratify him," adding, "What he paid me for them was not one fourth of their value; but I was fully satisfied, as I never was a dealer in statues in my life."[22] While in principle that might have been so, in practice everybody expected to get paid, and Belzoni was no exception.

The deal done, Forbin set out for Thebes, and Belzoni received another visitor to the consulate. He was a Major Moore, who was pausing in Cairo while carrying dispatches from India to London. To entertain him, Belzoni took the major to the top of the Great Pyramid and while there discussed the enigma of the neighboring second pyramid. "What a pity it was," he said, "that in an intelligent age like the present, it had not been opened, so that the interior remained quite unknown."[23] Others thought so too. Several Franks living in Cairo had proposed launching a subscription to raise £20,000 to fund blasting into the pyramid with gunpowder, a project to be supervised by none other than Bernardino Drovetti. As so often in planning archaeological projects, the will was way ahead of the wherewithal, leaving the big-bang solution on the drawing board. To Belzoni, therefore, the opportunity to upstage Drovetti and the French was mouthwateringly attractive, and a coup that left Henry Salt in the dark would be even more satisfying. But Giovanni needed a permit, and he doubted that the Pasha would give it to someone of such low station as himself. But there was no harm in looking into it—which he did. He was aware that many classically educated scholars had done so before him, but, he reasoned, "a man who thinks himself well-informed on a subject, often does not examine it with such precision as another, who is less confident in himself."[24]

Over time much of the pyramid's upper limestone casing had crumbled and fallen away, creating a skirt of rubble in places fifty feet high. Based on the relative heights of the entrances to the Great Pyramid, the debris extended well above the expected doorway. In Belzoni's theory, therefore, removing the rubble should expose the entrance—providing he knew on which side to look. The pyramid measured 707 feet square at its base, and the entrance could be as little as four feet wide. Over the millennia, nocturnal dew that forms in the spring and summer had cemented the fallen casing together; on one side, however, the debris was less compacted, suggesting that it had been disturbed. But no matter how good

Belzoni's guess might be, the necessity of a permit persisted. Although, in 1818, tourists trekking to the pyramids were few by modern standards, rarely did a Nile traveler neglect to visit them. Consequently, the sight of a large person shifting rocks could not long go unnoticed. A *firman* he had to have.

The ever-resourceful Belzoni settled on a lateral approach; rather than applying to the Pasha in Cairo, he made his request to the cacheff in whose jurisdiction the pyramids of Giza lay. As expected, the cacheff told him that he would be happy to allow digging, but first an authorizing *firman* had to be obtained. Belzoni then took that stipulation to the Citadel, where (as he probably already knew) Mohammed Ali was out of town. His deputy *(kikhyà),* therefore, provided the permit, and Giovanni was free to start digging. Remembering his previous waterwheel disaster, he feared that failure would "draw down on [him] the laughter of all the world." But, he reasoned, unless one tries, nothing is ever accomplished. So, with eighty hired fellahs, he began digging on both the north and the east sides of the pyramid.

Sixteen days of fruitless digging left the workers weary and most of their tools broken, until one of them noticed a chink between two of the pyramid's stone blocks. Closer investigation proved that one of the stones was loose and could be removed.

Belzoni, besides digging around the pyramid and pursuing his still-unfinished (and still unspecified) private business, had spent more than a month in Cairo without any expressed urgency to return to Thebes. Henry Salt, meanwhile, continued his unproductive digging in the Valley of Kings while daily looking with increasing irritation for the return of his coffin-shifting employee. The biographer Halls put it like this: "The protracted stay of Mr. Belzoni at Cairo began to occasion him a good deal of surprise. . . . Week after week however elapsed without any direct intelligence being received respecting the cause of his long delay."[25]

But Giovanni was not idle. Having pried out the loose stone and finding a passage choked with small rocks and sand, he spent the next four days shoveling it out. Progress was slow as the passage was narrow and the stones of its roof were in danger of falling once the supporting debris was removed. And they were not pebbles. A large block six feet long and four wide fell onto a kneeling Arab, but fortunately hung up on two other rocks and did no more than bruise his back. The dangers, as Belzoni saw them, were twofold: being crushed by falling rocks or having the passage

Drawing of Belzoni's first entry into Chephren's pyramid at Giza. Though almost certainly based on Belzoni's sketches, the image is autographed by the engraver Antonio Aglio.

cave in behind "and thus bury us alive." He concluded that the passage was the result of forced entry and not the original line of access. That depressing assumption had Giovanni considering abandoning the project, when he heard a shot fired from the top of the Great Pyramid. Tourists had spotted him.

Belzoni fired his own pistol in response and waited for the visitors to clamber down and was surprised when one of them had a name he already knew. He was Monsieur L'Abbé de Forbin, a cousin who had accompanied the "celebrated Count" to Egypt but had ventured no farther than Cairo. With him was a convent father superior, a French vice-consul, and an engineer, all of whom Belzoni invited to crawl through his tunnel—presumably without stressing the potential danger of doing so. But just like the Coptic fathers at Karnak, the experience gave the Abbé "less pleasure than a cup of coffee" he accepted in the shade of Belzoni's tent. The group's departure meant that Giovanni's secret was out, and within hours of the Abbé's return all the Franks in Cairo would know that Chephren's pyramid had been entered, and they would soon be on their way out to see it. And over the next several days they were.

Thus, just when Belzoni thought himself a failure, he was finding that he had become a celebrity and the center of congratulatory attention. But he knew that fame would be short-lived once academics began to belittle his achievement and perhaps even to condemn the damage he had done to the pyramid. On reflection, he had two choices: claiming victory while beating an honorable retreat, or getting back to work to find the real entrance. After giving his crews a day off while he studied the faces of the pyramid and rechecked his calculations based on what he knew of the Great Pyramid, Belzoni knew (or thought he knew) where to focus his diggers' attention. The next day, therefore, the workers returned with renewed zeal, not caring whether they found the entrance but delighted to again be paid by the Frank they privately called a *magnoon*—a madman. But Belzoni was not crazy, and on March 2, 1818, he found three stones that were part of the entrance to a granite-walled passage 4 feet high and 3'6" wide descending into the pyramid at a 25° angle, albeit filled with loose rubble from the roof. A day and a half of digging and hauling brought Giovanni to what appeared to be a dead end, the passage terminating or being blocked by a single, smooth-surfaced granite slab.

Meanwhile, back at Thebes, Henry Salt continued to curse the absent Belzoni, and having tired of fruitlessly shifting rubble in the Valley of Kings, was eager to move to somewhere more productive. However, as long as he stayed he could keep a watchful eye on his tomb and its prize sarcophagus. He figured that placing Arab guards at the entrance would not ensure its safety if someone like Drovetti came along with piastres in his pocket. Salt's solution, therefore, was to have a wooden door constructed to be held in place with iron hinges and intimidating bolts.[26] One assumes that it also had a lock and that Salt kept the key. His aim, he said, was to make the tomb available to travelers and to keep it so as long as he remained His Britannic Majesty's consul-general in Egypt.[27] Unfortunately, Salt was to live only nine more years—not long enough to prevent the hieroglyph-decorated door jambs at the bottom of the last staircase from being carried off, one to the Louvre and the other to the archaeological museum in Florence.

With the tomb secured, Salt and Beechey could turn their attention to sites on both sides of the Nile, marking them like gold-miners' claims and defying collectors of other nationalities to trespass on them. Where the consul and his secretary lived during these weeks of renewed searching is uncertain. Salt's letters give no clue, and Belzoni made no comment. Nevertheless, a tradition persists that Salt had a house built on top of the still largely dirt-filled Luxor temple, a house that would later be occupied by French engineers hired in 1836 to rob the temple of one of its two entrance obelisks. Recalling the Frenchmen rather than the English Henry Salt, the house came to be known as the Maison de France and would later become the home of the diarist Lady Duff Gordon (1864–67). Her editor stated that it was built "about 1815" by Salt and that Belzoni lived there during the Young Memnon project.[28] Neither can be true. Salt did not arrive as consul until March 1816, and would not make his first trip to Thebes until November 1817. It is true, however, that like the Arab villagers of Luxor, Lady Duff Gordon did live in a house atop the temple. She noted that its floor was composed of the temple's roof slabs and that peering between the cracks she could see "seemingly bottomless darkness."[29]

Back at his pyramid, Belzoni was equally in the dark, faced as he was with a tunnel that ended in a blank wall. Further torch-lit inspection showed that there were grooves to the left and right of the granite wall and another beneath it. The stone was akin to a medieval portcullis dropped to seal a gate. With much effort, this one was pushed up into its slot and propped from beneath to allow the search to resume. The passage continued for another twenty-three feet and then ended in a perpendicular shaft which led to another passage, thence to the main chamber. This room was cut from the natural rock but covered with massive slabs that created a gabled ceiling at the heart of the pyramid. As Belzoni entered and held aloft his torch of clustered candles, he expected to see a sarcophagus comparable to the granite monster still in the Great Pyramid; but the tomb appeared to be disappointingly empty. However, at the far end of the 46-foot-long chamber, a recess in the floor contained a large granite sarcophagus 8 feet long and 3'6" wide. The lid had been pushed aside and the interior filled with earth and stones. Why, and by whom remained a mystery that might or might not have been solved had Belzoni not found a charcoal inscription in Arabic on the west wall. A Copt later brought in from Cairo thought it read: "The Master Mohammed Ahmed, lapicide, has opened them; and the Master Othman attended this . . . ; and the King Alij Mohammed at first . . . to the closing up."[30] The names of

Antonio Aglio's finished rendering of Belzoni's entrance into Chephren's burial chamber, a description that does not accord with other accounts of this historic event. The drawing is dated "2nd March, 1818."

Arab kings being even less original than those of English monarchs, Alij Mohammed's reign has not been identified nor, of course, has the date of his entry into Belzoni's (Chephren's) pyramid.

Before Belzoni was through, he had traced a second original entrance lower than the first and found another empty burial chamber, this one much closer to the exterior. Modern Egyptologists have suggested that in the course of construction the location of Chephren's pyramid was shifted perhaps two hundred feet northward, leaving the original burial chamber too close to the exterior. Nevertheless, Belzoni's chamber was the real deal, and no one could deny that his opening of the second of the three acclaimed Wonders of the World was an achievement even greater than finding Seti's tomb. But what pleased Belzoni most was that instead of accomplishing it with a Drovetti-sized budget of £20,000, it cost him a mere £150.

That was the story of Chephren's pyramid as Belzoni told it, but as at the opening of Seti's tomb there was another eyewitness to tell it differently. Yanni D'Athanasi was scheduled to return with Giovanni to Thebes when the challenge of the pyramid presented itself. According to Yanni, it was he, as interpreter, who was instrumental in securing the *firman,* and he who supervised much of the digging. "This was in the month of February," Yanni wrote, "and Mr. Belzoni being invited to Cairo by one of his friends . . . returned thither the next day, desiring me to give him notice of the earliest indications I should meet with of the entrance. On this occasion he stayed away six days." On the fifteenth day of digging (still in Belzoni's absence), Yanni and his crew came upon one of the doorway's black granite pillars. The first to enter was an Arab laborer whose name was Argian (meaning "naked" in Arabic), "a man of gigantic height but as thin as a stock-fish," who was able to report that several chambers opened off the entry passage. Due to his size, Belzoni was unable to squeeze into the narrow tunnel and so prevailed upon Yanni to strip off his clothes and make the first educated exploration of the pyramid's interior. On emerging, Yanni described the sarcophagus chamber and noted that he had seen "several letters in the Arabic language."[31]

In writing his book, Belzoni omitted any reference to Yanni's participation either as a shoveling assistant or actual discoverer. It is hardly surprising, therefore, and certainly natural, that on reading the book Yanni should be somewhat piqued. He put it this way: "If he [Belzoni] had been a conscientious and a sincere man, as he boasted himself to be, he ought

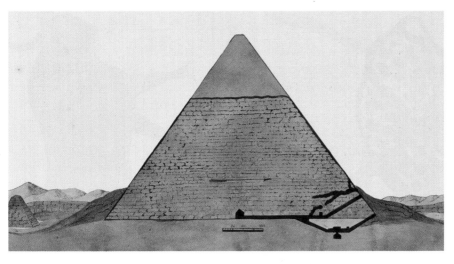

Belzoni's sectional view of Chephren's pyramid, showing both the false and the real entrances.

to have put forth the naked truth, without garbling the facts. . . . His memory cannot but suffer from it, for truth never long holds back from exposing and stigmatizing falsehood."[32]

By the time D'Athanasi published his attack, Belzoni was long dead and his claim to having made Chephren's pyramid his own was secure—as an 1821 silver medal struck in his honor attests, albeit depicting the wrong pyramid.[33]

12 ⟩ CONFRONTATION IN THE CONSULATE

THE COMPTE DE FORBIN'S exploratory expedition took him only as far as Luxor, at which point he encountered Lady Belmore's maid strolling through the ruins under a parasol and so concluded that the thrill had gone out of African exploration. Consequently, he turned round and headed back to Cairo. The whole adventure had taken him barely a month—approximately the amount of time Belzoni had devoted to Chephren's pyramid. A disdainful Giovanni later noted that "the attraction of a more easy life did not permit him to proceed any further into Africa."[1] Once back in Frankish civilization, the count did not linger long and quickly went on to Alexandria and to France. Before leaving, he met Belzoni at the house of the Austrian consul and heard about the disappointment of the pyramid's false passage. Forbin told Giovanni that he was wasting his time, but laughingly added that if he should find his way to the burial chamber, please send him a plan of it. Belzoni's thin skin and fragile ego did not respond well to such patronizing, and so when he did succeed he sent the count a copy of his drawing. One must conclude that he did so to thumb his nose at France's director-general of museums; but it was not a wise move. A French newspaper reporting the intrepid traveler's return had this to say:

> On the 24th of April, Mr. Le Comte de Forbin, Director General of the Royal Museum of France, landed at the lazaretto of Marseilles. . . . By a happy chance, some days before his departure from Cairo, he succeeded in penetrating into the second pyramid of Ghizeh. Mr. Forbin brings the plan of that important discovery, as well as much information on the labours of Mr. Drovetti at Carnak, and on those which Mr.

Salt, the English consul, pursues with the greatest success in the valley of Beban el Malook. The Museum of Paris is going to be enriched with some of the spoils of Thebes, which Mr. Forbin has collected in his travels.[2]

Belzoni had led with his chin but was enraged when he took the Frenchman's punch. The count had found nothing; his only spoils were the two Sekhmet figures he had bought from Giovanni, and the closest he got to penetrating the pyramid had been his cousin's crawl into the false passage. Belzoni, whose hatred of the French went back to his youth and their invasion of Rome, now had even more reason to despise them and their man on the ground, Bernardino Drovetti. Could he, Giovanni wondered, chalk up another victory by discovering the entry into the third Giza pyramid? He had seen that someone had been digging on the east side, and so chose the north face for what he termed "a cursory view."[3] His previous experience should have taught him that though the pyramid of Mycerinus was appreciably smaller than that of Chephren, the work of rock and rubble shifting could be equally taxing and time-absorbing—time which Giovanni was supposed to be devoting to Seti and Henry Salt.

Had Sarah not been away in Palestine, she might have encouraged her husband to be more circumspect, more willing to recognize his responsibilities, and less ready to take offense. But alone and brooding, Belzoni chose to take out his frustrations on the third pyramid. His disposition was made worse by his having received unspecified journals from Europe that lauded his discoveries but gave the credit to others while neglecting even to mention his name. "I must confess," he wrote, "I was weak enough to be a little vexed by this." He added that the cited individuals had no more to do with his discoveries "than the governor of Siberia."[4] Belzoni did not name the offending journals. In truth, reports of his successes were glowingly recounted in 1818 issues of the English *Quarterly Review*, whose publisher, John Murray, would later print Belzoni's own *Narrative*. Furthermore, when Count de Forbin published his journal of his travels in Egypt, he gave credit to Belzoni for opening the second pyramid and conceded that the world was under an obligation to him.[5]

Nigh on two centuries later, archaeologists still complain that they get inadequate credit for their discoveries. Only when something remarkable and preferably valuable is found do the newspapers show any interest, and when they do, the reporters frequently get names wrong, quote out of context, and fail to grasp the finds' real importance. Project funding often relies on government grants awarded to people called "principal investigators" who contribute their names but not their brawn. Nevertheless, as head honchos they become associated with the big discovery—no matter how real their modesty or loud their disclaimers. In short, the story of Henry Salt and Giovanni Belzoni is as old as archaeology itself.

Giovanni's paranoia is evident in his *Narrative,* which sometimes followed diary entries but at others jumped backward and forward as bitter recollections came to mind, making the chronology hard to follow. Henry Salt's missing months fall into that nebulous category. Thus we know that the Mycerinus excavation exposed much of the pyramid's north face, but there is no record of how long Belzoni took to do so. He noted only: "The removal of these blocks would eventually have brought me to the entrance to the pyramid, but it required more money and time than I could spare."[6] One might argue that he should have thought of that before he started. More pertinent, however, was his receipt of a letter from Salt saying that he had learned what his man was up to and was coming down to see for himself. The letter was brought by the returning Lord Belmore, who had completed his Nile odyssey and arrived in Cairo, his flotilla laden with a collection of antiquities which Belzoni considered "the largest ever made by an occasional traveller."[7] If his lordship was aware that the Wrath of God was following him downriver, it was none of his concern. Instead, he was happy for Belzoni to invite him into Chephren's pyramid to view the sarcophagus in whose contents a young visitor from Cairo had found a bone that at first was claimed to be human.[8] Later, to Belzoni's embarrassment, it proved to be bovine. But at the time of the Belmore visit, nothing marred Giovanni's big moment. He reminded his lordship that he, Belmore, had been the first Englishman to see the interior of Seti's tomb, and now he was the first to enter the second Wonder of the World. In addition to acting as Lord Belmore's Giza tour guide, Belzoni apparently gave him several substantial antiquities including a Late Period sandstone coffin and a large, black-granite statue of Sekhmet from ca. 935 BC, both eventually given to the British Museum.[9] Neither gift, so grandly given, was of put-it-in-your-pocket size, and one wonders whether they were part of the growing hoard stashed in Salt's name in the consulate's yard. One wonders, too, how and by whom they were moved to Belmore's boats at Boulak.

From Lord Belmore's yacht, his collection was transferred to a merchant ship bound for Malta. There the crates were opened and, because the island was in quarantine, were decanted without the inspectors touching them. Belmore described a "terrible wreck among my antiquities. . . . Many of the best of my small figures are broken to pieces, most of the papyri ground to dust, and everything lying jumbled together in the lazaretto, as so much rubbish."[10] Salt's shipment to Lord Mountnorris had suffered a similar fate "which occasioned no small degree of chagrin to his lordship."[11]

When Salt arrived in Cairo, he found his employee comfortably ensconced in the consulate's residence but in no better frame of mind than when they last met. Neither man recorded the exchanges that passed between them, but Salt had had the entire journey from Thebes to Boulak to think of something suitably pithy. Fortunately for their future relations, His Majesty's consul-general had an immediate official duty to distract him. Lieutenant-Colonel George Augustus Frederick Fitzclarence, the eldest of William IV's nine illegitimate children,[12] had just arrived from India carrying dispatches to London and had to be treated as an honored guest. With Belzoni still in residence, it followed that he would join the consul and the colonel after dinner. Doubtless to his host's irritation, Fitzclarence took an instant liking to Belzoni and thought him the most handsome man he had ever met. Basking in the colonel's admiration, Giovanni recounted every detail of his entry into Chephren's pyramid, thereby upstaging Salt's attempts to describe his own more modest discoveries at Thebes. Nevertheless, Fitzclarence would later write that by donating Young Memnon to the British Museum, Salt "made the whole population of Great Britain his debtor." But his praise for Belzoni was more direct, expressing amazement at his almost mystic ability to know where to dig, and declaring that "a nation like England should not miss the opportunity of making their own a man of such superior talents."[13] None of this prepared Giovanni for the master-to-man confrontation that would follow the colonel's departure. First, however, all three visited the pyramid, and Fitzclarence agreed to carry Belzoni's account of his achievement to England for future publication. For his part, Salt heaped praise on Giovanni for having accomplished the seemingly impossible. He could hardly do otherwise. He also offered to defray the £150 expenses.

Whether that was a guileless attempt to mend fences or the means to be able to say that the pyramid's opening had been under Salt's auspices and expense has never been explained. Belzoni, however, needed no explanation: Salt was trying buy the glory just as he had with Young Memnon and the Theban tomb, and Giovanni would have no part of it—and bluntly said so. His reputation for colorful language was such that that His Britannic Majesty's consulate almost certainly rang with undiplomatic invective. All that is left of it, however, is an agreement to disagree couched in legal terms:

> Whereas it appears that some erroneous ideas have been entertained by Sig. Giovanni Baptista [*sic*] Belzoni, with respect to the objects collected under the auspices and at the expense of Henry Salt Esq. in Upper Egypt, as being intended for the British Museum; and whereas it has since been satisfactorily explained to Sig. Belzoni that such ideas were altogether founded on a mistake, it has been agreed and determined, between the above parties in a friendly manner, to terminate, and they do hereby terminate, all differences between them by the present agreement.

In return and in recognition of Giovanni's zeal and discoveries, Salt was to pay him £500 in English money within one year from the date of signing: April 20, 1818. In addition, he was to cede to Belzoni another Sekhmet statue "now standing in the Consulate court-yard," along with the two he had already sold to Count de Forbin—implying that he had lacked the authority to do so. Salt also ceded the cover of a sarcophagus and "such other objects as he may be able to spare."[14] Although this last could open the door to further disagreements, it was the yet-to-be-salvaged Seti sarcophagus that would cause the most rancorous dispute. The agreement stipulated that whenever it should be disposed of, "the said Sig. Belzoni shall be considered as entitled to one half of the surplus of whatever price may be paid for the said sarcophagus exceeding the sum of two thousand pounds sterling. It being understood between the said parties, that the said Henry Salt Esq. shall offer the said sarcophagus to the British Museum, at a fair valuation, within the space of three years from the present date."

In plain English, Salt would sell the sarcophagus for whatever he could get for it, but if that was less than £2,000, Belzoni would get nothing. In April 1818, however, Seti's coffin was still the great treasure, and both

Salt and Belzoni had much higher figures in mind. In the presence of witnesses, G. Belzoni signed the agreement, and in May of the following year he received his money "in the final settlement of our accounts."[15] In the meantime, he was to return to Seti's tomb to fulfill his obligation to "do all in his power" to bring out the sarcophagus. Unwisely, Salt's new contract did not set a time limit, but it did include a clause allowing Belzoni to make an antiquities collection of his own, and that took precedence—as did an unscheduled research trip to the Red Sea.

Such squabbling over who owned what, and how many of the excavated objects should belong to the finder and how many to the person who bankrolled the search, still strikes sparks in the volatile world of treasure hunting. The difference, of course, is that archaeologists do not consider themselves treasure hunters. Howard Carter, who discovered the tomb of Tutankhamen, certainly did not. His sponsor, on the other hand, took a more possessive stance. Lord George Edward Stanhope Molyneux, fifth Earl of Carnarvon, began wintering in Egypt for his health in 1903 and, like his predecessors, amused himself digging for antiquities, albeit aided by a young hired professional, Howard Carter. Carnarvon, however, was unable to put shovel in the Valley of Kings because the American philanthropist Theodore M. Davis already had a government-approved digging concession, and not until he chose to surrender it could Carnarvon apply to take it over. The Antiquities Service required him to hire a professional archaeologist and proposed that it be Carter, but it also granted Carnarvon a share in whatever might be found. Having funded Carter's unrewarding work for four years, when the great discovery was made Carnarvon sought the share that was legally his. Carter, however, insisted that everything should stay in Cairo or in the tomb. The friends' consequent falling out became so volatile that Carter, who had a reputation "for not being the best tempered of men,"[16] ordered his mentor out of his house and told him never to come back. Carnarvon died before the dispute could be resolved, and when his widow tried to exercise the family's rights under the concession, the Egyptian government withdrew it, and later barred Carter from entering his own tomb.

A hundred years earlier there had been no Egyptian Antiquities Service; whatever *firmans* were issued were granted at the whim of Mohammed Ali Pasha or by provincial beys and agas, none of whom were interested in archaeological preservation. For the British in 1818, Henry Salt played the role of the wealthy Lord Carnarvon, and Belzoni was his untrained Howard Carter. It was fortunate, therefore, that Belzoni's tomb was virtually empty, for enterprising though Giovanni was, faced with the conservation nightmare that confronted Howard Carter, most of the treasures would have emerged ruined and worthy only for sale to the next rich tourist who wanted a bit of old Egypt to take home.

13 } OVER THE MOUNTAINS
AND THROUGH THE PASSES

LIKE GOLD MINERS prospecting in the Colorado Rockies, antiquities hunters in Egypt staked out their territories and hired guards to protect them from the competition. Thus when Belzoni returned to Thebes he found Drovetti's agents in control at Karnak, while across the river on the plain of Gournou Henry Salt had set aside a large area behind the gigantic Colossi of Memnon.[1] In late 1817, while Belzoni was attending to his little business in Cairo, Salt and Beechey were uncovering the remains of a vast temple that had been reduced to "the pedestals of many columns of very large diameter and in great numbers."[2] Such statuary as Salt had found was too shattered to be worth his taking away and so he quit, thinking the trove played out. Nevertheless, when Belzoni told Beechey that he planned to dig there, the latter insisted that the area was still set aside for the consul. Never one to be deterred by negativity, Giovanni started digging.

Two days into what Belzoni called his "researches," he came upon a large statue which he described as the finest he had seen. The seated figure was that of a man he took to be Memnon (Amenophis III), nearly ten feet high and carved in gray granite. Nearby lay an assortment of the mandatory lion-headed Sekhmets, all related to the building that future archaeologists would name the Amenophium. There is no record of Henry Beechey's response to seeing Belzoni invading—and successfully invading—his employer's concession, but by the end of June, Giovanni had "ceased all sort of researches." Having had second thoughts, he had decided that he "did not wish to encroach on his [Salt's] Theban territory."[3] Belzoni ruefully allowed that he had to be content to rely on the mummy plunderers of Gournou to help him make a collection of his own, which, he said, included "a few good articles, particularly in manuscripts, &c."[4] But buying was no substitute for digging and finding. Consequently, he shifted his activity from Thebes to Erment, where no one was claiming prior rights. But the digging proved unrewarding. Something new and exciting was needed to keep the restless Belzoni on his toes. Mohammed Ali Pasha provided it.

Two Copts returning from Arabia had crossed the Red Sea and claimed to have found sulfur mines in the mountains near the shore. Sulfur being one of the base components of gunpowder, the Pasha had sent several expeditions to the Red Sea coast, the last of them led by Drovetti's mineralogist friend Frédéric Cailliaud. The sulfur mines proved to have been either worked out or nonexistent, but Cailliaud did find potentially productive emerald mines as well as the ruins of an ancient town which Belzoni thought worth investigating. Although Cailliaud did not specifically say so, rumors were rampant that he had discovered Egypt's lost Red Sea port of Berenice. Built five hundred miles south of Suez, the port had been created during the reign of Ptolemy II (285–246 BC) to receive imports from Arabia and beyond. The inference, therefore, had to be that if Berenice had been rich in its heyday, it could remain so in ruins.

With Salt still in Cairo, Sarah waiting impatiently in Jerusalem, and Belzoni's copying work in his tomb virtually completed, this was an ideal time for a seaside vacation—albeit with a legitimate research component and a valid use of their employer's money. Henry Beechey agreed, and together they planned to go upriver first to Esna and then to Edfu before heading east overland. First, however, there was the Amenophium's statue to be shipped to Cairo along with Belzoni's purchases from the Gournouese. Beechey did not doubt that the statue belonged to Henry Salt: It was found in his concession area. Besides, Beechey would later report that when the statue was uncovered he heard Belzoni complain, "see how lucky I am excavating for others, and how unlucky when for myself."[5] Why, then, would Belzoni have carved his name beside its left foot (see pp. 2 and 264)? In May of the following year, Salt unequivocally considered it his. In a letter to his friend William Hamilton, he wrote, "I have a fine statue, got out of the ruins of the true Memnonium, about nine feet high."[6] Salt wanted Hamilton, as undersecretary for foreign affairs, to authorize a British navy transport to carry it home as an article for the British Museum—where it now resides.

The statue was heavy, as were several of Belzoni's smaller treasures,

Belzoni's view of the principal temple at Erment, dedicated to the falcon-headed god Montu. The domed structure in the right foreground is a Mameluke-era tomb.

and rented boats were designed to carry dates, olives, dhoura, and other much lighter produce. Loading the figure, therefore, was almost as taxing as shipping Young Memnon. Shortly before Belzoni's rented boat was due to leave Luxor, one of Drovetti's employees asked for a lift down to Cairo. Belzoni graciously acceded, but he would later wish he hadn't.

Dispatching a boatload of antiquities down the Nile in September 1818 was easier than sailing another up to Edfu. The river was in full flood, having risen higher than at any time in living memory. Belzoni wrote that "the rapid stream carried off all that was before it; men, women, children, cattle, corn, everything was washed away in an instant, and left the place where the village stood without any thing to indicate that there had ever been a house on the spot." A vast lake stretched from the mountains of Gournou on the west to those eight miles away to the east. The Colossi of Memnon rose out of the water "like lighthouses on some of the coasts of Europe." Appalled by what he saw, Giovanni declared, "I never saw any picture that could give a more correct idea of a deluge than the valley of the Nile in this season." Sarah would attempt to correct that omission by drawing a picture she titled *An Extraordinary Overflowing of the Nile,*[7] one that curiously shows the villagers wading about and by no means in extremis while ducks paddle upstream, evidently enjoying the water (see p. 174).

By the end of the month, the flood had reached the pyramids, providing Salt with a rare opportunity to visit them by boat. "As we passed the villages it was truly distressing to hear the cries of the inhabitants calling out for assistance, not being able to move their household furniture for want of boats."[8] He did not say that he provided any—but neither did Belzoni.

The Berenice expedition left Luxor on September 16 led by Giovanni and Beechey. With them went a new associate, young Dr. Alessandro Ricci from Siena, who had been employed by William Bankes and was now on Salt's payroll. Ricci was a skilled artist and would later help Belzoni with his work recording the details of Seti's tomb. Also part of the expedition were two Greek servants, one of them the always devious and self-serving Giovanni D'Athanasi, whose own account of the trip differed significantly from Belzoni's. Completing the company were a couple of Gournou lads to tote baggage, and an aged Arab miner who knew the way.[9] Two days later, they reached the town of Esna and were pleased to find that Khalil Bey, who had given Belzoni so much trouble during the Abu Simbel opening, had been shifted to a new administrative post and replaced by Ibrahim Bey, whom Belzoni called "the most civilized Turk I ever knew." He provided the necessary *firman* to be shown to the cacheff at Edfu, but was specific in its saying that when the expedition came to the mines, no one was to touch the emeralds. Giovanni figured that Ibrahim could not believe that the Franks would go so far into the deserts just to admire the mountains and the sand. Nevertheless, on reaching Edfu, the *firman* had the desired effect. Camels were there to be rented at one piastre a day; food and water were purchased and camel drivers hired. Belzoni had long since learned that in Egypt nothing ever went smoothly and on time, and the halt at Edfu was no exception. The camel drivers had to prepare bread for their journey, more camel food had to be secured, and the chief miner from the Pasha's emerald-digging gangs turned up on his way north and tried to discourage Belzoni from continuing until he returned. The warning ignored, the expedition mounted on sixteen camels set out on September 24 following an ancient but still-used trail punctuated by small ruined forts that had protected wells long ago dry and choked with sand. Dr. Ricci took sick and had to turn back.

When, eventually, the Belzoni caravan approached the sea, it came

to two still-yielding wells, one contaminated with salt water, causing Beechey to fall ill from drinking it, and the other putrid and brackish. The latter prompted Belzoni to observe that "there are few waters in the world better than that of the Nile; and now to have to drink the worst was such a change in one day, that we could not help feeling the consequences of it."[10] Two days later, the Nile water they had brought with them was found to be bad.

Today guidebooks are explicit in urging visitors not to drink the water without first boiling it for fear of developing bilharzias (hookworm disease), but as late as the mid-nineteenth century, Belzoni's opinion was still widely shared. "Nile water for drinking purposes is highly extolled: it is among waters what champagne is among wines," wrote Robert Chambers in 1862. Two centuries earlier, the historian Reverend Samuel Purchas reported that "Nilus water I thinke to be the profitablest and wholesomest in the world by being both bread and drink."[11]

In the light of such florid endorsements, it is hard to grasp why Belzoni's Nile water went bad. He offered no explanation, his single-minded intent being to keep his camels moving. Over mountains, through passes,

Sarah Belzoni's impression of the unusually destructive Nile flood of 1818.

and along rocky valleys, the Berenice expedition pressed on, still led by the old miner who from the start had been its hired guide. The prospect of reaching a Pompeii on the Red Sea was the ever-present carrot. Both Belzoni and Beechey expected to "distinguish the town by the lofty columns and architecture of some magnificent edifice." With their supplies running low, they concluded that once there they could remain for only a few days, during which time Beechey would concentrate on drawing the monuments, statues, and paintings, while Belzoni was to "run all over the vast ruins like a pointer, as fast as I could, to observe where anything was to be found or discovered." The plan was simple and, like all Belzoni's ideas, eminently practical. However, it did not include an unexpected halt. The old guide leading the caravan held up his hand for it to stop. The tired baggage-carrying camels promptly sat down.

Giovanni told their guide that they were not at a stopping place and that, it being four hours to sundown, he should continue into the ancient town site.

The old man replied: "This is it. This is the place where the other Christian was before."

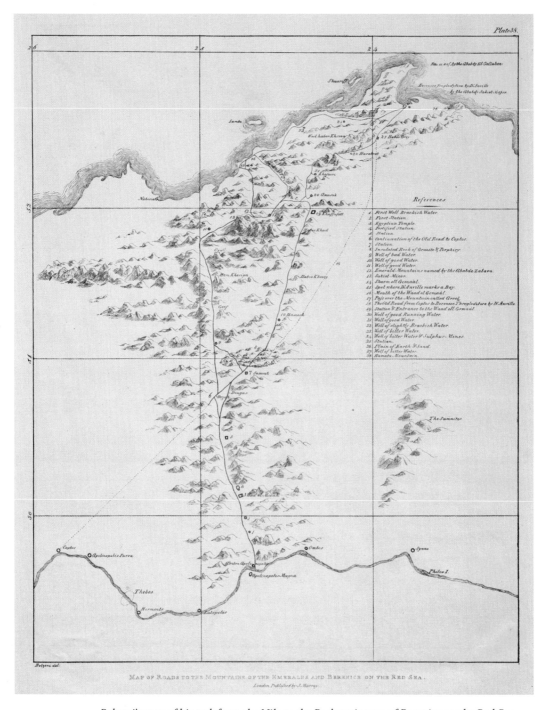

Belzoni's map of his trek from the Nile to the Ptolemaic port of Berenice on the Red Sea.

A temple encountered on the trail to Berenice, of interest only in that the watercolor drawing is attributed to Sarah Belzoni, who did not accompany her husband on that trek.

The Christian had been Cailliaud, the mineralogist, who had likened the town to Pompeii and claimed to have seen (and presumably counted) eight hundred houses. Was he suffering from a hallucination, or was this some devious French trick to lure the English away from Thebes? Belzoni's answer was to keep going to the sea—which they did. On reaching the shore and in sight of the Arabian Gulf, the two Christians "plunged into the sea like the crocodiles into the Nile, and found, that a bath after a long journey was very refreshing."[12] Two days later, on the morning of October 8, they came to bumps and hillocks in the sand that covered the remains of ancient habitation and in its midst found the partially buried ruin of a small temple. While there, Beechey copied several Greek inscriptions, one of which when translated read: "Of Berenice, and the sculptured animal; and having dug . . . of the river from the foundation; and . . . pence has dedicated them: with good fortune."[13] The source of the inscriptions is unclear, but there seemed little doubt that this little sand-shrouded town had been the port of Berenice. Although traces of buildings were visible behind and beyond the central area of streets and houses, Belzoni calculated that the core settlement had an east-west measurement of 2,000 feet and a north–south span of 1,600 feet and might have accommodated two thousand dwellings, none of them very large. Although the lack of Theban-style monuments did not suggest that Berenice was a potential source of portable treasures, early in the morning of October 9, Giovanni launched a test excavation in the sanctuary of the temple. It was, to say the least, a modest effort as no one had thought to bring a spade or a shovel. Equipped, therefore, with only a seashell, one of the Gourou boys was left to dig while everyone else went exploring along the coast to the south.

Although they had found the remains of a seaside settlement that possessed a natural harbor, Giovanni continued to question whether this really was the site of the fabled city. His only map of the Red Sea coast had been published a half century earlier by the French cartographer Jean Baptiste d'Anville and placed Berenice farther to the south—hence the renewed exploration.[14] On reaching what Belzoni believed to be the site shown on the map and finding no signs of buried buildings, he decided that he had gone the extra miles to prove that the little town with its temple was truly Ptolemy II's Red Sea port. Meanwhile, back at the temple, Mussa, the Gournou boy, was still digging.

Considering his substandard equipment, Mussa had done a remarkably diligent job. By the time Belzoni and Beechey returned, he was down about four feet through soft and sliding sand, revealing a limestone wall decorated with sculpted figures and hieroglyphs, as well as the top of a doorway. Mussa handed up a hieroglyph-decorated fragment of a tablet or stele made from reddish stone that was determined not to be of local origin. "We took it away," Belzoni declared, "as a memorandum of having seen an Egyptian temple on the coast of the Red Sea."[15] It was also the only artifact he had to take back to show how he had spent Henry Salt's money.

The expedition's return to the Nile was slow and thirsty, and although the human participants arrived safely, at least three of the rented camels did not. In the month that Belzoni had been away, the river's historic flood was over, the water having fallen as quickly as it had risen. The wet arable ground had been replanted and the mud-walled villages rebuilt. "By this time," Giovanni noted, "the drowned people were forgotten, and the only calamity remaining was the scarcity of provisions among the Fellahs." He added, "In all such cases the poor labourer is the last thought of."[16] While that is true in every country in every age, in Mohammed Ali's Egypt his nationalizing (or rather personal seizure) of plantations previously owned

Belzoni's only souvenir from Berenice, a terra-cotta fragment from an unidentified buried temple.

by the ousted Mamelukes left the fellaheen without spokesmen and without redress. Giovanni Belzoni, for all his faults, was a caring individual who believed in the Bible's admonitions and was kind to those who were good to him—at least when it was practical to do so. His relationship with the gentlemanly Henry Beechey has never been fully understood. Beechey was Salt's employee, but on the Berenice expedition he was content to let Belzoni be the leader. Much later, Beechey would have harsh memories of life with Giovanni, but in October 1818, learning what had been going on at Thebes in their absence was their jointly shared concern.

When they arrived at Luxor, Salt was already there, having brought with him a group he described as "consisting only of very *pleasant* and *agreeable people.*" Among them were William J. Bankes, who had a prior interest in securing the obelisk at Philae, and an old Prussian nobleman named Baron Sack, who was more interested in natural than ancient history. Salt called Bankes one of the most delightful companions he had ever met, and saw him as "high bred, well informed, and possessing an inexhaustible fund of humour, and the Baron full of little anecdotes."[17] Here, and elsewhere, it is clear that Henry Salt polished his persona by rubbing shoulders with well-bred and preferably titled men. He was also a poor judge of character. In the minds of many, William Bankes was a person to be avoided. He was arrogant, considered himself the life of any party, and talkative to the point of rudeness. One fellow guest recalled finding him "talking on my arrival at a quarter after seven, and it was his voice that concluded the conversation at eleven." Others referred to the "superior facetiousness of William Bankes" and found "his voice painfully unpleasant." In 1826, the London hostess Mrs. Arbuthnot declared that she never saw such bad taste in her life and thought Bankes was drunk. Two years later, she found his humor vulgar and tiresome.[18] An early college friend of Lord Byron, he flaunted a femininity that presaged his later disgrace. A pencil sketch of 1820 shows him draped in Turkish robes and striking a pose more suited to a Piccadilly prostitute.

Regardless of Bankes's propensity to overstay his welcome, Henry Salt was delighted to be the beneficiary of the visitor's ready wit and travel tales as well as the opportunity to bond with the friend of Lord Byron. It is unlikely, therefore, that the bedraggled return of Salt's employees from their unauthorized side trip fitted neatly into this atmosphere of gentlemanly bonhomie. Of the expedition to Berenice, Salt would say only that "all I know of it is, that it cost me several thousand piastres, being undertaken, as Mr. Beechey assured me before Mr. Belzoni's face—*on my account.*" He ruefully added that "Mr. Belzoni paid only for his own camel."[19] If young Mussa's "memorandum" fragment did anything to appease His Majesty's consul-general, the pleasure of it went unrecorded. Belzoni, however, thought enough of the shard to illustrate it in his *Narrative.*[20]

But was the Berenice trip Belzoni's idea? Salt's reaction says that it was, but not so Yanni D'Athanasi. In the latter's book, he stated: "Mr Salt gave me a letter, with orders to take it in person to Mr. Beechey, who was at Thebes. In this letter he directed us to set out without loss of time to discover the town of Berenice." Yanni added that the explorers were "Mr. Beechey, Mr. Belzoni, Dr. Ricchi [*sic*], and myself, accompanied by our servants."[21] One remembers that Giovanni in his *Narrative* had neglected to identify Yanni as anything but one of his two Greek servants. On balance, therefore, it is wisest to reject Yanni's account as the product of personal animosity.

The time that elapsed between the Salt party's arrival at Thebes and Belzoni's return is not recorded, but there evidently was plenty of time for the consul and his friends to pursue their researches on both sides of the river. Because archaeological posterity has been so hard on the inappropriately educated Belzoni, it is pertinent to examine how William Bankes, graduate of Trinity College, Cambridge,[22] was passing his time amid the mummified dead in the catacombs of Gournou. His assistant Giovanni Finati recalled their entering a chamber "three parts full of embalmed bodies, laid one upon another like a stack." In the hope of finding papyri among them, Bankes was delighted to come upon one "on the breast of the very first body that was opened by him." Finati added, "although we occupied ourselves afterwards for hours with the remainder, we could never discover a second."[23] One can well imagine the chaos that the two researchers left behind them in the tomb.

Finati, however, was not blind to the cavalier manner in which his employer and his associates were willing to treat the lesser legacies of Ancient Egypt. "I could observe," he wrote, "that it was not without regret that the antiquaries could inure themselves at first to imitate the natives of all that district, in applying to common purposes the wooden fragments and morsels of antiquity that abound (especially the mummy cases) as seats, and tables, and shelves, and even as fuel." Another traveler, Sir Frederick Henniker, who visited Gournou two years later, remembered that "the plain is strewed with broken bones, the coffins are used for firewood and the amomum or bitumen offends the nose wherever there is a fire."[24] Wallis Budge, an early keeper of the British Museum's Egyptian collections, observed that "the arms, legs, hands, and feet of such mummies break with a sound like the cracking of chemical glass tubing," adding that "they burn very freely and give out great heat."[25]

Although the smell of burning bandages and bones may have lingered in Henry Salt's nostrils as he contemplated how to control Signor Belzoni's independence and teach him respect for his employer's money, he doubted that a bare-knuckles confrontation would be the best approach. Salt was, after all, His Majesty's diplomatic representative in Egypt. Although, in the consul's opinion, Giovanni "still evinced symptoms of discontent," Salt decided that fence-mending would best serve them both. Consequently, they agreed on a new contract. Belzoni would continue to excavate on Salt's behalf but keep one-third of whatever was found. Salt would put up the money and underwrite the expenses. If there was a document to that effect, it has not survived to specify how one assessed a third of the antiquities or how much money was allocated. Nevertheless,

Belzoni considered the deal satisfactory. Salt, on the other hand, later complained that Giovanni "spent about fifteen hundred paistres . . . without finding, as he reported to me, a single article."[26] At the outset, however, everyone seemed willing to get along—until Bernardino Drovetti arrived at Thebes. He was not a happy ex-consul.

Drovetti, having been the French consul-general from 1804 until he was fired with the eclipse of Napoleon in 1814, still considered himself France's chief diplomat in Egypt and infinitely senior to Britain's new man, who had not arrived until 1816. That Salt should turn out to be a rival and an untutored antiquities collector added further cause for coolness. However, it was not monuments or mummies that riled Drovetti on that autumn evening, but the fate of his hitchhiking employee aboard Belzoni's Cairo-bound boat. Six days out from Thebes, he had fallen overboard and drowned—to the apparent dismay and regret of the crew. The accident had been reported to Salt, who was responsible for chartering the boat, and as such incidents were legally handled by the respective consulates, he saw no reason to launch an inquiry. Drovetti, then having no consular authority, did nothing. Now, however, with both men face-to-face amid the ruins of Thebes, Drovetti used the occasion to voice a complaint about the circumstances of his man's death.

Salt answered that he had heard of no occasion to investigate the matter.

"Then you should have!" snapped Drovetti.

"As the dead man was in your employ," Salt told him, "I'm surprised that you didn't make an application while you were in Cairo."

"I did not do so—for delicacy's sake." Drovetti's lame response "was received with general laughter" by the Englishmen, and did nothing to promote the bonds of friendship.[27] Nevertheless, Drovetti had something else on his mind. He knew that Seti's sarcophagus was still in his tomb, and he wanted to buy it for the Louvre, and so approached Bankes as a possible conduit to Salt. The latter's reply is not on record, but the audacity of the Frenchman (who, we remember, was actually Italian) must have generated both surprise and the satisfaction of refusing.

Several days later, Belzoni and Salt crossed the river from the Necropolis to Luxor on their way to inspect areas at Karnak that the consul considered his concessions. Drovetti probably saw them coming and met up with them at Luxor, where he proceeded to utter a warning in the guise of

Gallic humor. His agents had told him that they had seen a man dressed like Belzoni skulking amid the ruins who they believed meant to do him harm.

"Why would he dress like me?" Belzoni wanted to know.

"Because," Drovetti replied, "if the imposter did something bad, it would be you who'd get the blame."

Salt called the notion ridiculous, and anyone standing beside Giovanni would have known that no one was big enough to successfully impersonate the "Patagonian Sampson." Nevertheless, though suspecting that he was being set up for an unfortunate accident, Giovanni chose to reply in the same bantering tone: "I hope that before they shoot, your people will ask whether they are aiming at the real or the sham Belzoni. It would not be satisfactory to me," he added, "if the mistake was found out afterwards."

"There is no need to worry," Drovetti assured him. "The person has been sent away from Thebes and will not return again." So ended a very curious conversation. Drovetti then invited Salt and Belzoni into his "habitation among the ruins of Karnak" and there served them sherbet and lemonade. Belzoni talked about his Berenice expedition, and Salt explained that he and his friends were heading up to Nubia while Mr. Belzoni would be removing the Philae obelisk for Mr. Bankes, who planned to take it home to England.

Drovetti bridled at the news, claiming that the rogues at Aswan had many times agreed to bring down the obelisk on his behalf, but said so only to extort money. Belzoni, not being the most diplomatic of men, assured Drovetti that the Aswan rogues could not do so, because he, Belzoni, had already earmarked it for Consul Salt. The latter agreed that this was true, and that he, in turn, had donated the obelisk to William Bankes.

"Then, so be it," Drovetti conceded.

That Drovetti should so easily back away prompted Giovanni to conclude that the gift to Bankes was like Drovetti's present of the sarcophagus lid to him; neither, in his view, was retrievable.

"So when are you planning to set off?" Drovetti casually inquired.

"The day after tomorrow," Salt replied.

Always suspicious of anything Drovetti said or did, Belzoni suspected that the question was more than casual and that his readiness to surrender the Philae obelisk to Bankes was not as magnanimous as it appeared. In Giovanni's mind, therefore, getting to Philae with all possible dispatch was akin to his race across the desert from Hermopolis to Thebes. But Salt and his congenial friends were in no hurry. The trip upriver to Aswan would take them past several of Egypt's now famous temples and tombs and they intended to examine, discuss, and draw every one of them.[28]

Two days before leaving Luxor, Salt replied to a letter from Sir Joseph Banks regarding the possibility that the British Museum might invest public money in a campaign to secure even more treasures for its galleries. Salt told Giovanni that his name had been mentioned in that context and that his writing to the trustees might be a good idea. Belzoni thereupon wrote that he understood that Sir Joseph had wished such an arrangement to be advanced and that he could undertake it at a cost of a modest £1,500 per annum.[29] Although Salt did forward Giovanni's proposals, he noted that "Mr. Bankes, as well as myself, conceived they would not be accepted." Whether he undermined Belzoni's chances by saying as much in the covering letter to Sir Joseph is unknown. Nevertheless, when the upriver expedition set out, there was no sign of acrimony on Salt's part. The Berenice junket had been forgiven if not forgotten.

The party, Belzoni noted, was numerous and included Bankes, Salt, the naturalist Baron Sack, Beechey, the now-recovered Dr. Ricci, and a draftsman he called "Mr. Linon," a phonetic version of Linant. The nineteen-year-old Louis Maurice Adolphe Linant de Bellefonds had arrived in Egypt with the Compte de Forbin and was hired as a draftsman by Salt and later by Bankes. Although Salt thought to mention that the baron was chamberlain to the king of Prussia, other members of the party were cited simply as servants. One of them was Yanni (D'Athanasi), whose presence was mentioned neither by Salt nor Belzoni, but only in his own published account of his services to the consul. The same was true of Giovanni Finati, who had returned from Jerusalem with Bankes and contemptuously referred in his journal to the inclusion of "some inferior attendants."[30] Another anonymous servant was a drummer boy who had gone to Egypt with the British invasion force of 1807 and was taken prisoner at the disastrous Battle of Rosetta. Given the choice of death or becoming a Muslim, young Donald Thompson of Inverness changed both his religion and his name. As Osman Efendi, he dressed as a Turk and worked first for Burckhardt (and was with him at his death), then for Salt as an interpreter and excavator. One might uncharitably deduce that Consul-General Salt felt more comfortable in the company of the king of Prussia's chamberlain than with a Greek interpreter or an ex-drummer boy who spoke Arabic with a Scot's accent.

The odd but enthusiastic group set out from Thebes on November 16, 1818, aboard an equally exotic flotilla. Consul Salt, being the expedition's leader, had the largest boat; Bankes was aboard a light and shallow, fourteen-oared vessel called a *cangia;* the baron was on a smaller boat, and a canoe transported the food supplies of sheep, goats, fowls, geese, ducks, pigeons, turkeys, and donkeys that "accompanied the fleet with a perpetual concert." Belzoni neglected to identify his own accommodation, but it is likely that he shared a boat with M. Linant, Yanni, Osman, Finati, and the cook. He complained that they had only two kinds of wine and no ice, and that "our lives were a burthen to us from the fatigue and dangerous mode of travelling."³¹

After two days sailing, the expedition reached the great ruins at Edfu, its principal temple being dedicated to the falcon god Horus and of relatively late date. Replacing structures from the Old Kingdom, this building was begun in the reign of Ptolemy III (237 BC) but was not completed until 57 BC. Nevertheless, Belzoni called it a magnificent ruin and thought that if a traveler could repeat his visit every day of his life, there would still be more to see. He was less enthusiastic at discovering Drovetti's agents already there—with their crew busily digging. One of the supervisors had been another Piedmontese named Antonio Lebolo, whom Belzoni had previously confronted in the tombs of Gournou. For good reasons they neither liked nor trusted each other. But fortunately for Anglo-French civility, Lebolo had already left Edfu—apparently responding to a hasty courier's dispatch from his master sending him on his way to Philae. No evidence suggests that Salt or Bankes shared Belzoni's sense of urgency, and so after inspecting Edfu they continued their leisurely voyage, stopping next at the granite quarries at Gebel Silsila, where much of the rock was quarried to build the Theban temples. Before they got there, they passed a small boat heading downstream with Signor Lebolo aboard. Attempts to hail him were ignored, further convincing Belzoni that Drovetti's people were up to no good.

At Gebel Silsila, the travelers inspected several tombs, studied inscriptions, and found unfinished examples of the ram-headed sphinxes that flanked the avenues at Karnak and Luxor. As Giovanni noted, there was much to see there that "deserves the attention of the scientific traveller."³²

The outer pylon at the Ptolemaic temple of Horus at Edfu (view from the south). To the right is the carved figure of Ptolemy XII (80–51 BC) smiting prisoners in front of the hawk-headed Horus, who wears the double crown of Egypt.

But then, as today, visitors weaned on the wonders of Karnak or Edfu found Gebel Silsila noticeably short of grandeur, and so, after admiring the millennia-spanning labors of the ancient quarriers, the fleet reassembled and continued another fifteen miles upstream.

The next day, the expedition reached the far more visually impressive east-bank temple at Kom Ombo, part of which had eroded into the river. Built in the Ptolemaic Period on the site of at least one earlier temple, Kom Ombo was dedicated both to Horus and to Sobek, the crocodile god. Even in Belzoni's day, this sector of the Nile was infested with the creatures, and a chamber filled with their mummies still leaves an impression on modern tourists.[33] From the awed and excited reactions of his scientific traveling companions, Giovanni could see that they would linger longer at majestic Kom Ombo than they had in the quarries of Silsila. He therefore took advantage of a borrowed boat and, with Osman as his sole companion, headed toward Philae.

At Aswan, Belzoni's suspicions were confirmed. Lebolo had urged the aga not to let the English party touch the Philae obelisk. It says something for the aga that he remembered his commitment and refused to interfere. Lebolo therefore wasted no more time at Aswan and went straight

Kom Ombo's temple dedicated to Horus and to Sobek, the crocodile god (view from the south). Part of the outer court has eroded into the river, but the restored entrance to the vestibule and beyond it the hypostyle hall are still grandly dramatic. The temple was begun in the reign of Ptolemy III (246–221 BC), though improvements were being made as late as AD 218.

Mummified crocodiles stacked in and on clay coffins in a small chapel dedicated to the goddess Hathor. They relate to the worship of Sobek and were found in a cemetery at some distance from the Kom Ombo temple.

to Philae, where he told the sheiks and villagers that he had read the hieroglyphics on the sides of the obelisk and that they clearly stated that it had belonged to the ancestors of Bernardino Drovetti. That conclusive proof coupled with the distribution of gifts satisfied the local judge *(cady)* who wrote a decision confirming Drovetti's ownership. Lebolo left it with one of the Philae sheiks along with a note of his own—both to be handed to the English when they arrived. Lebolo's message was dated September 22, 1818, but as Belzoni noted that the date was only eight days earlier, one must conclude either that Lebolo got the month wrong or that Giovanni's editor erred. The voyage from Thebes having taken fifteen days, the note written on November 22 would, as Belzoni observed, have allowed Drovetti's men "time to do all this underhand work at their leisure."[34] Lebolo's note read as follows: "Le chargé d'affaire de Mr. Drovetti prie Messieus les Voyageurs Européens de respecter le porteur du present billet gardant l'obelisque, qui est dans l'ile de Philoe, appartenant á Mr. Drovetti. Philoe le 22 Sep^bre, 1818 Lebolo."[35] Giovanni assured the sheik that the obelisk did not belong to Mr. Drovetti, and then hastened back to Aswan to confer with Bankes and Salt. They invited the aga aboard the flagship, and without much (perhaps any) persuasion heard him agree that Belzoni had been the first to lay claim to the obelisk and had done so in Salt's name. He allowed, too, that he had been promised three hundred piastres (then about thirty Spanish dollars) when the English successfully removed it. With that resolved, Belzoni set about procuring a boat large enough to carry the twenty-five-foot block of granite and its bulkier but separate pedestal. He soon learned that two months earlier Drovetti's people had failed in a similar chartering attempt, the *reis* of the only available boat being unwilling to risk sending it through the rapids of the cataract. Now the river was considerably lower and the danger much greater. But at Aswan, as is still true today, money talked, as did a present of a fifteen-dollar watch to the aga given in Bankes's name.

The obelisk could be more easily loaded than Young Memnon, but the initial problems were identical. Belzoni had no hoisting equipment. There was no lumber to be had at Aswan, and such ropes as were available were made from palm fronds and probably rotten. Nevertheless, after procuring what Giovanni described as "a few sticks," he was able to move the obelisk, but not its pedestal. Bankes, however, insisted that he wanted both.

That problem was still unresolved when the aga of Aswan arrived at

Philae with a letter from Drovetti, secured under his own seal, ordering the aga to prevent anyone from removing the obelisk. Belzoni noted that the letter was translated by Osman "from whom we had no doubt of the correctness of its contents."[36] The flustered aga did not know what to do, but Henry Salt had no doubts. He instructed the aga to present his compliments to Mr. Drovetti and to tell him that like it or not, the obelisk was about to go.

As it turned out, however, Salt's assurance was to prove prematurely optimistic.

14 } PHILAE AND THE
GRAND ENGAGEMENT

NO ONE DOUBTED that if the man people called the Paduan Giant said he could accomplish some herculean task, he could and would do so. Consequently, William Bankes was confident that his obelisk had only to slide onto the waiting boat to be en route to England. But knowing that the rest of the party was eager to be on its way to Abu Simbel and beyond, Bankes was anxious to see the job done without delay. Belzoni, on the other hand, was not to be rushed. His growing reputation as an expediter was at stake, and the French were eager to see him fail. He knew, too, that getting the obelisk onto the boat was only half the battle; the really tricky part was maneuvering the heavily laden craft safely down the rock-strewn cataract at a time when the water level was low. Thus, to determine how best to do that, Belzoni returned to Aswan to review his options. Before leaving Philae, however, he instructed the local labor to use temple rocks to build a sloping jetty sufficiently far out into the river to allow the boat to ride at gunwale height.

There is no record of who was assigned to supervise this essential first step. The gentlemen travelers and their hired draftsmen were busying themselves tearing down Christian plaster from Ptolemaic walls and drawing whatever they exposed beneath it. In any case, none of them had any experience as jetty builders. In retrospect, Belzoni would confess that what happened "was entirely owing to my own neglect, by trusting a single manoeuvre to some who speak more than they can execute."

The jetty looked to Belzoni as though it was capable of supporting a load forty times heavier than the obelisk. However, he could not see that the stones at the sloping bank had been laid *on* it and not in it. Consequently, having no foundation, as soon as the weight of the granite shaft left the security of the bank, the jetty settled and propelled its burden into the Nile, taking several laborers with it. Both pier and obelisk, in Giovanni's words, "took a slow movement, and majestically descended into the river." The fellahs found it funny, but Belzoni was appalled. The loss of the artifact was bad enough, but the exaltation of Drovetti and his henchmen would ring in his ears for months to come, and he, Belzoni, would bear "the blame of all the antiquarian republic in the world." Fortunately, his client was away on the other side of the river when the accident occurred, allowing Giovanni time to consider whether there was anything he could do to redeem himself.

He could see that one corner of the shaft "was still peeping a little out of the water," while the rest of it lay submerged, creating an eddy that defined both its location and the shallowness of the river. Men standing chest-deep in the water might be able to get levers under it, and Giovanni, being an expert in the power of ropes and leverage, convinced himself that all was not yet lost.

Fellahs returning to their west-bank village had found Bankes and told him the bad news. Thus, his disposition on returning to Philae was less than sunny, though in a probably tight-lipped observation he allowed that "such things would happen sometimes." Giovanni, in a rare understatement, noted that Bankes "was not in a careful humour."[1] By this time, however, Belzoni felt confident that with two or three days of hard labor his employer's treasure could be retrieved. His account of this near-disaster and its aftermath occupy several pages of his *Narrative* and would stand as the definitive record were it not for the conflicting accounts by two other witnesses—the Giovannis Finati and D'Athanasi. Finati noted that "Mr. Bankes said little, but was evidently disgusted by the incident, and set sail within a day or two afterwards leaving me to witness Mr. Belzoni's further operations."[2] Yanni D'Athanasi said nothing about the circumstances of the accident, but did say that it was not Salt but Drovetti who gave the obelisk to Bankes.

More pertinent is Yanni's account of an alleged confrontation between Salt and Belzoni that led to the latter's dismissal—one mentioned by neither of them. Knowing that Yanni disliked Belzoni and that as an employee of Henry Salt he would trade on their association long after the latter was dead, the firing charge may have been hearsay or the product of wishful thinking. It is relevant, too, that Yanni made his claim eighteen years later, when fading memories could either fuzzy the edges or sharpen them beyond their worth. Nevertheless, he charged that while they were at Philae, Belzoni had told Salt that he wanted possession of the Seti sarcophagus as the price of his services. Giovanni needed it, he said, to be the centerpiece of his planned tomb reconstruction in London. Yanni concluded that "it may not be surprising to add that the explanations consequent upon this extraordinary demand ended in the dismissal of Mr. Belzoni from his employ under Mr. Salt."[3]

Although Finati was to stay on at Philae while the rest of the party continued south, he wrote nothing about any cataclysmic dispute with Salt that might have led a volatile Belzoni to quit and leave Bankes's obelisk at the bottom of the river. Instead, Finati said only that the task was accomplished "with great skill though not quite without injury." He went on to provide a graphic description of the laden boat's descent through the rapids: "The great boat wheeling and swinging around, and half filling with water, while naked figures were crowding upon all the rocks, or wading or swimming between them, some shouting, and some pulling at the guide ropes, and the boat owner throwing himself on the ground, scattering dust upon his head, and hiding his face. The danger, if any, was but for a few seconds, the equilibrium was recovered, and the mass glided smoothly and majestically onward with the stream."[4] The drama over, Finati headed upriver to tell Bankes the good news.

"And the pedestal?" Bankes may have asked.

Finati could not say. But Yanni could—and would. While negotiating the cataract, Belzoni had off-loaded the rock and left it on a sandbank, where it later settled to be swallowed the next time the river rose. Four years later, Yanni salvaged it and hauled it overland on a journey that would end in the garden of a grateful William Bankes.[5]

There is no evidence in Henry Salt's letters that Belzoni had been fired. On the other hand, there is nothing in them that discusses Bankes and his nearly lost obelisk. Perhaps because Salt had ceded it to his friend, and Bankes was paying Belzoni to do the job, there was nothing for Salt to impart. The deal was that Giovanni should see the obelisk safely to the Mediterranean, the timing of the journey being left to his discretion. Armed, therefore, with his new contract with Salt and with the acquiescence of Drovetti, Belzoni was free to dig where he chose in Karnak and to keep a third of what he found. At the same time, however, he was still under contract to get Seti's sarcophagus out of his tomb and down to the

The William Bankes mansion at Kingston Lacy in Dorset, with Belzoni's obelisk set up in front of it (view from the south).

sea. Christmas 1818, therefore, found the obelisk's boat moored at Luxor, and Giovanni back in the Biban-el-Maluk and unexpectedly reunited with his wife.

Sarah had been in Syria when she received her husband's letter telling her that something had come up to prevent him from joining her.[6] As the letter does not survive, there is no way of knowing what, if anything, he suggested she should do; but with or without his blessing, Sarah returned to Thebes and to their apartment previously set up in the mouth of Seti's tomb. Together they "passed the solemnity of that blessed day [of Christmas] in the solitude of those recesses, undisturbed by the folly of mankind."[7] Giovanni, being a Paduan, referred to the following day as the Feast of St. Stephen, but in England it was Boxing Day and the time to give annual gifts to servants. But Sarah had none to give, though her husband did have one unnamed Greek servant who would accompany him to Karnak on what was to be a pivotal day in his life.

For the frustrated Bernardino Drovetti, who had tried and failed to prevent Bankes's obelisk leaving Philae, the sight of it moored at Luxor had to be galling. Belzoni noted that it was "rather too close under their noses, as they expressed themselves."[8] Whether that thought occurred to him as he crossed the Nile on that St. Stephen's Day morning has to be mere speculation—but not at Luxor. Drovetti was back at Karnak, watching and waiting for his rival to arrive.

Riding a rented donkey and accompanied by his Greek servant and two Arabs, Belzoni rode the mile from Luxor to Karnak intending to mark out one of the plots of ground that had been agreed on during the previous visit with Salt and Drovetti as accessible to the English. On his way, Giovanni received an Arab's warning to stay away from ground "where other Europeans were." Melodramatic though the warning sounded, Belzoni had it in mind when he came to his first digging site and found Drovetti's men at work there. Although the Greek noted that the area "was our share," Belzoni told him to keep quiet and not to meddle. Together they walked on without remonstrating or even acknowledging the incursion.

Drovetti, who was lodged in some mud huts within the temple ruins, appears to have been waiting for Belzoni to protest and thereby ignite a confrontation. But when Giovanni failed to take the bait, something less subtle was needed. Drovetti then waited for Belzoni's return and dispatched a running and shouting Arab, who approached him complaining that he had been beaten by Drovetti's men because he had been faithful to the English, or, as Belzoni added, "as far as an Arab can be." If Giovanni already suspected that he was being set up and that defending the faithful Arab would fire the tinder, he chose not to do so and continued on his way. He was within three hundred yards of the temple's great pylon when he saw about thirty Arabs running toward him led by someone he knew all too well. It was Antonio Lebolo with his Piedmontese cohort Rosignani, whom Belzoni called the "renegado Rossignano" but neglected to say why.

"What business had you to take away an obelisk that doesn't belong to you?" Lebolo demanded. "You have done so many things of this kind. But you won't do any more." With that he seized the bridle of Belzoni's donkey with one hand and grabbed his waistcoat with the other. Several Arabs pinioned his servant and, in spite of his struggles, snatched his pistols from his belt. Simultaneously, Rosignani leveled a double-barreled gun at Giovanni's chest and threatened that it was time to pay for all the ills he had done them.

Lebolo was more specific. "Mr. Drovetti had promised me one third of the price the obelisk would have fetched in Europe, had you not stolen it from Philae," he shouted. "And one of our people was drowned on board the English boat—and nobody did anything about it!"

Belzoni figured that if he got down from his donkey he would be set upon and killed. It was safer to stay there. "If I have done anything wrong," he replied, "I'll be ready to account for it." But nobody was listening: "Their rage had blinded them out of their senses."

From the back of his donkey, Belzoni elected to "look on the villains with contempt" while ordering Lebolo to let him pass. However, before the stand-off could turn uglier, another group of Arabs arrived, with Drovetti and his pistol-toting servant at their head.

"How dare you stop my people from working!" snarled Drovetti.

"I have no idea what you're talking about," Belzoni retorted. "I have been extremely ill-used by your people, and you must answer for their conduct."

"Get down off that donkey!" Drovetti ordered.

"No, sir, I will not!" The words were hardly out before Belzoni heard a pistol discharged close behind him. That did it! Giovanni dismounted and resolved that it was "high time to sell my life as dear as I could." In a later description of the event, Richard Burton would tell how Giovanni "defended himself in a characteristic way, by knocking down an assailant, seizing his ankles and using him as a club upon the foemen's heads." "This novel weapon," Burton added, "in the Samson style, gained a ready victory."[9] Heroic though this sounds, it is best to assume that Belzoni's account, written less than two years after the confrontation, was likely to be more reliable than Burton's tale garnered from "living authorities" sixty years later.

Drovetti stepped back saying, "Well now, let's not be hasty," or words to that effect. "You're in no danger as long as I'm here." Lebolo, taking his lead from his boss, agreed absolutely. It may have been the gunshot or merely the shouting of Drovetti's gang that brought a crowd of Karnak villagers to Belzoni's defense. "Those wild Arabs, as we call them, were disgusted at the conduct of the Europeans, and interfered on my behalf," he wrote. Warming to his point, Belzoni asked, "What ideas must have been formed in the minds of those people of the civilization of Europe, by the conduct of such villains?" It is unlikely that such thoughts had much longevity. Drovetti and his colleagues would be continuing to dig at Karnak and other Theban sites for several more years, and the villagers needed their work and his pay. The traveler Edward de Montulé, who was at

Thebes during the fracas, would write that he envied Drovetti, "who is daily the witness of fresh discoveries," adding that "the Arabians, by whom he is adored, uniformly convey to him the results of their labours."[10]

Montulé evidently liked Drovetti and was the beneficiary of his hospitality. He recalled seeing Arabian chiefs "seated at the French Consul's [table?], expressing in passionate terms the inimical sentiments which they nourished against the colossus (as they termed him) of the left bank." Nevertheless, Montulé concluded that Drovetti, Salt, and Belzoni were not to blame for the animosity and placed it on the shoulders of their agents, who expected to be rewarded in proportion to the value of whatever they found. Thus Drovetti's people raged against "the *ravisher* of the Obelisk at Philé," and prompted Montulé to note that the "Natives of a country, fertile in revolutions and assassinations, are always disposed to have recourse to means the least honourable and the most sanguinary." He concluded with a reminder that this had not been a confrontation between the French and English, "everything having passed *between* these Italians."[11]

The ostensibly near-fatal confrontation between Drovetti and Belzoni, which Montulé called the "grand engagement," was to become one of the enduring legends in the early history of Egyptian archaeology. Although it is true that when anyone brandishes a gun something bad can happen, this was a manufactured drama that could have had international consequences. The French diplomat Drovetti knew that and cannot have forgotten his previous joke, made in the presence of the British consul, about the threat posed by a bogus Belzoni. If that came true, Salt would almost certainly charge Drovetti with murder. Regardless of his suspected villainies, Drovetti was no fool. His drama performance at Karnak was in all probability no more than melodrama intended only to scare Belzoni away from Thebes.

None of this was actually witnessed by Montulé, who that morning was on the west side of the river at Gournou. His London publisher described him as "not only the most recent Traveller in that Country of exhaustless wonders, but also one of the most intelligent, inquisitive, and amusing."[12] Whether he was also innately acquisitive or whether the desire to obtain souvenirs blossomed once he saw everybody else blandly looting is hard to say. He described himself as "a traveller, and in pursuit of curiosities,"[13] but he did not say that he planned to take them home. Nevertheless, on his way to visit Belzoni's tomb, he bought a female mummy and its double case, plus other unspecified objects. Unlike his host, Montulé evidently had qualms, asking: "Whence has it arisen that all these tombs are thus violated? If any perfect still exist, I sincerely wish they may escape the research of the curious antiquary; to them the learned are become objects as much to be dreaded as Cambyses, for the sarcophagus's [*sic*] and mummies which they contained, would inevitably take the road to London or Paris."[14]

While the Karnak engagement was being played out amid its ruins, Salt, Bankes, and possibly the noble baron had continued upriver. In January 1819, they were at Abu Simbel, where Henry Salt was seeing for the first time the temple that he considered he had bought and paid for. Since its first opening, much more sand had blown down from the desert behind, again obscuring most of the flanking colossi. Spurred on by Bankes and aided by villagers more friendly than they had been to Belzoni, the visitors spent three weeks clearing sand from one of the figures. After finding a Greek inscription on the leg of the huge statue to the left of the entrance, Bankes insisted on attacking its companion to the right—even though it meant reburying the first. Before they were done, both Bankes and Salt made sure that they would be remembered. Their inscription reads:

> THIS TEMPLE WAS
> OPENED AUGUST 1 1817
> BY ORDER OF
> [name defaced]
> H.B.M. CONSUL GENERAL
> IN EGYPT
> THE SOUTHERN COLOSS
> US LAID OPEN TO ITS BASE
> BY Wm BANKES Esq [date obscured][15]

The name of Giovanni Belzoni being conspicuously absent, we are tempted to draw conclusions. On the one hand, we may deduce that on such auspicious occasions only the name of what today is known as the "principal investigator" gets recorded; but on the other, we might guess that the sarcophagus-related confrontation at Philae was still feeding a mean streak in Henry Salt's nature. If his name, roughly scratched under that of Belzoni at the Ramesseum, was in his hand, it is likely that the much more robust Abu Simbel inscription was cut by Beechey chipping away to his boss's dictation. Bankes, however, applied his own memorial to the leg of the southern colossus, but all that is left of it reads: Wm BANKES OPENED . . .[16]

Back at Thebes, the Philae obelisk was still tied up at a Luxor wharf in range of Lebolo's vengeance, making the Belzonis' departure a matter of urgency. Because the Karnak confrontation had prevented him from renewing his excavations, Giovanni had only small artifacts to take aboard—with one exception. Seti's sarcophagus was still in his tomb. He had put off this seemingly ingenuity-testing task as long as he could, but now it had to join Bankes's obelisk on its way to the sea. The tomb, one may remember, had a thirty-foot-deep pit at the end of the entry passage dug in part to discourage robbers but also to trap water that might otherwise run down into the tomb.

The twentieth-century archaeologist Howard Carter studied rainfall in the Valley of Kings and concluded that violent storms hit the area every ten years, cascading water down from the desert through the valley's ravines and gullies in huge quantities and at a tremendous rate. The storms over, the water disappeared into the ground as quickly as it arrived.[17] Local Arabs who had experienced these events noted that a cascade pouring down the scarp vanished without any dwindling runoff, and it was this phenomenon that allegedly led one of them to suggest where Belzoni should dig for Seti's entrance. Although he denied it and claimed that the "Fellahs who were accustomed to dig were all of the opinion, that there was nothing in that spot," the water clue became a factor when he considered how to get the sarcophagus out of the tomb.

The pit was thirteen feet wide and twice the length of the sarcophagus. But by the time Belzoni came to move the coffin, the gulf was no longer a barrier. He had filled it with rocks from the sealing wall and from other debris he had cleared from the tomb's passages and chambers. Consequently, his description of the extraction was relatively brief. Giovanni noted that the sarcophagus, being "so slender and thin" that it could break at a touch, presented him with a challenge that was quickly overcome. Successfully crated and hoisted onto rollers, Seti's last treasure was hauled to the Nile, heaved on board, and laid beside the obelisk for their trip to Cairo.

Belzoni said that he had been aware of the rain problem, and declared (contradicting both Carter and himself) that "at present it rains in Thebes every year, and so [he] began to dig a canal at the tomb's entrance to carry it off, but halted it at the arrival of Salt on his first inspection."[18] While Belzoni was away on Project Obelisk it did rain, and with the protective pit filled, some of it seeped into the tomb. The resulting dampness being absorbed into the porous limestone walls caused paint to peel and corners to crack. In one chamber, an entire figure fell away, and though it was broken into three pieces, Belzoni observed with some satisfaction that he had saved it from further destruction. He did not say whether his rescue included carrying the three pieces to his boat. He deplored the damage, nonetheless, and feared that within a few years it would get much worse. He was right. Today the interior of Belzoni's Tomb (as it is often called) has lost the brilliance that we see in the watercolored drawings so wonderfully captured by Dr. Ricci and by Belzoni himself.[19]

The rain that Belzoni noted in the fall of 1818 was not to be a once-in-ten-years event. Discussing the tomb, Giovanni's critic Yanni D'Athanasi wrote that "a terrible rain which fell at this place in 1819 injured everything." Yanni went on to charge that "Mr. Belzoni with his much reputed architectural knowledge, ought to have reflected that the Egyptians had not made this well as an ornament to the tomb, but in order to preserve it from rain water."[20] Answering a rhetorical question as to whether the sarcophagus could have been removed without the pit being filled up, he declared that four sarcophagi could have been brought out without doing so. But D'Athanasi, of course, had his own axe to grind, being a favored employee of Henry Salt, the man whose arrival had caused Belzoni to cease cutting his water-diverting canal.

As Drovetti had intended, the contretemps at Karnak had shaken the usually unflappable Belzoni. The hostility of Drovetti's men had made renewed digging potentially life-threatening; and his work in the tomb was done. If it was true also that he had been fired by Salt, Giovanni was a man with no future in Egypt. No doubt he reviewed his predicament with Sarah and both agreed that it was time to return to England to make the most of his fame. He had his tomb exhibition to mount, a book to write, and a collection to sell. He also had his share of the profits from the sale of the Seti sarcophagus to tide them over. For all those reasons, this seemed to be the moment to exchange his tattered oriental robes for the garb of a London celebrity and to be listened to by the gentry of the Society of Antiquaries and the trustees of the British Museum. Nevertheless, he wrote,

"I must confess, that I felt no small degree of sorrow to quit a place which was become so familiar to me, and where, in no other part of the world, I could find so many objects of inquiry so congenial to my inclination."[21]

With everything aboard that the Belzonis owned and had acquired, their boat pushed off from the Luxor quay on January 27, 1819, and arrived at Boulak without incident on February 18. On their way they were passed by a *ganja* belonging to Salt's friend the Reverend William Jowett who carried Arabic Bibles to distribute to needy Muslims. Traveling with him was Nathaniel Pearce, who was to join Salt in Nubia. Pearce was the young man Lord Valentia had left as a potential agent in Abyssinia when exploring the Red Sea in 1810. He had been there ever since as a British agent, and had written to Salt asking to be allowed to come out. After seven years of living among the Abyssinians, Pearce looked like one of them and could barely make himself understood in English. But Belzoni liked him and regretted that they could not spend time together. More important was Pearce's impression of the Belzonis—particularly of Mrs. Belzoni. "I shall never forget the kindness of this lady," he wrote after telling her about his Abyssinian wife, Tringo,[22] whom he had left at the consulate and who declined to eat non-Christian food. Sarah told him that when she reached Cairo she would see to it that Tringo had "something killed for her by a Christian before her face."

"This treatment," wrote Pearce, "was so different from what I had hitherto experienced from Europeans at Cairo, that I could not leave them without feeling a sincere affection for them, and wished that my voyage could have been with beings so humane and as affectionate to a fellow traveller. They [the Belzonis] often said 'We know what it is to travel, every one is for himself in this part of the world, but we think it our duty to help others when it is in our power.'"[23]

Nathaniel Pearce's midriver encounter with the Belzonis provides the only record of Sarah's character outside her loyalty to her husband. Although brief, clearly Pearce's was an opinion uncolored by the criticisms of Henry Salt or by tales yet to be told by Beechey, Yanni, Finati, and the rest. With that said, however, it may be argued that working with colorful people can leave a very different impression than can a chance meeting with them in mid-Nile.

The Belzonis arrived in Cairo, stayed for several days at the consulate, and then went on to Rosetta, where the obelisk, sarcophagus, and numerous other antiquities were off-loaded and sent to Alexandria for shipment to England. Among them was the fine sarcophagus lid which, thanks to Drovetti's muted generosity, Giovanni had found at Gournou undisturbed by previous robbers, and which he declared had been recovered on his own account.[24] There is no record of the rest of that planned shipment, but the always-venomous Yanni declared, "I say nothing here of the specimens of antiquity which Madame Belzoni collected on her own account, and which she had no right to do, as both Mr. Belzoni and his wife were engaged and acted in the service of Mr. Salt."[25] Yanni specifically mentioned forty papyri that had been secretly shipped out without Salt's knowledge or proprietary claim. As D'Athanasi's charge was not published until 1836, there is no knowing when the papyri were exported. But if they accompanied Young Memnon, their acquisition could stem from the time in 1816 that Sarah had spent in the tomb homes of the women of Gournou. Yanni was not then at Thebes, but attributed the information to a friend of Giovanni's who had helped in the papyri's dispatch to Europe.

On seeing the antiquities safely to Alexandria, the Belzonis had intended to take the first available ship to England, but complaints that Giovanni had forwarded to Salt regarding the attack on him at Karnak had forced the consul to act on his behalf. Consequently, Peter Lee, the English vice-consul at Alexandria, lodged a formal complaint with his French counterpart. That somebody was doing something was gratifying to Belzoni, who, nonetheless, had "very little hopes to have any redress, as no such a thing ever happened in those countries, in particular against such people."[26] The legal proceedings were complicated by Drovetti being in Alexandria, where he lodged a countercharge against Henry Salt. The matter, therefore, had to be shelved until Salt returned from Upper Egypt. Not knowing when that would be, Belzoni left Sarah in a rented house in Rosetta and mounted a time-filling expedition westward from the Delta to the district of the Fayyum, where, in the Twelfth Dynasty (ca. 1991–1786 BC), the arable area around Lake Moeris had been developed into the breadbasket of Ancient Egypt.[27] Many towns and their temples grew up there, most of them dedicated to the crocodile god Sobek, whose earthly brethren abounded in the marshes around the lake.[28] Beyond it and deep in the Libyan desert was the fabled oasis of the god Ammon, which reputedly had never been visited by a European and therefore presented the kind of challenge on which Belzoni thrived.

He left Rosetta on April 29, 1819, taking with him a Sicilian servant and a Moor returning from Mecca who, being a *Hagg*, might prove useful as a man worthy of admiration and respect. Although, having crossed the lake, they came to numerous villages and told their sheiks that they were not treasure-hunters but only seekers after old stones (an unlikely story in the minds of their listeners), yet old stones were virtually all that Belzoni found. On May 5, while on the way to the village of Zaboo, his camel slipped and rolled down a twenty-foot bank on top of him. The accident left him severely bruised and unable to ride. He was still in severe pain when he returned to Cairo to find Salt back in his consulate, confined there due to the quarantine imposed against a renewed outbreak of plague. On the night of May 12, Belzoni breached the curfew and visited Salt as he had "business to transact with the consul." That was the extent of Giovanni's explanation, but Salt was more expansive. After settling Belzoni's claimed accounts, Salt gave him £200 and on the following day reviewed his collected antiquities and gave Belzoni all the items he could spare, "which he gratefully accepted." In Salt's opinion, Giovanni "seemed quite a satisfied man, and expressed a hope in parting that we should continue friends."[29] On returning to Sarah at Rosetta, Belzoni found that the legal machinery he had set in motion had a life of its own. Drovetti was charging that it was not Belzoni who sought redress, but Salt who had launched the complaint. Drovetti's successor as the French consul, M. Russel, was ready to dismiss the case in favor of his countryman, but Salt refused to drop the complaint against Lebolo and Rosignani. It was they who had physically attacked, if not an Englishman, at least a Paduan under the official protection of His Majesty's Government. The case would go forward—though not with Russel in the judge's chair. He departed for France leaving his vice-consul, Mr. Tednar Divan, to hear the evidence.

According to Belzoni, Mr. Divan had never visited Thebes but longed to do so. He saw the Karnak case as an official opportunity for an evidence-seeking trip and to get someone else to pay for it. He announced, therefore, that if Belzoni wished to proceed with the action, he would have to deposit 1,200 Spanish dollars to cover the judge's travel costs. Giovanni wryly enumerated them: "clerks, stewards, witnesses, boats, barges, canjars &c., and all this at my expense." He refused, but demanded a face-to-face meeting with Drovetti in the presence of the English and French consuls. When thus confronted and asked what he, Belzoni, had done to earn Drovetti's animosity, the answer was blunt. Giovanni had been guilty of absconding with the Philae obelisk. "I could scarcely believe," he would write, "that a man who held a situation once as a consul, should forget himself, and show an open inveteracy against an individual, merely because he was fortunate in his undertakings."[30] Just as Belzoni had feared, he could expect little justice from a French judge; nevertheless, the man's decision came as a surprise. Vice-Consul Divan determined that as the two defendants were Piedmontese and not French, if Salt and Belzoni wanted a decision, they should go to Turin to seek it.

In the course of this unsuccessful litigation, the patched-up relationship between Salt and Belzoni deteriorated. Salt wrote that "the Alexandrian air brought on his fever again,"[31] prompting accusations from Giovanni that the consul was taking credit for his discoveries. Had Salt thought about it, he might have replied that he who pays the piper calls the tune. Instead, he expressed bemused dismay that their relationship had broken into an open rupture, adding that in a last act of friendship he had paid all Belzoni's expenses incurred in the Karnak lawsuit.

While it was yet summer, the crated sarcophagus was loaded aboard the brig *Diana*, a ship belonging to Mohammed Ali's infant navy and being sent to England for refitting. The obelisk, too, may have been stowed aboard and was ultimately bound for the garden of William Bankes's father at Kingston Hall,[32] albeit without the pedestal which Yanni would later hoist from the Nile.[33]

Giovanni Belzoni's on-site contribution to Egyptian archaeology was over. "At last," he wrote, "having put an end to all my affairs in Egypt, in the middle of September, 1819, we embarked, thank God! for Europe."[34]

15 } BINGHAM RICHARDS AND
THE "CHRISTIE-SORT OF LIST"

SEPTEMBER 1819 STARTED WELL for Henry Salt. A bout of ophthalmia
that had brought him close to blindness had passed, and the tiresome
Belzonis were ready to leave Egypt. Moreover, after a two-week court-
ship, Salt was to be married. His biographer recognized that by English
standards the decision was both surprising and precipitous—but under-
standable. Halls's justification said much about contemporary European
life in Cairo, though he, himself, had never been there. "The want of accomplished female society in Egypt," he wrote "is one of the most serious evils that afflicts that demoralized and profligate country; and the few
European women who occasionally visit its shores, come and go like birds
of passage; so that when a fair occasion of this nature offers, a man must,
like Salt, be sudden in his proceedings and determination, or the prize
will surely elude his grasp."[1]

Before reaching for it, Salt was said to have had a son by an Abyssinian woman named Mahbubeb, but he avoided the responsibility of par-
enting by giving the boy to his servant Osman, nee William Thompson.
Although proof of that paternal giveaway is lacking, Henry Salt's need for
female companionship was such that he even wrote to Lord Mountnorris
saying that his "affections are strong" and his need for a wife much in his
mind.[2] Salt was thirty-eight and his prize a sixteen-year-old girl from Leghorn whose parents were in Alexandria on business. Her father's surname
was Pensa, but nowhere in Salt's correspondence do we even learn her
first name. She was, he said, "very young and amiable" and had been res-
cued by him from a distressing, but unspecified, situation.[3] The marriage
was performed in Alexandria with William Bankes and Henry Beechey

in attendance, both on their way home to England. Their departure thus robbed Salt of his closest companions and must have cast a shadow over the happy day. That shadow lengthened before it was out when the groom was stricken with a return of an intestinal malady that was to keep him near to death for the next two months.[4] His financial health was not much better. The £5,000 left him by his father had been invested in Belzoni's work in Upper Egypt, in Captain Caviglia's work at the pyramids and Sphinx, and in assembling the collection of antiquities whose sale would offset the outlays. Thus, Salt's shipment of his collection to England was one of those "fingers-crossed" undertakings which in the dangerous days of sail caused breaths to be held and prayers uttered.

With Nathaniel Pearce (Salt's protégé from Abyssinia) installed at the consulate as Salt's social assistant, in February 1820, it fell to Pearce to supervise the shipment. From the outset something evidently went wrong. Writing from Rosetta, Pearce informed Salt that the collection had been "in imminent danger . . . of going to the bottom of the Nile."[5] As it is only Salt's relieved response that survives, we have no details of that near-disaster.

After seven debilitating years in Abyssinia, and the death of his African wife early in May, Pearce was anxious to return to his family in England. Consequently, Salt made arrangements for him to accompany the collection. But, as had to be expected in nineteenth-century Egypt, nothing happened quickly. Having supervised the collection's move from Rosetta to Alexandria, Pearce had returned to Cairo. At the end of May, he was back in Alexandria to embark, "having taken charge of many valuable antiquities for the British Museum, and some other interesting articles for different noblemen and gentlemen in England."[6] He was already aboard waiting to sail when the captain concluded that he lacked both a sufficient cargo and a wind in the right direction. There would be no sailing until September. The disappointed Pearce went ashore, developed a fever, and died on August 12.

Salt had requested that a British naval transport might provide free passage for his collection, claiming that, as it was destined for the British Museum, it already was the property of the nation. Although the collection was not to be an outright gift, the ship *Dispatch* belonged to the British navy and did sail, as expected, in September.[7] Whether the captain realized that his instruction to help the consul would run to ninety-two crates is anybody's guess. He may also have had to find room for Bankes's obelisk, which had languished in an Alexandria warehouse since Belzoni had left it there two years earlier.

Giovanni and Sarah had not gone straight to England; instead, they had sailed to Venice en route to visiting his family in Padua. With his showman's instincts to the fore, in March 1819, he had heralded his visit by writing to the mayor and sending him a pair of Sekhmet statues as a gift to the city. He wanted them set up at the east door to the Palazzo della Ragione. However, their arrival in June presented an unexpected problem: the recipient was liable to import duties. Although the customs officers had no idea what the figures were worth, they thought that if they were objets d'art, it could be a lot. A referral to the region's Austrian governor produced two art experts, who, though knowing nothing about Egyptian antiques, sagely appraised the gifts at a nominal fifty lira apiece. Thus Padua avoided the embarrassment of having to shell out for a gift the city did not want. Nevertheless, by the time the figures were unpacked in the town hall and the mayor and his aides had debated how and where to display these barbaric gifts in this very Christian and medieval city, Belzoni's was a name to conjure with. As a son of Padua he was a celebrity of some sort and worthy of civic recognition. This was an era in which medals were struck for achievements that had nothing to do with valor. In England, they served as school prizes, promoted political candidates, were both anti- and pro-slavery, expressed support for the shamed Queen Caroline, and much else. A medal for Giovanni, therefore, seemed a good idea, and not all that expensive, only one being struck in gold.[8] Six more were made in silver and sixteen in bronze, none of them ready for presentation before he and Sarah left for Paris. Peter Clayton has noted that the bronze medals were minted to enable Belzoni to give them away to "professore de arti et di science," one of whom was Thomas Murdoch, whose relationship with the donor is unknown. Although a Fellow of the Royal Society who lived in fashionable No. 1 Portland Place and married a lady from Madeira, Murdoch's only surviving claim to fame seems to be his name engraved on Belzoni's medal.

As the Belzonis' fame continued to grow, Padua's city fathers realized that this son of a barber had public-relations possibilities. Tourists might come to see where the great man was born, and so a birthplace was designated—No. 2946 in via Paolotti. A stonemason was hired to provide a marble tablet with a suitable inscription. It read: IN QUESTA CASA IL

Above: *One of the sixteen bronze medals struck at Padua designed by L. Manfredini de-picting the pair of Sekhmet statues donated by Belzoni. The edge of the illustrated example is inscribed "GIOV: BELZONI TO T. MURDOCK F.R.S: 18 JUNE 1821." (Courtesy of Peter Clayton). Below: The ca. 1821 medal designed in England by an anonymous well-wisher. (Courtesy of Peter Clayton)*

5 NOV, 1773 NACQVE BELZONI. The correct date was 1778, but a few years either way were of little consequence. Besides, as the visitor Richard Burton observed in 1878, the house was too modern to have been the birthplace.[9] Much more impressive was an honorary medallion set up in the Palazzo della Ragione after Giovanni's death. Sculpted in Carrara marble and six feet in diameter, it depicted the bearded and turbaned head of the famous son of Padua. The inscription read: I. B. BELZONIVS. VETER. AEGIPTI MONVMENT. REPORTER.

Burton noted that in addition to the roundel, the city had commissioned

Left: *Beechey's head and arm from Karnak. (© The Trustees of the British Museum).* Opposite: *Young Memnon (Ramesses II) installed in the British Museum's sculpture gallery. Clearly visible is the hole reputedly bored by the French, who had intended to use gunpowder to blow the head from its shoulders. (© The Trustees of the British Museum).*

a statue of heroic proportions, almost ten feet tall and attired in an inappropriately fancy costume. "This work of art," wrote Burton, "has two merits. It shows the explorer's figure exactly as it never was, and it succeeds in hiding his face from a near view." The statue was in plaster and the precursor to a bronze casting that was never made. Burton was no more impressed by the building that housed it. "I find it," he declared, "a forecast of a nineteenth-century railway station."[10] Easy enough though it is to deride the quality of these Paduan memorials, in England Belzoni's only public memorial was to be the name he carved himself on the base of the British Museum's Amenophis statue.

By the end of March 1820, the Belzonis were in London looking for a publisher for the large book he had been writing in Italian titled *Narrative of the Operations and Recent Discoveries in Egypt and Nubia.* They found him in John Murray, whose *Quarterly Review* had already published notices of Belzoni's exploits at Abu Simbel and at the pyramid of Chephren. Murray (known as JM2) was the son of the Scottish publisher John Murray,[11] whose London business had flourished in the late eighteenth century and provided a base for JM2 to develop a respected and still existing publishing house. Murray had an eye for literary talent—in spite of the fact that he had only one, having lost the other to a writing master's errant penknife.[12] He was to be the publisher for Lord Byron, Jane Austen, Sir Walter Scott, and many more literary luminaries. Giovanni was not one of them, but he had celebrity status and potential sales appeal, and more

important, John Murray was interested in the expanding world of travel. As one such pioneer, Belzoni had already made his way into what Henry Salt called the "Temple of Fame."[13] Young Memnon was on display at the British Museum, and the great Seti tomb exhibition was on the drawing board, both of which were likely to sell books. JM2 was an enthusiastic yet wary publisher, and so printed only one thousand copies of Giovanni's first edition. He was taking a chance on underwriting a manuscript by an Italian with a volatile personality who began it by declaring, "As I made my discoveries alone, I have been anxious to write my book by myself, though in so doing, the reader will consider me, and with great propriety, guilty of temerity."[14] Regardless of the fact that he did not make his

The Piccadilly façade of William Bullock's Egyptian Hall, ca. 1830, formerly the London Museum and later an exhibition hall. (Courtesy of Peter Clayton)

discoveries alone, the book had a rough-cut liveliness to it that fit well with the public's image of the intrepid explorer on the fringes of Darkest Africa. Consequently, a second edition in 1821 sold as briskly as the first, spurred on by the publicity generated by the opening of Belzoni's London exhibition on May 1.

Still needled, perhaps, by his antipathy toward Drovetti, Belzoni was eager to have his *Narrative* published in France and so went to Paris in the autumn of 1821, where he met a bookseller named Galignani and the publisher-editor M. Depping, who agreed to make a French translation and publish it. Depping, however, overstepped his editorial bounds when he censored bits that were anti-French, cut passages from Sarah's essay that he thought *choses insignificantes,* and added material by Burckhardt and other travelers. M. Depping sent Giovanni page proofs and was surprised when the author reacted "in a severe and sometimes very rude style." Depping concluded that Giovanni had "become peevish and jealous in consequence of his disputes in Egypt" rather than that he was responding to overly aggressive editing.[15]

When Belzoni arrived in London, he had no idea where he would mount his exhibit, but fortune favored him. The grand Egyptian Hall, built in Piccadilly in 1812 at a cost of a princely £16,000 to house the ethnographic collections of the showman William Bullock, was now vacant. In spite of the success of Bullock's topical Napoleonic Wars exhibit that included Bonaparte's carriage and attracted 220,000 visitors, in 1819 he sold his collection of stuffed animals, birds, and armor and converted the building into rentable exhibit galleries.[16] With its Denonesque Egyptian façade and location in the middle of fashionable London, no better venue could be imagined. Although the building originally was known as the London Museum, the word "Museum" was removed from the front and "Exhibition" substituted. The name change was immaterial, however; Belzoni was turning the core of the building back into a museum where, under its glass-domed skylight, visitors could marvel at the fifty-foot cutaway model of Seti's tomb, complete with scaled copies of all those murals that he and Ricci had so laboriously copied in the candlelit depths of the Biban-el-Maluk sepulcher. The centerpiece, however, was Belzoni's full-scale reconstruction of two of the tomb's main chambers into which visitors could walk and share something approaching the wonderment he had experienced when they were first opened. To enhance the effect, the "apartments were to be illuminated by artificial lights."[17] But as modern gallery designers well know, every successful exhibition (with or without artificial lighting) needs its metaphorical elephant—that unique "wow" factor that stays in memory long after the doors close. Giovanni knew better than anyone what it was. Without Seti's alabaster sarcophagus, his reconstruction was an empty shell, yet with it, all London would be lining up in Piccadilly. And the *Diana* had docked at Deptford.

Remembering that Salt had requested a British ship to carry his collection and that the *Diana* belonged to Mohammed Ali, gaps in the documentary evidence leave one wondering which crates and obelisk were on the *Diana* and which on the navy's *Dispatch* transport. When Bankes learned that his obelisk had arrived, he took his friend the Duke of Wellington to Deptford to see it. In a letter postmarked September 22, Bankes wrote that the duke was so impressed that he had offered to have the obelisk transported to Kingston Hall on a gun carriage. In the same letter, Bankes noted that he had also seen the Seti sarcophagus that "had just arrived on a frigate belonging to the Pasha."[18] It may be inferred, therefore, that the obelisk did not travel aboard the *Diana.* It is possible, however, that when Bankes and the duke inspected it, the crate had already been off-loaded, whereas at Belzoni's insistence, the sarcophagus was still aboard. Logic suggests that as the sarcophagus could not yet be construed as belonging to the British Museum, it should not travel free on a British navy ship. With even greater validity the same argument can be applied to the obelisk.

Henry Salt's London agent, Bingham Richards, had the unenviable task of cataloging the antiquities which, once off-loaded from the British *Dispatch* and Mohammed Ali's *Diana,* were to be deposited at the British Museum. All were to be kept together until their collective value could be determined by the museum's trustees. The sarcophagus was to be treated no differently. But Salt was in Cairo and Belzoni in London, and Belzoni had other ideas. He went first to Deptford, where the *Diana* was berthed, and demanded that the Turkish captain should delay turning the sarcophagus over to Richards until he, Belzoni, had been in touch with the British Museum regarding a loan of it to his Egyptian Hall exhibition. But first he wanted it appraised.

In the world of antiques and antiquities, valuations are arrived at on the basis of recent sales of comparable objects. But there had been no prior market for sarcophagi or, indeed, for most of the relics Salt was shipping to the British Museum. Would a coffin of painted wood be of equal value to another of alabaster? Could a lesser sarcophagus of alabaster with a mummy still in it be more valuable than a better coffin without its occupant? Salt had written that he would leave it up to the museum authorities to provide the answers. But as the collection included everything from life-sized statuary to a packet of beads, no one was in a hurry to come to a decision. Meanwhile, a sarcophagus sent by Salt for Lord Mountnorris had inadvertently been turned over to the museum, which declined to release it. Knowing this, Belzoni was reluctant to see Seti's coffin go that route. Salt, all the while, was waiting for a price to be put on his collection and for it to be sold and paid for. To further that end, Salt sent his old friend William Hamilton a catalogue of all he had shipped or was still to be loaded from Thebes. In order to help the British Museum's trustees render a fair assessment, he put his estimated values beside each item—a step arrived at by consulting fellow collectors in Egypt.[19] Bernardino Drovetti was one such advisor, but drawing from pockets much deeper than Salt's, his estimates were high—too high for the museum trustee Sir Joseph Banks, who considered the price list a submission whose consideration was beneath everyone's dignity.[20]

Before Salt left for Egypt, Banks had urged him to discover and retrieve antiquities for the museum, as had Lord Mountnorris (at that time still Viscount Valentia), but now having done so, Salt discovered that the trustees' enthusiasm had waned. In a letter to him from Sir Joseph dated February 11, 1819, he learned that rather than giving Young Memnon prominence in the museum, the curators had "not placed that statue among the works of Fine Art." Banks went on to question "whether any statue that has been found in Egypt can be brought into competition with the grand works of the Townley Galleries," and, if not, Salt's prices were "very unlikely to be realized in Europe."

Charles Townley was an English rural landowner with enough money to embark on the Grand Tour of classical Europe in 1772, and thereby became hooked on Roman and Greek statuary, which he brought home in considerable quantities to grace his Park Street home in London.[21] Although many of his treasures turned out to be late Roman copies, after Townley's death in 1805 the British Museum purchased the collection for a hefty £20,000. It thereupon formed the centerpiece of the national collection of classical sculptures. This being the Age of Enlightenment and of young gentlemen still learning Latin and Greek, the Townley Marbles represented the best of what art appreciation was all about—until 1816, when Lord Elgin's marbles were extracted from his garden shed and sold to the museum for £35,000. Stripped from the Greek Parthenon by Elgin's employees between 1801 and 1812, the sculptures were the real deal and immediately outshone the Townley Collection.[22] Nevertheless, there were critics who dismissed the Parthenon marbles as "a parcel of old rubbish for which ten thousand pounds would be an exorbitant price."[23]

The purchase of the Elgin Marbles and the way they were obtained had caused a public outcry and spawned charges of condoning vandalism, the kind of publicity that no museum enjoys. Furthermore, the British economy was ailing; there was chronic unemployment; the price of bread had risen; and radical politicians were demanding parliamentary reform, all of which led in August to the infamous Peterloo Massacre.[24] In short, this was no time to ask Parliament to vote more money to buy relics for the British Museum. In a letter of February 16, William Hamilton wrote from the Foreign Office advising Salt "not to dip too deep in search of the hidden treasures of Egyptian sculpture, for in these economic times, John Bull may be easily induced to withhold his purse-strings, even at the risk of losing the unique monuments which you have discovered."[25] Sir Joseph Banks's letter written two days earlier chided Salt for his "very great miscalculation." His old friend and mentor Lord Mountnorris also wrote a reproving letter prompting a mortified Henry Salt to reply that it seemed that his list "has gone nigh to stamp me with the character of a Jew," and that "he was considered worse than Lord Elgin."[26] Mountnorris had sneeringly described the catalogue as a "Christie-sort of list,"[27] and evidently wanted to distance himself from anything so crass. Salt wrote letters of apology to Hamilton, Mountnorris, Charles Yorke,[28] and Sir Joseph Banks. In them, he stressed his willingness to cede the entire collection (excluding Seti's sarcophagus) to the museum at its own evaluation—though noting that he hoped that it would allow him £4,000 in recompense.

Banks agreed that Salt's apologetic explanation for having written the list was acceptable, though huffily adding that "he does not appear to me to establish on any good ground his reasons for having originally sent it."[29] Although it had been Sir Joseph who, with Mountnorris, had first put the collecting idea in Salt's head, they had since drawn a distinction between the kind of marble sculptures whose poses could be copied by naked art-school models and the stiff stances offered in granite by the Egyptian figures. Wrote Halls, "We are too apt in England to erect an individual, who has raised himself to distinction by any particular branch of knowledge, into a supreme judge of every other pursuit." Banks, said Halls, was one of them. "His knowledge of the Fine Arts was exceedingly limited," wrote Halls, "and yet on these subjects, as well as on those he really did understand, his authority seems to have been regarded as paramount."[30] Fortunately for everybody, Sir Joseph died on June 19, 1820.

Bickering and posturing over the price that the British Museum might or might not pay for the Salt Collection went on for years. Meanwhile, however, Giovanni wanted the sarcophagus for his exhibition. While he continued his efforts to prevent it going from the *Diana* to the museum, in August 1821, he appealed to the under secretary for foreign affairs, Joseph La Planta, to persuade the museum's trustees to grant him a year's loan of the sarcophagus, after which he would transfer it to the museum. Belzoni told Bingham Richards that William Hamilton had already agreed to the proposal.

It appears that Hamilton had had a meeting with Belzoni, whom he had not previously met, and found him an engaging and pleasant person. But when Hamilton got wind of the fact that Belzoni was using his name to promote his cause with the trustees, he wrote: "Gentlemen, I cannot take upon myself to authorize *any* deviation from Mr. Salt's instruction respecting his sarcophagus, nor was I aware of Mr. Belzoni's intention to make such a claim. I am, gentlemen, your obedient servant, William Hamilton."[31]

By this time, Bingham Richards was likely to have been wishing that the *Diana* had foundered and taken the Seti crate down with her. In a letter to Hamilton, he explained his dilemma. His instructions from Salt had been to deliver the sarcophagus to the British Museum and to offer it for sale—while bearing in mind that Belzoni would be due 50 percent of the sale price over £2,000. If the museum voted to let Belzoni have it, somebody would have to be responsible both for the bill of lading and the crate. Richards explained that if such a decision should be reached, he "cannot object to it, but must claim some guarantee, or indemnity, as may be satisfactory, for having given up the possession of this valuable article."[32] Five days later, Richards received a none-too-cordial note from Belzoni accusing him of having lodged complaints with Hamilton. The note ended, "Though it is immaterial to me to whom you complain, I beg you for the future to be more cautious in making use of my name on such unfounded insinuations and intrigues."[33]

The question still in everyone's mind was how valuable was this valuable article? In May 1819, Salt had written to the trustee Charles Yorke, stating that Drovetti (using William J. Bankes as a conduit) had made an offer of 10,000 Spanish dollars, which he rejected, as he said, being determined not to place himself "in the light of a dealer."[34] That figure translated into about £2,000—not enough to give Belzoni his cut, a restraint unknown to Richards until Giovanni showed him the signed agreement. Richards was an accountant and knew nothing about the value of an old Egyptian coffin. Although Giovanni had estimated it at about £20,000, Salt had urged Richards to get £2,000 for it. But with Salt in Cairo and Belzoni larger-than-life in London, Richards was caught in the middle, trying to be fair to both men. Meanwhile, he sought the advice of his father, who suggested that the signed agreement might be a forgery. Whether it was real or false, however, Richards had no choice but to follow Salt's original instructions. Richards Sr. ended by telling his son that by deviating from them, "you might be liable to an action for damages by the Trustees of the British Museum."[35] The crate, therefore, was finally off-loaded from the *Diana* and carted to the museum to join the rest of the still-to-be-appraised collection.

In an attempt to propel the museum's trustees into a purchasing decision, Belzoni announced that he had a foreign buyer for the sarcophagus who was prepared to pay £3,000 for it. The ploy backfired. On May 11, 1822, the trustees voted to "decline the alabaster sarcophagus, on account of the very high value put upon it by Mr. Belzoni."[36] However, Richards did not hear of that decision until September, when he received a letter from William J. Bankes urging him to accept Belzoni's buyer's £3,000 offer as "the sole means of silencing so troublesome and vexatious a claimant who I am very sure would be capable, should it be otherwise disposed of, of harassing Mr. Salt with lawsuits that might lead into great expense." Bankes added that the trustees at their meeting estimated the sarcophagus's value at "considerably under one thousand pounds."[37] Bankes evidently felt no gratitude to Belzoni once he had received his obelisk.

Although the coffin controversy had dragged on for three years, denying Belzoni the use of it in his exhibition, he had enjoyed celebrity life in London as the great explorer. His publisher, John Murray, had taken him under his literary wing and had even secured him a ticket to the coronation of George IV in July 1821. The accession had been wracked with scandal, as the new king's estranged wife, Caroline of Brunswick, had been enjoying herself in Europe with a disreputable Italian named Bartolomeo Bergami and had led George to try to divorce her by laying her dirty linen before the House of Lords in the hope that it would prevent her from becoming queen. Popular sentiment in favor of Caroline reached fever pitch when Bergami was blamed for having led the lady astray. As often happened when Giovanni emerged from the Egyptian Hall, crowds of well-wishers gathered to cheer him, but one day the fans grew into a riotous mob after someone mistook him for Bergami and chased him up Bond Street. Queen Caroline had insisted that she should accompany her husband at his coronation but found the doors of Westminster Abbey shut in her face and four bouncers waiting to drive her away. That interruption had barely subsided when John Murray and his guest arrived, tickets in hand. Whether or not the doormen thought Belzoni was Bergami is unknown, but they refused the pair entry until Giovanni used his bulk to push the bouncers aside.

Belzoni's friendship with John Murray survived the coronation embarrassment. Both were famous in the London of 1821, and each used the other to promote their books. At his house in Mayfair, Murray often invited the current literary lions to tea at events labeled his "four o'clock friends," and Belzoni undoubtedly was included. He was there again for a private party on New Year's Eve attended by the well-known poet and novelist Isaac D'Israeli and his young family, plus the Irish poet and folklorist Thomas Crofton Croker, whose account of Belzoni's unexpected behavior on that occasion was later published.[38] To those whose works he printed, Murray was known as "Glorious John." He also brewed a particularly potent punch, which, on this occasion, he tasted and then made a sound akin to that of a puppet showman trying to attract an audience. Moments before, he had given each of his guests a New Year pocketbook; in his, Isaac D'Israeli[39] composed four penciled lines, which he then handed to Crofton Croker. They read:

> Gigantic Belzoni at Pope Joan and tea,
> What a group of mere puppets, we seem beside thee;
> Which our kind host perceiving, with infinite jest,
> Gives us Punch at our supper, too keep up the jest.[40]

"Very true—Excellent!" Croker replied.

"Will you permit me to partake of your enjoyment?" asked Belzoni.

"Why, certainly," Croker answered, handing him the book.

When Belzoni read the lines, his face flushed and his eyes blazed. He struck his forehead and muttered, "I am betrayed!" and abruptly left the room. He had associated the puppets and the potable punch with the Punch of Punch and Judy shows and by extension his past career on carnival stages. When this unintended slight was explained to Murray, "the great publisher knew for the first time, that the celebrated Egyptian explorer had been an itinerant exhibitor."[41] While it is true that in his book Belzoni avoided any reference to his theatrical past, it is surprising that Murray would not have asked him about his years in England before going to Spain. Furthermore, on the day that the mob mistook him for Count Bergami, he was accompanied by an old acquaintance, Cyrus Redding, who was then the editor of the *New Monthly Magazine*. This was the same Cyrus Redding who had been a Plymouth newspaper editor when Belzoni had had a disagreement with Mr. Foote, the Plymouth theater manager. Redding would later recall that "Foote wanted to screw the Italian too hard in his bargains."[42] Belzoni's past may have been anathema to his post-Egyptian persona, but it had to have been, at best, a poorly kept secret.

When the great tomb exhibition opened in May 1821, Belzoni was at the height of his fame. The medal struck for him in Padua had arrived,

The great tomb exhibit in the Egyptian Hall, 1821. (Courtesy of Peter Clayton)

and although its obverse featured only the two Sekhmet figures he had donated to the city, another medal designed in England by an unnamed well-wisher honored his opening of Chephren's pyramid. Few would have noticed that the rendering was that of the Great Pyramid of Cheops.[43]

Just as an international bout of Egyptomania followed the discovery of Tutankhamen's tomb, and today a successful movie leads to numerous licensed or unauthorized products flooding the toy and souvenir markets, Belzoni's exhibition generated its share of knock-off products. In January 1822, a ladies' fashion magazine noted that "A favourite dress for the evening is a white satin slip tied behind of the Belzoni or Egyptian plaid." The editor huffily added, "We cannot forbear remarking the absurdity of the term Egyptian to the Scotch word plaid, when given to the chequers on a mummy's tomb of two thousand years ago."[44] Lacking an agent or a business manager, Sarah and Giovanni almost certainly earned nothing from such exploitation. They did, however, promote their own show in every way possible, including the hiring of billboard carriers to walk the city streets. They were called "peripatetic placards," and included a massive, pole-carried sign announcing "Belzoni's Egyptian Tomb at the Egyptian Hall" under an imaginary painting of the entrance to the tomb.[45]

Meanwhile, the controversy over the Seti sarcophagus continued to drag on and with it the museum's refusal to put a price on the rest of the collection. In 1822, Salt wrote to Richards telling him, "I hope to get four thousand pounds from Government, or otherwise I shall feel myself aggrieved. Should it be five thousand, I shall be highly satisfied," he added.[46] Salt had previously written to the trustees and repeated the "unconditional offer" that he had made to Sir Joseph Banks. However, he ended by saying, "I throw myself entirely on your liberality, and shall be perfectly satisfied with whatever you may determine in my favour."[47] This, of course, differed from feeling aggrieved if the museum offered less than £4,000. Still with nothing resolved, on January 8, 1823, an exasperated Bingham Richards wrote to Under Secretary of State Joseph La Planta, pointing out that Salt's agreement with Belzoni about the price of the sarcophagus could be ignored if the government would grant Salt £5,000 for the entire collection including the sarcophagus, that figure representing £2,000 for the bulk of the collection and £3,000 for the sarcophagus, thereby matching Belzoni's unnamed foreign buyer. Such a decision, Richards wrote, would not only reimburse Salt for his investment but also serve as "a testimonial of the desire of the Trustees that the British nation should possess the best Egyptian Collection extant." Although the claim sounded like advertising from a modern patriotic car dealer, the proposal seemed capable of satisfying everyone.

A month later, Richards was summoned to the museum "to confer with the sub-committee respecting Mr. Salt's Collection." There were five trustees present, of whom Henry Bankes was the only member with a prior interest in Egyptian antiquities.[48] The committee heard that Belzoni had an offer that would be accepted as soon as the museum released the sarcophagus. This the committee agreed to do and asked Richards whether he would accept £2,000 for the rest of the collection. Richards felt that he had no alternative but to do so in the hope that, at the next general meeting of the trustees, £3,000 more could be voted to save the sarcophagus from the ignominy of being shipped abroad.

Although the biographer J. J. Halls would dub the subcommittee's proposal "a miserable offer," Richards had explained that he "was led to believe that the leading and principal Trustee was averse to any purchase on the general grounds of economy and the *want* of interest in Egyptian antiquities." With that in mind, he grasped at the offered straw, citing "the old mercantile adage of 'Better to make a sale and repent, than to make no sale and repent." On March 17, Richards received a copy of a resolution by the General Meeting of the museum's trustees authorizing him to remove the sarcophagus whenever he chose. All he now had to do was to get Belzoni to name his buyer, a task that was to prove no easier than selling the rest of the collection. First, however, he had to inform Henry Salt of the way in which the deal with the museum had turned out. But communicating by letter was a slow process, and another year would pass before his client replied.

Salt had been ill through much of the winter. In March, a fire near Mohammed Ali's palace caused a magazine to explode that sent Cairo's Franks running—some to take refuge in the British consulate for fear that the flames would spread to the main arsenal and demolish the city. That did not happen, but it put an additional strain on the sickly Salt, as did the quarantine due to the return of the plague that was estimated to be taking 250 lives a day. On April 10, his wife gave birth to a second daughter who lived for only three days, and two days later she, too, died. On May 2, Salt wrote two letters to Richards, one telling him of his wife's death and his own continuing illness, and the other blasting him for his handling of the collection.

"I cannot understand upon what grounds you are acting. When there was a moment for taking a high tone, when the Trustees offered the miserable sum of two thousand pounds for the whole of my Collection, excepting the sarcophagus, you made no opposition; accepted the money, and compromised me completely." Salt went on to aver that he had not insisted on getting £3,000 for the coffin and "never laid any extravagant value" on it. "Nothing vexes me so much," Salt added, "as the circumstance that you should have by this line of acting, given the Trustees reason to suppose that I have been in collusion all the time with that prince of ungrateful adventurers—God knows, on the contrary, that I have always believed his offer to be a fictitious one, and that I have but one wish, never to have my name coupled with his. Why then ground your demands on his offer?"[49]

After so many months of silence, such a tirade (of which there was a good deal more) must have come as a shock to the long-suffering Richards, but being a reasonable man, he almost certainly read the second letter in the context of the first. Nevertheless, Richards still had Salt's power of attorney to handle the sale of the sarcophagus—regardless of Belzoni having a legitimate lien on it. But neither Richards nor Sarah, nor anyone else, knew that the Great Explorer was already dead.

16 } HARD TIMES

SARAH BELZONI HAD PLAYED no public part in the sarcophagus wrangling, being only the wife of one of the players. Nevertheless, throughout it all she had been loyally by his side—albeit when he wanted her. Although Giovanni had sent to Padua for his brother Francesco to help install the Egyptian Hall exhibit, he did not arrive until it was open. James Curtin with his experience in theatrical construction would have been a help, but after leaving Sarah in Jerusalem, he had taken other work, and was currently serving as a dragoman accompanying two reverend gentlemen spreading the Word in Ethiopia.[1] It is highly likely, therefore, that Sarah was the tomb project's principal foreman, carpenter, and scene painter. Once the show opened and the reviews were in, the price of admission dropped from half a crown to one shilling (in London slang "a bob a knob"), the excitement of success waned, and the ever-restless Belzoni needed new heights to climb. Consequently, he took off on an itinerary that drew him to Paris and to St. Petersburg for his meeting with the tsar, thence to Scandinavia and eventually to Copenhagen, in each country seeking opportunities to mount more tomb exhibits and to enjoy the hospitality and recognition afforded by civic leaders who claimed to have heard of him. Once again Sarah had been left behind. Indeed, she only learned where he was and what he was doing from letters he wrote to his publisher, John Murray.

Through the winter and spring of 1821–22, Giovanni's brother Francesco was in London and available to be useful, but there is slight evidence that Sarah did not like him, perhaps because he was enjoying himself at his brother's (and Sarah's) expense.[2] By the year's end, ticket sales at the Egyptian Hall were falling off, and in a wild winter storm the rotunda sprang a leak and rain seeped down, damaging the tomb's water-absorbing plaster of Paris reliefs. The show was scheduled to close on April 1, and an agreement had been reached with Sotheby's auction house that most of its contents would be sold. Belzoni, however, was still in Russia. In one of his letters to Murray, he asked him to monitor the sale if it should it take place before he, Giovanni, returned, adding that Francesco would welcome the advice. In another letter to Murray, Belzoni mentioned that in writing to Francesco he had told him to retain several specified objects.[3] Where, one might ask, did Sarah fit into this fraternal scenario? Her only known comment was to Murray expressing surprise that she had not received a letter of her own.[4]

By mid-May 1822, the traveler was back in London enjoying more publicity generated by the *Times.* However, in the June 3 issue, the writer was Belzoni himself complaining that he had been insulted and then arrested by three Bow Street Runners whom he called "thieves catchers." This is what had happened: A much-anticipated gala was to be held at the King's Theatre as a charity for "relief of the distressed Irish" for which advance tickets had to be purchased. By the time Belzoni returned to London, tickets were no longer available, denying him the opportunity to "behold an assembly of the beauty and magnificence of this country, and to contribute at the same time to that charitable purpose." It turned out, however, that the theater's owner still had a hundred tickets (probably turned in by "no-shows") that he wanted to sell at ten guineas each. Whether this was a scalper's price or the original cost of admission is not known, but in his letter to the *Times,* Giovanni complained that only two of the ten guineas would actually be applied to the relief of the Irish poor—a complaint with a twenty-first-century ring. The ticket Belzoni bought had previously been issued in the name of the Countess de Grey. It was hardly surprising, therefore, that an astute ticket checker at the theater noticed that he was the wrong sex to be a countess—and a great deal too tall. Two policemen took him into custody, where he was stared at by the crowds of distinguished ticket holders still entering the theater, leaving him exposed, he said, "as I had been in a pillory." Eventually one of the gala's sponsors, the Earl of Ancran, came to Belzoni's rescue, and not only vouched for him but gave him his ticket. Unfortunately, the wheels of justice had already been set in motion, and a half hour later the three Bow Street Runners seized him and hauled him before a magistrate, Sir Richard Birnie, who declared him guilty of being a gate crasher. Several people said they recognized the Great Explorer, the Lord Mayor of London among them, and finally Belzoni was released to enjoy what was left of the evening. As he explained in his letter, Belzoni considered that he had been "subjected to people who should have protected me."

Earlier in the same letter to the *Times*, Giovanni had given a hint toward the direction of his next move, saying, "I am going out of England within a few weeks, and probably a long time will elapse before my return."[5] Whether or not his unpleasant experience at the King's Theatre played any part in his decision to leave England no one knows, but it is certain that one man who knew lived in Cambridge and was destined to be a primary source for the last chapter in Belzoni's life. The man was the Reverend George Adam Browne, an idealistic but somewhat naïve don and junior bursar of Trinity College whom Giovanni may have met through a Masonic Lodge of which he had been a member since 1821.[6] Belzoni gave Browne his power of attorney to act for him in his absence in regard to the still-unresolved affair of the Seti sarcophagus. Browne passed the signed document to the solicitor-general, Sir John Copley, to whom Bingham Richards wrote seeking access both to it and to the name of Belzoni's unidentified buyer. In June 1823, Browne was staying in London and wrote to Richards saying that he did not know the name of the person but had no doubt that the individual "would readily offer two thousand pounds to you for the sarcophagus." Browne ended by saying that he would be seeing Copley later in the week and would urge him to "interest Parliament in behalf of Belzoni." He hoped that the Commons would advance £2,000 to Salt and £500 to Belzoni, enabling the sarcophagus to remain in the British Museum "where so splendid a relic ought to be."[7]

Richards then left it to Browne to contact Belzoni to obtain the name of the anonymous buyer. After five months of silence, Richards wrote again to Browne and even asked Henry Beechey to call on him in Cambridge. To this Browne replied that he had written to Belzoni via the British consul in Tangier, who had returned the letters unopened to Sarah Belzoni in England. "I only think it would be an act of the greatest injustice to the person who discovered the Tomb, and the valuable sarcophagus it contained, if in the sale of the said sarcophagus he is to be entirely overlooked," Browne wrote. He added that he had done what he could to impress the British Museum's trustees "with a proper sense of what is due to Mr. Belzoni's merits," but found them less receptive than he had hoped.

His appeals to members of Parliament fared no better, and so with regret he had no choice but to let destiny take its course.[8]

The Reverend Browne's role in all this is obscure. He was not a traveler who had become hooked on Egypt by sailing the Nile, but he did know two other Trinity clergymen who had. Those were the men who had hired James Curtin as their dragoman and brought back a mummy which they presented to the Fitzwilliam Museum. Browne considered that "together with its case, it is one of the most perfect and beautiful that can be found in any known collection."[9] Although mummified beauty is not recognized by every museum visitor, Browne became the conduit for another more easily admired Egyptian treasure that would come to the Fitzwilliam Museum. The red-granite lid of the sarcophagus from the tomb of Ramesses III had been included in the shipment from the *Dispatch* and mistakenly deposited in the British Museum's yard when inventory taker Richards failed to recognize that the allegedly three-ton slab was not Salt's.[10] Following Giovanni's instruction, Browne undertook to have it carted to Cambridge (see p. 76). The circumstances surrounding this large and heavy gift (if, indeed, it *was* a gift) are obscure. That Belzoni should donate one of his principal treasures when selling it would have brought him much-needed money is another unsolved mystery. The Reverend Browne knew the answer and so did the Fitzwilliam Museum, but neither was telling.

We know that Belzoni was an astute individual with a well-developed opinion of his own worth. It seems possible, therefore, that his lust for academic acceptance led him to believe that the museum or the university would bestow some honor or that his being inducted as a Mason into a Cambridge Lodge was payment enough.

Belzoni's June announcement that he intended to be away from England for some unspecified time turned out to mean that he was going to Paris to open another tomb exhibit. However, he was back in London by the year's end, and in a letter to Bingham Richards written on New Year's Eve, he repeated that he had "just arrived to pay [his] last visit to England, at least for some time." In his biography of Henry Salt, Halls unkindly printed the letter exactly as written—perhaps to infer that Belzoni was an untrustworthy and uneducated foreigner. Giovanni was still blaming the chairman of the British Museum's trustees for their failure to settle the sarcophagus sale, declaring that if he "is still obstinate in refusing to retourn the properiety of other, I am determined to troy how far the low of Ingland can be inforced against injustice and harogance."[11] Giovanni ended by wishing Richards a happy new year. It was to be the last communication he would receive from the Great Explorer.

In a letter written from Paris in October 1821 to his publisher and friend John Murray, Belzoni was inspired to wax poetic:

> Britains farewell my friends adieu
> I must far away from the happy shore
> My hart will remain hever with you
> Should I the dear land see no more
> I scoff at my foes, and the Intrigoni
> If my friends remember their true Belzoni.[12]

It seems clear that by this time Giovanni was planning to travel a good deal farther than Paris, a notion likely to have been previously put into his head by Murray and thereby stirring memories of conversations with Burckhardt and his goal to reach the source of the Nile. A later traveler, Richard Burton, wrote of Belzoni that he "prepared to carry out the dream of his life—a plunge into the then unexplored depths of the African continent."[13] However, as is well known, the dream of Giovanni's life was to be a successful hydraulic engineer in a civilized land.

A previous explorer named Mungo Park had suggested that the River Niger flowed eastward, in which case it might be linked to the Nile. Burckhardt, therefore, intended to join one of the slave caravans returning to the fabled city of Timbuktu and there reach the river and follow it wherever it went. Park had been right; at Timbuktu, the Niger *was* flowing east, but soon after the town of Bamba, it turned south and eventually spilled out into the Gulf of Guinea as the Rio Fermoso. If the Niger and the Nile had a common or adjacent source, half of Africa could be commercially exploited—at least that was the hope of the Association for Promoting the Discovery of the Interior Parts of Africa, founded in 1788 by its first president, the cantankerous Sir Joseph Banks. A map published in the same year demonstrated how little was known about the interior behind the coastal fringe of West Africa. Most of that was then claimed by the Portuguese and the French and known to the English by their marketable commodities as the Grain Coast, the Ivory Coast, and the Gold Coast, and collectively known as the Slave Coast.[14]

In the same year that Banks founded the African Association, he also created the Linnean Society to cultivate the science of natural history. The Scottish surgeon Mungo Park (whose portrait bears a striking resemblance to Thomas Jefferson) was a founding member of both. In 1794, he volunteered to follow Major Daniel Houghton's failed attempt to chart the course of the Niger, approaching it from the Gambia River to the north. July 1, 1796, found Park at its bank, where he was able to follow its course from the village of Ségou downstream to Silla before the lack of supplies forced him to give up. Park tried again in 1803, this time with government backing. Three years later he reached Timbuktu, but afterward, while riding the Bussa rapids in his boat *Joliba* (the local name for the river), he was attacked by natives armed with bows, arrows, and throwing spears. As he tried to evade them, the boat overturned and Mungo Park drowned.

In Park's absence, his account of his first expedition was published in London and read by the African Association of which John Burckhardt was a member. Sir Joseph Banks then prevailed upon the association to bankroll Burckhardt in trying to reach the Niger from the Nile. In 1816, John Murray published Park's *Travels in the Interior Districts of Africa: Performed in the years 1795, 1796 and 1797,* thereby renewing interest in the elusive river. Just as in a later generation it made patriotic sense for the British flag to be the first raised atop Mount Everest, so in the early nineteenth century an Englishman should have the honor of reaching the source of the Niger. It also made sense that a hero who could solve the mystery of Chephren's pyramid and write a best-selling book about it would be just the chap to open the interior of Africa. It mattered not that the city of Padua claimed him as its own; Giovanni Belzoni was a proven Anglophile and would give the glory to Britain. His verse had said as much.

It was time to go. The Paris exhibition had not been a success, the rent of the property far exceeding the profits;[15] the London show had closed; he had no job; and there were magistrates and policemen in the city to whom his good name meant nothing. It would take a grand new enterprise to put Belzoni back on his pinnacle. If Sarah thought otherwise, her objections have gone unrecorded. Instead, she insisted on going with her husband, regardless of where it might take them.

Unlike Mungo Park or Burckhardt, Giovanni could not count on support either from the British government or from the African Association, both of whom knew him as the man who was giving the national museum such trouble over a stone coffin that nobody seemed to want. According to Richard Burton, he had been able to borrow £200 from Briggs Brothers, Henry Salt's bankers. It is likely, too, that as Mungo Park's publisher, John Murray contributed to defraying the expedition's expenses. Nevertheless, Belzoni was about to run into debt and put his life at risk on behalf of his adopted country.[16]

At the start all went relatively smoothly. On arriving at Gibraltar, Giovanni met the agent representing the emperor of Morocco, who passed the word to his master that this was a person worthy of a *firman*. The British consul at Tangier was equally ready to help, and an audience with Emperor Mulay Abd ar-Rahman added a level of dignity unequalled since Alexander of Russia gave Giovanni his ring. The Belzonis then went on to the port of Fez, where Giovanni prepared himself to cross the Atlas Mountains into the El Areg Desert, where, with the emperor's blessing, he would join a caravan bound for Timbuktu. He would allow his wife to venture no farther. As she had at Philae, Sarah was to stay and await his return. If after an unrecorded time he did not, she was to leave Fez and catch the next boat back to England. Perhaps Belzoni had a premonition that the project might not turn out well and so was prompted to make his will using the London bankers Briggs Brothers as his executors. In the will, he left £200 to Sarah, but the rest of his meager property was to be divided into thirds between Sarah, his ailing mother, and his brother Domenico.[17] Among the listed items were Giovanni's share of the Seti I sarcophagus sale and the tsar's diamond ring. The will ended by directing that if nothing was heard from him after five years, the sealed document should be opened and executed.[18]

In a letter to his Cambridge friend the Reverend Browne, Belzoni noted that Jewish merchants with influence at the emperor's court were concerned lest a European country should poach on their lucrative monopoly of trade in central Africa. Whether that opposition prompted the emperor to revoke Belzoni's permit to join the caravan is unproven, but revoke it he did. Consequently, a new approach was needed, one not dependent on favors from the emperor of Morocco. After returning to Gibraltar, Giovanni sailed to Tenerife and there waited for an English warship that could carry him to the coast of West Africa. It proved to be HMS *Swinger* under Captain Filmore, who was to command the English presence in the Gulf of Guinea. Unfortunately, however, Giovanni's plan to follow Mungo Park up the Gambia River did not work out. Captain

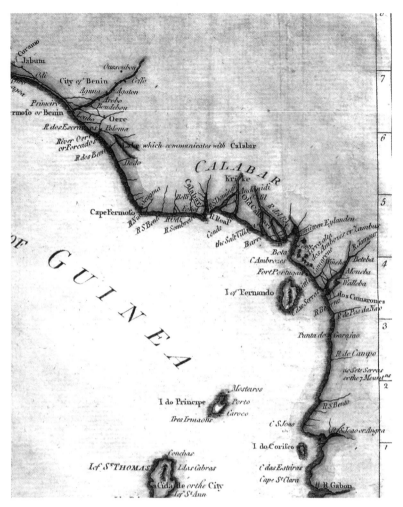

Detail of the Benin coast derived from a map by Jean Baptiste Bourguignon D'Anville labeled "Map of the Coast of Guinea" and published in London in 1788.

Filmore's orders were to sail south toward the Slave Coast and the British fort near the mouth of the Niger.

The fort stood on the north end of the island of Fernando Po, where, in 1861, the previously quoted Richard Burton was to become a reluctant British consul. He considered it the worst posting in the Foreign Office's fiefdom and was well aware that it had a reputation as "the white man's grave."[19] But so was the rest of the West African coast, into which Belzoni was about to venture, known as the Bight of Benin. A contemporary seaman's song began:

The Bight of Benin! The Bight of Benin!
One comes out where three goes in.

At Fernando Po, Belzoni transferred to the Liverpool-based brig *Castor*, whose mercantile officer (supercargo) William Fell and crew were happy to welcome the famous traveler and gave him three hearty cheers when he left on his journey upriver. A previously supplied letter of introduction to a Benin merchant named John Houtson provided both a companion and a guide. But soon after they reached the city of Benin, Belzoni suffered the onset of a bout of dysentery that neither opium nor castor oil would overcome. Nevertheless, Benin's king having agreed to provide an escort and carriers who would take him on to Houssa, Giovanni, without Sarah to dissuade him, pressed on until sickness sapped the last of his strength. The merchant companion left him and went back to Benin, but there alerted John Hodgson, the captain of another trading brig, the *Providence*, who set out to find the sick explorer.

Hodgson did so, but realizing that Belzoni was near death, he acceded to Giovanni's request that he be taken back to the coast where he could breathe sea air. On December 2, they got as far as Gwato (or Gato), where he recovered enough to drink a cup of tea and write two letters, one to his executor, Samuel Briggs, and the other to William Fell of the *Castor*, asking him to dispose of the expedition's supplies of food and medicines. In writing to Briggs, Belzoni specified that "all the travelling apparatus" should go back to England on the *Castor*. The letter ended in an uncharacteristically tender note, pleading, "console my dear Sarah; tell her I cannot write to her—she has been to me a faithful and good wife upwards of twenty years. I die at last a beggar; and if my friends should agree to do any thing for her and my family, I wish it to be divided between my wife and my mother."[20] The letter would take nearly five months to reach England. In belatedly printing it, the *Times* noted that it was then in Sarah's hands, having been given to her by Samuel Briggs "as it must always afford her a source of consolation."[21]

One may be forgiven for wondering why, if Belzoni could write two business-related letters, he could not write to Sarah? The answer may be that he had always been an undemonstrative husband and that even now that he was dying he could only express his hidden feelings through a third person. Sarah's love, however, was evident in her last letter, written on August 4, 1823, after her return from Fez to London. She was, she confessed, "much troubled in mind on your account the manner we parted in so unexpected neither saying farewell." Later in the letter, Sarah warned him "not to trust my people or make use of their letters," adding that "The trustees of the B.M. refuse to buy the sarcophagus excepting at a Price not beyond seven hundred pounds." She ended by urging her husband: "do not be too venturesome[.] recollect poor Mungo Park[.] if you find too many difficulties turn back before it is too late. . . . I am far from happy[.] we must hope for the best[.] God will I hope and trust[,] either prosper you in your undertaking or cause your safe return[.] once more farewell[.] be cautious. May God Bless and Protect you[.] trust in him my dear jo-vanni and happy return to England."[22]

Giovanni died at Gwato in Benin on December 3, 1823, where William Fell and sailors from the *Castor* buried him six feet deep "at the foot of a very large tree" near the residence of Ogea, the local governor. Captain Hodgson of the *Providence* read the funeral service and with eighteen of his men saluted the Great Explorer with three volleys of musketry. Guns on the *Providence,* the *Castor,* and the American schooner *Curlew* added their voices.[23] William Fell, supercargo of the *Castor,* ordered his carpenters to create and erect a wooden monument reading:

Here lie the remains of
G. BELZONI, Esq.
Who was attacked with Dysentry On the 20th Nov.
at Benin on his way to Houssa and Timbuctoo
and died at this place on the 3rd December, 1823.

The inscription ended with a request: "The gentlemen who placed this inscription over the grave of this intrepid and enterprising traveller, hope that every European visiting this spot will cause the ground to be cleared, and the fence round the grave to be repaired, if necessary."[24] By 1862, when Richard Burton visited the grave site, neither the marker nor the fence had survived, although old men at Gwato still talked about "Belzoni's tree."[25] A local rumor had it that Governor *(Cabocdeer)* Ogea had poisoned Belzoni, and, wrote Burton, "what lends colour to the charge is that he afterwards tried the same trick upon a European trader and failed." Burton got his information from another Gwato chief, "also, by the by, a noted poisoner," who said that Ogea had acquired many of Belzoni's papers, pages from which had been seen by European merchants. Alas, Burton was unable to find them.[26]

After Sarah returned from Fez, she went to Paris to see what could be done to salvage the fortunes of the tomb exhibition, and if that was not possible, to try to sell its elements. Failing that, she planned to bring it all back to England, thence to Edinburgh and Dublin (both cities she well remembered) and finally on to St. Petersburg. Once the exhibit opened in Russia, she meant to cross Europe to Alexandria and, as a *Times* correspondent put it, "there pursue her course up the Nile to Chandi in Nubia where she will await the arrival of the different Caravans, in order to gain the much-wished-for intelligence of Mr. Belzoni's movements."[27]

Once Sarah learned that her Giovanni was no longer alive, she realized that she had inherited deep financial trouble. Something needed to be done to preserve the Belzoni name as a source of income. The lithographs that had accompanied his book had been rapturously received. As those had sold well, it followed that a portrait engraving of the Great Explorer should find a ready market. Two years later, therefore, Sarah commissioned a new portrait that surrounded him with what the *Times* called "symbolic ornaments," notably Young Memnon, the head of Ramesses II; the giant arm from Karnak; and the Amenophis statue from the Amenophium, all backed by the pyramids (frontispiece). Also included were the Seti sarcophagus and the Bankes obelisk, both entwined with a snake whose symbolism may relate to Salt, Bankes, and the British Museum's trustees. An advance print was placed on the entrance table at the University Club, where members were invited to inscribe the signatures of "such members as are willing to become purchasers."[28] The number of copies sold has not been recorded, but clearly Sarah needed more help. To that end, with the assistance of the returned James Curtin, she put together a new but smaller exhibition in Leicester Square that was billed as a memorial to her husband.[29] She hoped that it could feature the attention-grabbing "elephant" that Giovanni had been denied.

By then the sarcophagus stand-off had been resolved. Addressing a letter to Joseph La Planta at the British Museum, Bingham Richards wrote, "I beg to inform you that I have disposed of the Alabaster Sarcophagus deposited by me in the British Museum to John Soane Esq., & that I shall immediately after the Easter recess take the necessary steps to remove it from the museum to that Gentleman's residence in Lincoln's Inn Fields."[30] The relieved Richards had previously written to the trustees transmitting the same good news.[31]

John Soane was already a well-established London architect with both

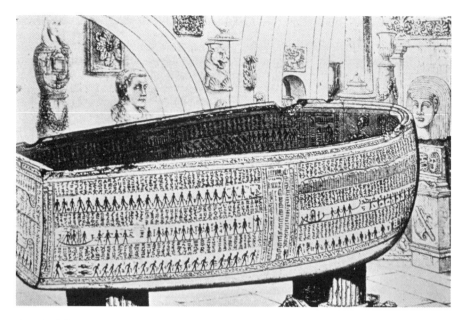

Seti I's alabaster sarcophagus as exhibited in Sir John Soane's basement, ca. 1824.

the taste and the money to buy the sarcophagus as his own toy to add to his already significant collection of Townley-era sculptures and ancient architectural bits and pieces. He also inherited the continuing correspondence that bedeviled the sale. On February 9, 1825, the Reverend Browne again entered the lists, sending Soane a copy of a notice in the *Cambridge Chronicle* from the previous December. Though almost certainly provided by Browne, the paper announced that Sarah's exhibit would open in London in the spring, voicing the possibility that the sarcophagus "will decorate the chamber itself, as the conditions of its sale to Mr. Soane expressly allowed it to be repurchased by Mr. Belzoni or his heirs at the sum originally agreed upon in Egypt."[32] Browne's covering letter also stated that trustee William Bankes[33] told Richards "most clearly" that this post-sale proviso was part of the deal. Browne added that "of course Mrs. Belzoni is anxious to make the new exhibition as complete as possible, & the Sarcophagus would effactually contribute to render it so."[34]

Soane was prompt to reply, assuring Browne that "there was no understanding at all between Mr. Bingham Richards & myself as to the relinquishment of the Sarcophagus." He concluded by saying that he could not imagine "from what source Mr. Bankes derived his information."[35] The likelihood that Soane would even lend the sarcophagus to Sarah was remote. Before receiving it, he had written to the museum delaying delivery because the "Catacomb preparing for it cannot be completed before Tuesday evening."[36] The "Catacomb" was in reality Soane's basement, illuminated by a small rotunda that offered little light on a dull day. The sarcophagus remains there in what is now the Sir John Soane Museum, albeit protected by a hideously framed glass case.

Wealthy collectors fall into two groups: those who keep their acquisitions quietly, even miserly, to themselves, and the others, who want the world to know what they have—and probably what they paid for it. John Soane stood somewhere in the middle, eight months elapsing before he threw a party for Belzoni's box. On Saturday, March 26, 1825, he "received a distinguished assemblage of the patrons and lovers of the arts . . . for the purpose of gratifying them with a view of the splendid monument, and other antiquities, by lamp-light." There were no "Please Do Not Touch" notices, and while "viewing this curious relic of antiquity," some of the guests "when touching it with their hands, seemed to feel sensations of awe, inspired, no doubt, by the reflection that it once contained the dust of a powerful monarch, of whom no other trace remained." The awed touchers included "a numerous party of ladies and gentlemen of rank," but the following Monday's report in the *Times* made no reference to the presence of Mrs. Belzoni.[37]

Although news from England took a while to reach Australia, the exploits and death of Belzoni attracted a surprising amount of newspaper attention. On Friday, October 28, 1825, the *Colonial Times & Tasmanian Advertiser* carried a report that began: "Yesterday [April 2] Mr. Soane, the fortunate possessor of this inestimable curiosity opened his house in Lincoln's Inn-Fields, to his friends and other persons versed in antiquarian lore." The sarcophagus, said the correspondent, "was discovered in Egypt by the indefatigable Belzoni, and was brought to this country, where we grive [sic] to say, a false economy prevented it being made public property."

To Sarah's rueful disappointment, her exhibition both opened and closed without the sarcophagus that could have brought it success. According to the *Morning Herald*, however, Soane was no villain and "promptly set the example . . . to aid Mrs. Belzoni in her trying difficulties, that he did, without hesitation, what the Government had declined or hesitated to do—While so many thousands were given to Lord Elgin [& others?] for 'Marbles' Mr. Soane gave Mrs. Belzoni 2000 guineas for the fine, perfect, and celebrated *Sarcophagus,* brought to this country by that most enterprising & remarkable traveler of modern times."[38] Mr. Soane, of course, did nothing of the kind, the money having been deposited with Bingham Richards to be sent in toto to Henry Salt in Cairo. The sale brought Sarah nothing. Nevertheless, Soane had been generous, prompting her to acknowledge with gratitude "his very handsome contribution in relief of her present distressed situation." She added an apology that she had not immediately answered Soane's letter because it was delivered "while she was engaged with some Gentlemen who had called to view the Tomb, whom she was unable then to leave."[39] Sarah did not specify the size of Soane's donation, but it may have been the fifty pounds revealed in a list of contributors printed in the *Times* on November 12 and 15. Among them were John Murray (who should have felt some guilt at encouraging Belzoni back to Africa) at another fifty pounds; the banker and executor Samuel Briggs at twenty-five; William J. Bankes at twenty, likewise the *Morning Herald;* and a "Lady who visited the Tomb with her children, five pounds." "Four youthful admirers of Belzoni" gave ten shillings each, and an anonymous benefactor volunteered one pound.

A previous edition of the *Times* had praised "the warm interest excited throughout the benevolent portion of society" and rejoiced that "some of the most respectable bankers in town are ready to receive subscriptions on the joint behalf of that amiable lady." The column went on to note that "some persons of the highest character and distinction have declared their anxiety to promote in this instance the cause of humanity and science."[40] Other unnamed gentlemen would set up a committee to help Mrs. Belzoni. Among those serving on it were to be the lord mayor of London, the Rev. G. A. Browne, and his friend the Rev. Bernard Hanbury, who had given his mummy to the Cambridge museum. Another news report had it that the government had been moved to grant Sarah £200, but three weeks later the statement was retracted.[41] The government would, in fact, give her nothing for another twenty-five years, and then only a token £100 per annum from the Civil List. Among the many who tried to help Sarah was a Scottish lawyer named William Rae Wilson who had traveled in Egypt and who subscribed "his mite with regret that I could not make it 100£." He ended by saying that no greater respect for Belzoni's memory could be shown "than in drying up the tears of his afflicted widow . . . by constituting a proper fund to purchase her an annuity for her comfort, and make her heart sing for joy in the evening of her life."[42]

Regardless of such worthy and moving appeals, in 1828 Sarah was still trying to raise money to pay off her debts and put bread on her table. But the *Times* was close to being right when it declared that Belzoni's name "is, we fear, well nigh forgotten," adding that "as far as our feeble authority may extend, the memory of a good man, and a man of genius shall not perish from the earth." Those laudable sentiments preceded an announcement on behalf of Sarah that she intended to publish new lithographs of her husband's tomb paintings to be issued in several parts and which, in all, would contain eighty plates. But there was a hitch: The project could not go forward unless at least two hundred subscribers would step up in advance. The paper's reporter, however, did not doubt that three times that number would be aboard in a very few days.[43] Alas, he was wrong; there was no stampede, and Sarah's publication never got beyond its promotional brochure and the six prints lithographed for her by Charles Hullmandel.[44]

Giovanni Belzoni is remembered as much for his watercolored lithographs as for his *Narrative*, and admiring viewers are led to suppose that these fine renderings were created almost photographically in the places depicted. However, there is reason to suggest that some, if not most, of the views were completed in London before or during the exhibition year. How, one might ask, could eighty new plates materialize after the artist was dead? Among the six extra plates published in 1822, one is better known than the others, namely the moving of Memnon at the Ramesseum (see p. 70). Why, if this iconic picture already existed, was it not included in the original set of illustrations? That the folio includes a view of the temple on the trail to Berenice attributed to Sarah, although it is a site she never visited, suggests that this lithograph was created from Belzoni's unfinished sketches.[45] Three more carry Sarah's credit, including the view of the Nile in flood with ducks happily swimming against the flow (see p. 174). It would seem, therefore, that Sarah deserved more artistic credit than she was allowed. That assumption could explain the curious blue bloomers that Ramesses II is shown wearing in the temple at Abu Simbel. Was that feminine detail another finishing touch from Sarah's hand?[46]

Although the public memory of Belzoni and his accomplishments was fading toward oblivion, his name lived on. In April 1827, a race horse named Belzoni lost to the colt Fleur-de-lis, and a month later a similarly named passenger and cargo ship was outward bound from Calcutta.[47]

In every generation there are opportunists eager to milk the fame of others. One taking advantage of Giovanni Belzoni was Sarah Atkins, who claimed to have secured his permission to write a children's book titled *Fruits of Enterprise*, which reduced his *Narrative* to a stilted question-and-answer format by a mother to her four priggish, clean-collared children.[48] The responses of the boy, Bernard, ranged from, "What a troublesome thing selfishness is, mamma!" to, "How very droll Mahomed Ali must have looked when he was standing on that little stool!" Although the dialogue was as wooden as a cricket bat, the tract went into at least twelve editions. In the flyleaf of one copy of the twelfth, in a well-scrubbed little hand, Master Hugh Cholmley Bucchann wrote his name and the date "14 January, 1855." Sarah Atkins had made another sale.

17 } SAVING SARAH

That the cares of to-day may vanish to-morrow,
And with joy, drive away dull grief and sad sorrow:
The traveller's poor "Widow" appeals not in vain.
Each Briton attends, hears—her cause will maintain.

An anonymous well-wisher,
Times (London), November 15, 1825

THE FAILURE OF Sarah Belzoni's lithographic venture ended her attempts to resuscitate her husband's memory. She had no money, and most of the artifacts she had retained from her exhibit appear to have been sold, and so, with no public persona, she disappeared from newspaper records. In 1833, she left London and rented a house in Brussels, where she remained until she was sixty-eight.[1] Why she chose Belgium is unknown, any more than is the reasoning which, in 1857, prompted her subsequent move to St. Helier on the island of Jersey. We know only that seven years earlier, friends in England were again pressing the government to grant her a pension. Writing from Clapham, one who signed himself "Humanitas" pointed out that visitors to the British Museum would see "several precious relics of Egyptian sculpture for which the British nation is indebted to her husband," and gentlemen would be "disturbed by the self-reproach that they had left the old widow of him by whom these acquisitions were made to pine away in destitution." The writer continued in the same clumsy vein, and ended by stating that the Royal Geographical Society was among those who had agreed to receive subscriptions.[2] A year later Charles Dickens wrote his helpful, but highly inaccurate essay, which was to be printed on both sides of the Atlantic.[3] Well-meaning people read it and undoubtedly thought Sarah a deserving cause but were relieved of any responsibility to dip into their purses once Her Majesty's Government elected to give Sarah her widow's mite of a pension. There is no record that she ever returned to London to visit Giovanni's gifts to the nation or to inspect John Soane's catacomb and Seti's sarcophagus. There is, however, a hint that something of Sarah still lingers. Carved in faint lettering on the rim of the sarcophagus one can see the inscription Disc [ed] BY BELZONI. That preface is not found on his other inscribed statuary, suggesting that Giovanni did not write it. The likelihood, therefore, is that Sarah, fearing that Drovetti or Salt might seize or sell the sarcophagus, carried a candle back to the burial chamber and by its flickering light hurriedly wrote the words. Thus, the Soane Museum's modern visitors viewing the sarcophagus may well be within a few inches of reliving that moment in 1818, when, in the darkness of the tomb, Mrs. Belzoni unintentionally immortalized herself in her usual unassuming way.

Sarah's notebook indicates that during her years in Brussels she corresponded with relatively educated people and was ready to share her ideas on religion, English royalty, and the pope. Shortly after arriving there, she wrote a rather curious letter to the novelist and political activist Sydney Lady Morgan, who also was in Belgium in 1833.[4] Sarah had never met her but had read her books and articles. One of the latter prompted Sarah to write to her concerning the Temple of Solomon, which "On my arrival in Jerusalem, 1808 . . . was then under repair." The letter accompanied three gifts, one of them a "spoon that I bought in Grand Cairo, 1837, which the Grand Turk's people eat their rice with." Sarah's letter was dated Sept 25, 1833, and published in *Lady Morgan's Memoirs* in 1862, whose editor, William Hepworth Dix, apparently did a poor job of transcribing. In 1808, Sarah was somewhere in the British Isles helping her husband with his stage act. In 1837, she was not in Grand Cairo but in Brussels. No doubt in reading her undeniably difficult handwriting the dates should have been seen as 1818 (when she was in Jerusalem) and 1817 (when she was in Cairo). That the dates were so obviously incorrect serves as a reminder that (*a*) an editor must be conversant with the context, and (*b*) that anything written before the invention of the typewriter can be misread.[5]

Sarah's other gifts to Lady Morgan were a cross made from wood of the door of the Temple of Solomon and which had "received the benedic-

The British Museum's Egyptian sculpture gallery, ca. 1840. Belzoni's Young Memnon faces Beechey's head of Amenophis III. (Courtesy of Peter Clayton)

tion on the holy *Sepulchre,* under my own sight," and an Egyptian basket platter. This, Sarah explained, "was made above the first cataract of the Nile, *Nubia.* Fruit of the *date tree, the inside is dissolved, and made into beads*" may have been one of the gifts sent to her by the wife of Daoud Cacheff on Belzoni's return from Abu Simbel.[6]

Sarah's postscript to her 1833 letter to Lady Morgan offers more: "I have often longed to see you," she wrote, adding, "that wish is at last gratified." She recalled, "In 1822, I passed the Simplon, two days after you had passed, and was much mortified at having missed seeing one who had charmed me so often." The Simplon Pass over the Alps had become the northern doorway to Italy when, between 1800 and 1807, Napoleon constructed a military carriage road through it. By 1822, with Napoleon long gone, his road had become a much-traveled tourist route. What the Belzonis were doing on it remains unstated, but the journey may reflect an unrecorded visit to his family in Padua. One might wonder, too, how, prior to 1822, Sarah had been charmed so often by Lady Morgan whom she clearly had never met?

According to one biographer, Sydney Owenson (subsequently Lady Morgan) was born on a packet boat somewhere between England and Ireland in 1776. However, that has been repudiated in *The Dictionary of National Biography*, which puts her birth in Dublin in 1783. She was the daughter of the Irish actor Robert Owenson. After several false starts, she came to prominence with her widely read and much-praised novel *The Wild Irish Girl*, which was published in 1806—when Sarah Belzoni was on tour with her husband. The possibility that Sarah was born in Ireland rather than in Bristol is suggested by the title of the 1806 book. Was she, too, a wild Irish girl? Lady Morgan's writing was not everyone's cup of tea, and both in articles and in her books she lauded Irish patriotism, and in doing so made herself a pariah among English Tories. Like many small people (she was said to have been only four feet tall), Lady Morgan made a great deal of noise.[7] It may, therefore, have been her Irish radicalism that drew Sarah Belzoni to her.

In the autumn of 1833, Lady Morgan was staying at the Hotel de Flandres in Brussels. Since she was a literary celebrity, her presence there would have been widely known—prompting Sarah to leave her a fan-style note. On a September day prior to the twenty-fifth, Lady Morgan responded by paying Sarah a visit, thereby providing posterity with a sad portrait of the still-grieving widow.[8]

"I found her occupying a little back room," wrote Lady Morgan, "on the second floor of a small house in a dreary suburb.[9] Her only window commanded a view of the red-tiled roofs of the city of Brussels; and beyond, an illimitable prospect of its environs. The disconsolate companion of the most heroic of all modern travelers was still in faded weeds [widows' black mourning] and intently occupied in reading from a very fine folio Bible. A large coffin, covered with hieroglyphics stood open and upright before her:—it contained the most perfect mummy perhaps in existence. The walls and floor of her little room were covered with fragments, drawings deemed holy, in holy land."[10]

Sarah expressed surprise by the visit and added that she thought herself "beyond the reach of sympathy or notice." She explained that she had only called on Lady Morgan as a mark of respect because her husband in their last journey over the Alps had read her passages from her ladyship's book titled *Italy*. The news that the noble Belzoni had read the book must have been music to the ears of its author, who had been the recipient of one of the worst literary reviews imaginable. Written for Giovanni's publisher, John Murray, it began:

> It may be expected that we should say something of this book,—we shall take the liberty of explaining why we shall say very little.
>
> In the first place, we are convinced that this woman is utterly *incorrigible,* secondly, we hope that her indelicacy, ignorance, vanity, and malignity, are *inimitable,* and that therefore, her example is very little dangerous,—and thirdly, though every page teems with errors of all kinds, from the disgusting down to the most ludicrous, they are smothered in such Boeotian dullness, that they can do no harm."[11]

To put this scabrous tirade in its context, one must remember that Murray was a Tory and a defender of the nation's Protestant religion. Lady Morgan, on the other hand, was a feisty and outspoken Whig, and like her father, who had been a member of the Irish Volunteers demanding constitutional independence, she was what in modern terms might be called a bleeding-heart liberal. Sarah, being of a like mind, was naturally drawn to Lady Morgan's writing, and she, in turn, saw Madame Belzoni as one of the world's downtrodden and a victim of the establishment's cruel indifference. She was, in short, a person who in her poverty could be exploited to further Lady Morgan's political agenda. More altruistic, however, were Lady Morgan's stated reasons for the visit; she intended to create a new Saving Sarah fund either in Brussels or upon her return to England. However, the would-be benefactor "found it difficult to keep her [Sarah's] attention fixed to her own destitute position; her mind continually wandered to the unmerited misfortunes and unrequited services of Belzoni. She said she wanted nothing more than the means of leaving Europe and laying herself down in the tomb 'under the shade of the avasma' at Gato."[12]

Sarah showed Lady Morgan the prospectus and originals of the series of lithographs of Seti's tomb that she still hoped to see published, and she volubly enthused over the mummy. It was, she said, that of a priestess,[13] and because of its fine state of preservation, an object of great value. In her letter to the editor of the *Athenaeum,* Lady Morgan enclosed a copy of the publishing prospectus and added that she was going to do what she could to get the Belgian nation to buy the mummy. This was the same prospectus that Sarah had been unsuccessfully touting in 1828, and again

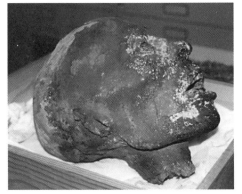

Sarah Belzoni's mummy photographed before being dissected and destroyed in 1939. The head had been reattached. (© IRPA-KIK, Brussels)

Above: *The damaged coffin of Sarah's mummy in the process of conservation in the Brussels Museum. (Photo courtesy of Jeannine Johnson Maia).* Below: *The unwrapped head survives in the Brussels Museum collection. (Photo courtesy of Jeannine Johnson Baia)*

it went nowhere. It appears that Lady Morgan's efforts (if she made any) on behalf of the mummy were no more successful. Her ladyship, however, had her own nest to feather and used the *Athenaeum* letter as fodder for her next novel, titled *The Princess,* in which her readers would be reminded of the impoverished widow in her Brussels backroom.[14]

It is hard to imagine sharing one small room with a mummified priestess, but if Lady Morgan is to be believed, Sarah Belzoni had taken her bereavement to the edge of eccentricity and perhaps beyond. One is left with an impression of a grieving widow alone amid a clutter of dust-collecting relics from years long gone—the embodiment of Charles Dickens's Miss Havisham. In truth, however, Sarah was not without friends in Brussels. One of them was the antiquary Martialis Reghellini, who attempted to provide her with financial help by trying to sell the mummy to the Académie Royale des Sciences et Belles-Lettres. But the Académie, having no existing Egyptian collection, rejected the offer. Reghellini later sold it to the Musée Royal d'Artillerie d'Armes et d'Antiquités,[15] making Sarah's mummy the first acquired by a Belgian public collection.[16] The painted coffin survives but is in appalling condition and is no longer exhibited. As for the mummy, it was consigned to the autopsy table in 1939 and subsequently discarded save for the severely damaged head, which when unwrapped, was found to be missing the back of its cranium. The coffin and mummy were initially deemed to be unrelated, and Sarah's priestess turned out to be a fifty-year-old male.

A note written in Sarah's hand that accompanied the sale implied that both mummy and coffin had been found together in the Biban-el-Maluk (Valley of Kings). But true or not, the question of why Sarah took this questionable treasure with her when she moved her possessions to Brussels is still a puzzlement. Perhaps it had been thought insufficiently important to attract a buyer when the artifacts from the Belzoni exhibits were auctioned. Perhaps, too, Sarah knew that the mummy and the coffin were not found together and that they were run-of-the-mill antiques, yet talked them up to her Brussels visitors in the hope that someone who did not know one mummy from another would take the bait and buy it.[17] There is no doubt, however, that Giovanni and Sarah thought their "priestess" to be of above average interest and value, prompting him to paint a watercolor of the mummy. But did he do it in Egypt?[18]

Nothing in Egyptology is as simple as it may first appear, and Sarah's coffined legacy is no exception. Her identifying note adds: "This mummy, with others, was conserved by this voyager as one of the most beautiful specimens of the art of embalming, and was undoubtedly a [momie de premiere classe] described by Herodotus. . . . The arms and legs were not contained in the same envelope, but instead are bandaged separately." Although this technique was popular in the Ptolemaic and Roman Periods, as early as the Twenty-fifth Dynasty (ca. 750–656 BC) individually wrapped limbs were sometimes concealed within an outer mummiform linen wrap. It is possible, therefore, that this was stripped off by the Arab finders in search of jewelry and anything else that was saleable.

Similar uncertainties also surround the wooden coffin which bears the name Boutehamon, an important Theban scribe who lived in the Twenty-first Dynasty (1085–935 BC).[19] The name, however, was fairly common and the construction of the coffin could place it anywhere in the Third Intermediate Period (1000–800 BC), perhaps making it as much as eight-hundred years older than a Ptolemaic mummy.[20] This supposes, of course, that the late dating of the mummy is correct. But is it?[21] Adding to the confusion, the Turin Museum possesses two outer and inner coffins bearing the Boutehamon name, the latter containing a mummy, all presumably part of one of Drovetti's collections.

One might expect that Belzoni's on-the-spot drawing would settle the sequence, but this, too, has its problems. It shows the left arm over the right, the reverse of the arm positions on the actual mummy—a very unlikely error. Making that even more surprising, the painted interior edges of the coffin visible in the drawing are to be seen on the surviving wooden box as, too, is the treatment of its laminated sides. Unfortunately, Belzoni's carefully watercolored drawing is undated, leaving open the possibility that it was rendered in London after the mummy and coffin were made ready for the first exhibition. The paper has no watermark, but it appears to be the same as that used in the drawings of the London exhibit, which are now in the Bristol City Museum. The inference, therefore, is that the drawing was made after the mummy reached England.

There is no denying that an "as found" illustration could have given the exhibit the authenticity of modern in situ photography. However, a contradicting clue is provided by shading around the foot of the coffin, suggesting that it was drawn standing up—as it was when Lady Morgan saw it in Sarah's Brussels room. It seems fair to suggest, therefore, that to give the mummy a gee-whiz presence as a highlight of the London exhibition, Belzoni intended to publish a promotional brochure for which

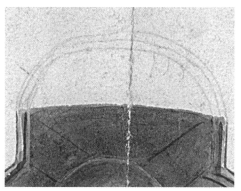

Giovanni and Sarah's prize mummy and coffin drawn standing at the time they were to be exhibited at the Egyptian Hall. Note the square treatment of the mummy's neck. The coffin interior is decorated with winged serpents. (© Bristol Museums, Galleries & Archives)

Detail of the coffin's squared head end showing the faintly penciled arch of its original shape. (© Bristol Museums, Galleries & Archives) he needed an illustration. As the mummy's arms were crossed one upon the other, obscuring the right hand, for the purposes of publicity it made sense to separate them. With that degree of artistic license accepted, rearranging the arms altogether was a logical extension. If this interpretation is correct, the watercolor would not have been exhibited alongside the real thing, but used on posters and brochures or copied onto the backboards of sandwich men.

The London artist George Scharf made sketches of this itinerant advertising and in 1821 drew a poster carrier for Belzoni's exhibition. The artistic rendering of the billboard is paralleled by a watercolor in the Bristol City Museum's Belzoni Collection. If that was created for promotional purposes, it is reasonable to argue that the standing mummy was used elsewhere for the same reason.

The standing-up clue is but one of three that raise a bevy of hitherto unaddressed questions. The Belzoni drawing has an unusually flat headboard, but Amber Druce at the Bristol Museum has drawn my attention to faint traces of a penciled arch which would have given the coffin a much more conventional shape. Equally faint traces of interior decoration within the arch imply that this missing element was part of the coffin as first drawn. No less curious are lines around the mummy's neck which suggest that the head was set into the shoulders—a technique deviating from the normal neck wrappings.

Sarah's contention that her mummy was one of the most beautifully wrapped of any she had seen may have been the result of her not having examined many Ptolemaic examples or not knowing that the outer wrapping had been removed. As mummies go, this one did not live up to its billing; instead, it has the look of a prop left over from a Boris Karloff movie. At the time of the autopsy, the right hand was missing and the back of the skull was shattered, but nothing in the subsequent report explained these very evident deficiencies, the writer being content to note that they had disappeared "during the mummy's tribulations."[22]

Sarah's note also differs from the rest of the historical record. "This mummy," she wrote, "which has been in the Brussels museum for several years, is the property of Madame Belzoni, widow of the famous voyager, who would like to sell it for 2000 francs." It seems probable that she had put it on approval at the Musées Royaux D'Art et D'Histoire, whose trustees debated at length the high price (as had the British Museum over the Seti sarcophagus), finally paying 400 francs for it in May 1847.[23] That equated to a modest thirty English pounds and was consistent with prices realized by Greco-Egyptian mummies at the auction of Henry Salt's third collection in 1836.[24]

Although it is hard to believe given its present flaking condition, the coffin had been of good quality, and is decorated both outside and in with images relating to the *Book of the Dead;* along with other death-related gods, the enthroned figure of Anubis is depicted aboard his celestial boat sailing on a sea of scarabs atop an undulating serpent. The bottom of the coffin is split, and pieces are missing along with the whole of the shaped head end.[25] What remains of the interior decoration appears to relate to the wings of the serpent goddess. Pursuing the fate of both coffin and mummy does not advance the sad story of Belzoni's widow, but as they are the only surviving memorials to Sarah's later life, they deserve our attention.

The most elaborate part of any ancient Egyptian coffin was its zoomorphic lid, which, to the Gournou Arabs, was most easily removed, transported, and sold—leaving the mummy and the bottom of the coffin until a mummy-seeking collector should be found. It seems likely that Belzoni was one of them, for when he had his drawing made, the coffin lacked its lid. Lot 986 in Salt's 1836 sale provides a parallel clue. There the auctioned mummy was said to be that of a priest, but the coffin's hieroglyphs were read as relating to a king. In his annotation of the sale catalogue, Giovanni D'Athanasi wrote: "In justice to the memory of the late Mr. Salt, it may be stated, that he never saw the case or the mummy it contained; both having been accidentally purchased of an Arab." D'Athanasi went on to allow that the "coffin was originally that of the king whose name is described upon, though it is at present tenanted by the mummy of a priest, of much later date."[26] Consequently, the bidding on Lot 986 was neither fast nor furious and the coffin was knocked down to the British Museum for a mere £12 15s.

It is known that the Belzonis had two mummies in their 1821 show, and that after much of the collection had been sold, one or both were shipped to the failed Paris exhibition. In the absence of the Seti sarcophagus, at least one mummy was needed for Sarah's second London exhibition, and it is likely that hers was the one that eventually went with her to Brussels. The coffin had to have been intact when it arrived there, and must have been sufficiently well preserved to merit Lady Morgan's admiration. Furthermore, the Brussels museum would not have bought it had it been in

Opposite: *A page from the Belzoni Collection at the Bristol City Museum, thought to have been drawn in London as an 1821 exhibition advertisement.* (© *Bristol Museums, Galleries & Archives*). Right: *A promotional signboard for Belzoni's exhibition drawn by George Scharf in 1821.* (© *Trustees of the British Museum*)

anything like its present sorry condition. At the time of the purchase, the Royal Museum of Art and History's small collection was housed on the third floor of the "Porte de Hal," the only remaining medieval gate in Brussels.[27] In 1942, the Belgian Egyptologist Jean Capart recalled that while he was still a child, his father had shown him the mummy before it was moved from the gatehouse gallery around 1889.[28] It requires no elasticized stretching of one's imagination to see workmen hired to move the collection to new quarters dropping the coffin and its contents on their way down the worn medieval steps from the third floor. The head end of the coffin broke off, leaving the mummy unprotected. Its head then snapped at the neck and bounced away down the stone stairs, with the resulting damage discovered only when the mummy was unwrapped in 1939.[29] I had come to believe that sequence until, at Amber Druce's urging, I more carefully studied Belzoni's drawing. The damage had occurred *before* the drawing was made as had the breaking away of the head. I may have had the sequence right, but my dating was wrong. The "accident" happened en route to England or in London ca. 1820, and not in 1889 in Brussels, in which case both Giovanni and Sarah must have known that theirs was a doctored coffin. And there is more.

The square-cut neck of the mummy shown in Belzoni's drawing may not be the product of an accident, but may represent, instead, the uniting of a body with another's head. Heads were in greater demand than awkwardly shipped intact mummies. In a letter to Lord Mountnorris, Henry

Salt explained that captains were reluctant to allow intact mummies on their ships, then added brightly, "If I get a good head, you may depend on having it."[30] William Bankes was another who added a head to his collection—having severed it himself. "The tomb," he said, "was full of painting & sculpture, out of a noble sarcophagus of red granite . . . I removed the Head." Bankes added that his trophy was "sufficiently perfect to show that it is of a young person & not of a negro race."[31] In short, there were a great many headless mummies, and Belzoni's may have been one of them.

The 1847 sale of Sarah's "priestess" coincided with the arrival in Brussels of a young man from Ropperville in Lorraine who had moved there to complete his medical education. While a student physician, John Adam Weisse (perhaps in the role of a doctor) met Sarah through a shared interest in hieroglyphics and the notion that they might be related to the mysteries of freemasonry. She was then living in a rented house near the Boulevard de Waterloo and paying the rent by letting most of it out to lodgers.[32] Sarah showed Weisse some notes scribbled by her husband as well as an essay written by herself wherein she may (or may not) have suggested that Seti's tomb was really a Masonic temple. Thirty years later in New York, Dr. Weisse published a book he titled *The Obelisk and Freemasonry according to the Discoveries of Belzoni and Commander Gorringe*, in which he discussed his meetings with Sarah in Brussels and found her, contrary to Lady Morgan's description, strong, active, and having a keen interest in Egyptian antiquities and wanting to visit the ruins of Mexico.[33] A hint that she dabbled in spiritualism is to be found in her notebook, in which she wrote, "the spirit even I held unconscious intercourse with other minds and [science?]?" Spiritualism had become a popular pseudo-science in the 1850s, and it is possible that a person whose life centered on a long-dead husband would be drawn to it.

On January 10, 1870, at the age of eighty-seven, Sarah Belzoni made her will. She was then living on Bellozane Road in St. Helier, a street name remarkably similar to her own and perhaps her reason for choosing to live there. Two days later, she died. Attempts to locate her grave have proved elusive, as has much of her life. In my correspondence with Mrs. Joan Porter of the Jersey Wildlife Preservation Trust, she noted that she thought that as Sarah "was married to an Italian-sounding gentleman, perhaps she was a Roman Catholic," and so contacted the largest Roman Catholic church in the town in the hope that its records would hold the answer.[34] The suggestion was logical, but Sarah's notebook said otherwise. One of the few easily read entries reveals: "I am not what is called a religious person, for too often religion is used as a cloak to hide some depravity or other." Remembering that Lady Morgan found Sarah "intently occupied in reading from a very fine Bible," one may be forgiven for asking why? As this apparent harmony with heaven did not match Sarah's religious opinions, one might construe that her Bible reading was no more than a theatrical exhibition of piety intended to impress the devoutly Catholic Lady Morgan. And there are other questions.

If her ladyship's visit to the small second-floor room was a surprise, how did she get there? In her novel, Marguerite (Morgan) "led the way up a narrow staircase, and was followed by Sir Frederick Mottram to a small landing place on the second story." Setting aside the fictitious Sir Frederick, who let her into the house and told her where to find Sarah? Marguerite "put her finger, in token of silence and then opened the door of a back room, unheard by its sole occupant."[35] Even a junior law student would ask why, as an unannounced guest in the house, she did not knock on the door—if only to be sure she was not intruding on someone else? Perhaps the whole incident is colored by Lady Morgan's gratuitous adjective: *devoutly* reading—which can only be observed if the reader is, indeed, unaware of the visitor's presence. The same student barrister would say, "I put it to you, Lady Morgan, that you saw the Bible in the room and used it as a literary prop to make Sarah appear more deserving of public sympathy." It is true, nevertheless, that she did have an interest in the Bible's contents, hence her visit to the Holy Land. On her way back to Egypt, she had been persuaded to peddle the Bible in Arabic to potential converts, but that did not imply that she was devoutly reading it as a Catholic. On the contrary, in a later entry in her notebook, Sarah spoke well of the French Protestant church, telling a correspondent, "I am sorry that you do not understand English as the Anglican Church would be better understood by Roman C."[36]

The Jersey archaeologist John L. Hibbs searched the Protestant cemeteries in St. Helier but found nothing. It does not follow, however, that Sarah was buried elsewhere. People without surviving relatives to mourn them rarely aspire to headstones. That Mrs. Porter's search of the Jersey newspapers also drew a blank is similarly explainable; Sarah had no one to submit an obituary. In her will, all of Sarah's worldly goods were left to her goddaughter, Selina Belzoni Tucker, then living at Cheltenham. The English Census of 1881 showed a Selina B. Tucker to have been born at

Portsea, Hampshire, in 1822. She is the only Selina B[elzoni] Tucker in the census listing and was born when Sarah Belzoni was still in England.[37]

In 1900, the Bristol City Museum acquired, through a Mr. C. E. Wilson, a collection of Belzoni memorabilia that included the enigmatic coffin drawing, Sarah's notebook, Giovanni's sketchbook, and incomplete models of his exhibits in London and in Paris.[38] So who, one might ask, was Mr. Wilson? Nobody at the museum could find any record of him or of his gift—if gift it was. Was it possible, therefore, that the collection had been part of Selina B.'s inheritance, and not, as has been suggested, the result of a direct connection between C. E. Wilson and Sarah?

If the unmarried Selina had been living in Cheltenham prior to Sarah's death, she may have moved south to Walcot (now a suburb of Bath) by 1881. This Selina B[elzoni] Tucker lived with her older spinster sister, Sarah A. Tucker, at No. 11 Hanover Street, a lodging house owned by another old lady, Maria Morgan. Selina was dead before the census of 1901, but had she lived, she would have been seventy-nine. Maria Morgan, on the other hand, would have been ninety-two. It is possible, therefore, that the deaths of either or both of them would have precipitated household disbursement—this at about the time that Mr. Wilson passed the Belzoni materials to the Bristol Museum. Was he, perhaps, only a secondhand furniture dealer with a business in Bath? However, there may have been an earlier direct connection between Sarah and another Mr. Wilson—the one who in 1825 had subscribed his mite to the Help for Sarah Fund and enthused over her husband's accomplishments. *The Dictionary of National Biography* states that William Rae Wilson died in London in 1849 and that his second wife outlived him. It does not mention children by either spouse, but it remains to be determined whether a son or grandson could have been the donor C. E. Wilson.

The Tucker sisters had both been born in the vicinity of the British naval base at Portsmouth, Sarah A. at Stebbington in 1820 and Selina B. two years later in Portsea. In 1795 a watchmaker named John Tucker was a resident of Portsmouth, but whether he also made two daughters is a question whose answer can only be culled from unpublished parish records. This and other pertinent questions are posed but remain unsolved. Were Sarah and Giovanni Belzoni in Portsmouth in 1822, and what was their relationship with the pregnant Mrs. Tucker? Why did Selina not give her middle name when responding to the census taker? Was she simply following her senior sister's lead in filling out the form, or was she embarrassed by having a forgotten foreigner's name? Speculation, however idle, is always intriguing, and leaves one wondering whether it was only a coincidence that the two old sisters were living in the house of Maria Morgan, who, given her age, could have been the stepdaughter of Lady Morgan.[39] However, any historian will warn that arbitrarily connecting genealogical dots is a temptation strenuously to be resisted.

18 } SIGNIFICANT OTHERS

AT THE AGE OF EIGHTY-SEVEN, Sarah had outlived nearly all her husband's contentious contemporaries. The first to go had been Henry Salt, who died, still in office, in 1827. His health had been poor even before he arrived in Egypt and grew worse as ophthalmia and intestinal problems took their toll. He had hoped to be able to retire on a pension as had his predecessor, Colonel Missett, but was informed by the Foreign Officer that the colonel's had been a permanent position whereas his was not. Therefore, he could expect no pension. He noted that his ten-year term as consul-general had expired, that his friend and colleague Peter Lee, the consul at Alexandria, had died, and that he, Salt, had been holding both posts for the past eighteen months. Writing from Alexandria to Lord Mountnorris, he complained (very reasonably), "I am kept here much against my will, and to the detriment of the service, as the Pasha now stays entirely at Cairo, and is surrounded by French agents and partisans."[1] With no replacement for Lee forthcoming, Salt had two consulates to maintain, but no money coming from London. He had earlier written that the expenses incurred by a consul exceeded the salary as every traveling gentleman expected to be lodged or entertained at the consulate.

Following the death of his wife in 1824, Salt felt compelled to send his daughter, Georgina, to her grandparents in Leghorn, he being unwilling to let her "continue to be exposed to the danger of this detestable country."[2] God, he said, had left him nothing but to continually deplore the loss of his wife. In another letter to Bingham Richards, Salt ended it by admitting, "I should be most happy if I could get away from this dreadful place, even on my leave of absence, but much more so on a pension, *however moderate*."[3] A letter to Lord Mountnorris on the same day called on his friends to assist him. "I am entitled to a pension," he wrote, "but I fear it may be difficult to prevail on Mr. Canning to do me the favour of letting me retire." George Canning was then Britain's foreign secretary before becoming prime minister in April 1827—but he died in August without responding to his consul's plea.

Although Sir Joseph Banks was already dead, Salt continued to feel betrayed by his friends among the British Museum's trustees, declaring that he would have "no more of *dealing* with the British Museum—the *Soanes* are the people for me."[4] Since his falling out with Belzoni and the museum, His Britannic Majesty's consul-general in Egypt had concentrated more on digging than on diplomatic drudgery. He had sent to his brother-in-law, Pietro Santoni at Leghorn, a collection which he valued at £4,000 and called "the finest collection of papyri existing, the best assortment of Egyptian bronzes, several paintings in incaustic, and rich in articles of gold and porcelain."[5] Santoni was instructed to act as Salt's agent to seek a purchaser among continental governments. By the end of July, he was able to report that he had been visited by none other than Jean François Champollion, renowned as the founder and "father" of Egyptology. Two years later, King Louis XVIII would appoint Champollion conservator of the Egyptian antiquities at the yet-to-be-opened Louvre in Paris. In short, there was no more informed critic to favorably review Salt's second collection than M. Champollion. Salt had told Santoni that he would be satisfied to get 150,000 francs for it, and must have been delighted that the offer was for 250,000. Curiously, however, Salt never told the long-suffering Bingham Richards that he had obtained so noble a price. Instead, he was still asking him to encourage friends to prevail upon by-then Prime Minister Canning to grant him a pension, adding, "I am thoroughly tired of Egypt."[6]

Although Richards's surviving correspondence with Salt makes no reference to the sale, we know that he was aware of it, having received the good news from Santoni, who commented: "As to the Directors of your Museum, they have, in truth, conducted themselves very ill, in every respect, with regard to our friend. Salt might well have been to his country what Champollion is to France."[7] Perhaps Salt felt shame that he had sold out to the French for 250,000 pieces of silver.

The departure of the Belzonis to England had left the door open to the duplicitous Greek, Yanni D'Athanasi, to become Salt's man in the sand, and it was he who assembled the Leghorn collection. Included in it was the granite sarcophagus of Ramesses III, whose magnificent lid Giovanni had brought home as part of his share and had donated to the Cambridge museum.[8] Salt had inherited Yanni as a servant interpreter from Colonel Missett. He wielded a shovel at Abu Simbel, salvaged the pedestal for Bankes's obelisk, and opened several relatively unimportant tombs. However, one of them was thought to be that of a royal scribe, making Salt happy to say that he had extracted a statue of the scribe and his wife, his color stand, his pallet, and "a scarabee, set as a ring, with his name." From another tomb Yanni had removed a chair inlaid with ivory and ebony, and from yet another the remains of a twenty-one-string harp. Additional loot included small statues in wood, stone, and bronze which Salt determined to be "a better collection than I have before seen."[9] After the sale of the second collection (whose French francs translated into £10,000), Yanni continued in Salt's service, gathering a third collection, part of which Salt shipped to Leghorn three weeks before his death. Eleven years later, it came under the hammer at Sotheby's auction house in London, the catalogue prefaced by a long account from Yanni describing his discoveries at Thebes and elsewhere. He claimed that his service had been secured by Sotheby to authenticate the sources of Salt's treasures, but nine-tenths of the 1,269 lots had no attributions, while those that did were of little archaeological value. Thus a group headed "Various Objects in Bronze principally found at Thebes" included one from Memphis and two from Abydos. Another group, "Sculptural Tablets [subtitled] Taken from the sides of the Tomb at Abydos," starts with one from Thebes.[10] Just as Salt's first collection had resulted in so much hard feeling, ownership of the third was not entirely unsullied. In his preface, Yanni declared that he had formed the collection albeit under Salt's direction, and had "with his executors an equal interest."[11]

Although the Salt catalogue with its D'Athanasi introduction was not published until a year after the sale (complete with prices realized), the presale catalogue ends with a list of thirteen lots described as "Miscellaneous Antiquities The Property of the Late Mr. Belzoni." Among them was listed "The Skeleton of a Mummy disengaged from the bandages, in its case, with a glazed front," this probably a relic of Giovanni's and Sarah's exhibitions. Lots 1277 thru 1281 were "Sitting Female Figure[s] in Granite, with the Lion's head, *damaged.*"[12] One of them may be the incomplete Sekhmet figure that still stares down on Bond Street from the entrance to Sotheby's auction house.

A broken head and torso of the lion-headed goddess Sekhmet over the entrance to Sotheby's auction house in London's Bond Street.

A brief biography in *Who Was Who in Egyptology*[13] states that Giovanni D'Athanasi made a collection of his own which he brought to England and sold in a seven-day sale at Sotheby's in 1837—two years after the eight-day Salt sale of June 1835. However, Yanni's 1836 preface to the third Salt collection has as its frontispiece a granite sphinx, one of two which "now form the principal objects of Egyptian Antiquity at St. Petersburgh," and which came from the dig behind the Colossi of Memnon which Salt had previously claimed as his own.[14] Yanni's 1837 sale was handled by Leigh Sotheby, who advertised that he had a mummy from the collection on view at his house prior to it being "unrolled in the large room at Exeter Hall, Strand." In his advertisement, Yanni wished to "Respectfully inform the Public" that this was not just another mummy from Thebes, but came from Memphis.[15] Whether the public knew the difference or cared is debatable.

Unwinding mummies had become a popular entertainment in the 1830s and began with doctors performing belated autopsies whose presentations could claim a modicum of legitimacy, but later devolved into ghoul-ish spectacles. Thus, for example, Lord Londesborough sent out invitations telling the lucky recipients that he would be at home at 114 Piccadilly on June 10, 1850, where a mummy from Thebes would be unrolled at half past two.[16] As high-end mummies were likely to have had ceramic or precious metal amulets wrapped between the bandages, the exercise was akin to English children pulling Christmas crackers to extract their goodies. What, if anything, Yanni's mummy yielded was not the point. His published announcement flaunted his name in bold letters for all London to read. Giovanni D'Athanasi may have detested his namesake, but from Belzoni he had learned the art of self-promotion and antiquities salesmanship. The rest of his collection was sold in 1845, after which he slipped from sight and died in 1854; one unconfirmed report suggested that he was killed in a Cairo riot.[17]

The third Giovanni (as in Finati) returned to Cairo in 1829 and is believed to have opened a hotel, but of his fate, like that of Yanni, nobody is sure. In 1830, however, Salt's friend William J. Bankes helped Finati publish his journal and in a preface praised his truth and fidelity. Three years later, Bankes's endorsement became a liability after he was arrested for indecent behavior in a nocturnal encounter with a Guardsman in London's Green Park. At his trial, Bankes testified that it was all a mistake, and that there was no way that he could be guilty of "a charge of so horrible a nature." He testified that he had met a soldier in the uniform of the Foot Guards and asked whether he knew someone in the regiment whom Bankes also knew. Later in his trial, Bankes declared that it was not until they were arrested that he realized that the man was a soldier. That rather apparent contradiction was deemed less important than were the supportive affidavits from powerful friends—among them the temporarily out-of-office prime minister Arthur Wellesley, Duke of Wellington.[18] To the relief of the duke and the rest of William J.'s society chums, Bankes was found not guilty.[19] However, being nice to strange soldiers in the park seems to have been a habit. In 1841, a constable's bull's-eye lantern again invaded Bankes's privacy. This time, he gave a false name and tried to bribe the policeman. Five charges of indecent behavior and being a "person of a wicked lewd filthy and unnatural mind and disposition" did not sound good, and after being arraigned and scheduled to stand trial, he hastily fled to France and then to Italy, remaining a fugitive until his death in Venice on April 15, 1855.[20]

Bankes's principal legacy remains Belzoni's obelisk, which still stands on Yanni's pedestal in the garden of his mansion now known as Kingston Lacy (see p. 193).[21] To give Bankes his due, no one doubts that when he saw the fallen shaft lying beside the river at Philae he thought he could interpret cartouches on it that related it to one of the Pompeys and to a Cleopatra—of whom she was the seventh and he, her brother, the unlucky thirteenth. Like the Rosetta Stone, the base carried an inscription in Greek which Bankes had believed could be used to break what, in 1815, was still the hieroglyphic code. Although his flight prevented him from ever returning to enjoy the fruits of renovations at Kingston Lacy, the collections of his own Egyptian drawings as well as others by Linant and Dr. Ricci are preserved there by the British National Trust and provide an unrivaled pictorial record of their travels.[22] Along with the obelisk, the Kingston Lacy gardens display an Eighteenth Dynasty granite sarcophagus found by D'Athanasi and a surprise present from Henry Salt. Bankes had asked him for a set of canopic jars but apparently never received them. By any traveler's standards, Bankes's collection of antiquities was small and unimpressive and today lacks its "elephant." In a letter to Lord Byron, he gloated that he had acquired an artifact that "could hardly fail to interest your imagination." It proved to be the head of the mummy that he had separated from its sarcophagus and which he thought to be that of a Theban king. To preserve it he proposed to seal it in a blown-glass ball.[23] What became of it, nobody now knows, although it is likely that a later generation found that it provided more food for imagination than the family needed.

In the 1880s, a new science was born, the brainchild of Sir Francis Galton, who called it "eugenics," a word derived from the Greek word meaning "well born." He described it as "the study of agencies under social control which may improve or impair the racial qualities of future generations either physically or mentally."[24] What part mummified Egyptian heads played in this new anthropological study is unclear, but the British Egyptologist Flinders Petrie is said to have sent hundreds to Galton at the University College of London.[25]

Greek inscriptions on the obelisk's pedestal that Yanni had retrieved from the Nile did play a small part on the road to deciphering hieroglyphics, but in the end it did no more than dot i's and cross t's for Champollion's great discovery.

Salt, too, had made strenuous efforts (albeit with modest results) to unlock the secrets of the hieroglyphs and sent home several letters out-lining his theories, which seemed to coincide with those of the physician Thomas Young, both yielding pride of place to Champollion. Salt sent his numerous drawings home with Bankes to be shared with other like-minded antiquaries. In 1825, he formalized his ideas and published an *Essay on Dr. Young's and M. Champollion's Phonetic System of Hieroglyphics, with some additional discoveries.* In a letter written in the previous year to William Hamilton, he explained that he had become a complete convert to Champollion's system "that had made so much noise in Europe, yet which appeared to me so absurd." Salt allowed that although Champollion had forestalled him by publishing his *Précis du systême hieroglyphique,* he considered that he and Champollion had independently arrived at the same conclusions. Consequently, his essay would confirm the correctness of both.[26] Not all orthographists have agreed, although Salt was able to interpret several names and hieroglyphic letters not previously recorded by Young and Champollion.[27]

Throughout his life in Africa, Salt kept detailed notes on his travels and opinions. His friend William Coffin[28] was in Cairo at the time of his death and was told that they were all to be sent to John Halls. Salt ex-plained to Coffin that the pile of papers "contains a work upon Abyssinia, Egypt, and Arabia, which has employed me for years, and on which I rely for my future fame. It is to go to Halls," he added, "for he will do me jus-tice." But it never did.

When Salt knew that he was dying, his papers were packed into sev-eral boxes for shipment. But when Coffin returned to the consulate to do as he had been asked, he found that the boxes left unsealed and with-out shipping instructions had been ransacked "and scattered in confusion about the floors of the apartments."[29] Unfortunately for posterity, Halls never discovered whether Coffin rounded them up or what became of them.

Henry Salt had also considered himself a poet in the age of Shelley and Byron, when poetry was considered an appropriate activity for educa-tionally well-rounded gentlemen. In his months of mourning for his wife, Salt wrote a descriptive poem of twenty-one cantos titled simply *Egypt.* Modestly identified only as "A Traveller," he added that "the only satisfac-tion he can promise himself consists in the gratification of those friends to whom it is dedicated." He had it privately printed in Alexandria (the first to publish in English) at his own expense and gave copies away to his friends in England. Their gratitude may have been more polite than enthusiastic when they opened the little volume and began to read:

> EGYPT, renown'd of old, demands my song,
> High favour'd land, where Nilus sweeps along
> His course majestic with full flowing stream,
> And back reflects to day the sun's bright beam.
> Sweep on in triumph, noble river, sweep[30]

The poem may not have been of poet laureate caliber, but it was written from the heart by a widower who was only beginning to realize that he hated his job, his failing health, his betrayal by his government, and his rejection by the trustees of the British Museum.

The rival who must have kept Henry Salt awake at night was neither a poet nor an orthographist. Bernardino Drovetti was not even a Frenchman—even though he had been Napoleon's French consul-general in Egypt until his master was ousted in 1814. Drovetti was reappointed in 1820 and remained there until 1829, all the while focusing his attention less on his diplomatic duties than on garnering antiquities by methods often as foul as they were fair. Like Salt, he made three large collections: the first was bought by the king of Sardinia in 1824 to form the basis of the important Egyptian collection at Turin; the second went to the Louvre, and the third to Berlin. However, it was a papyrus bought by Drovetti at Gournou in 1822 that was to become his lasting memorial. Legend has it that he shoved the rolled and brittle papyrus into his saddlebag and carried it back to Luxor, by which time it was already disastrously damaged. With few people yet able to read hieroglyphics, Drovetti unknowingly had in his hands the greatest portable document of Egyptian history. Written in hieratic script, it listed the name of Egypt's kings from the first to the end of the Seventeenth Dynasty and when written may have extended to the Twentieth and the reign of Ramesses II. Stored in a wooden box, it became part of the collection that Drovetti sold to the king of Sardinia, who subsequently gave it to the Palazzo dell'Academia delle Scienze.[31] By then the fragile papyrus was in 160 tiny fragments that scholars, from Champollion onward, have struggled to reassemble—with varying degrees of success. Lacking both its beginning and end, the tentatively restored document is known as the Turin King List or the Turin Royal Canon. Drovetti lived long enough to learn the importance of his purchase, but having seen his collection brought to his home city and purchased at an adequate price of 30,000 francs, he may not have cared. His sharp and belligerent mind eventually deserted him, and he died in a Turin asylum in March 1852.

Other contributors to the Belzoni saga faded into obscurity to be missed only by their families and friends. After leaving Salt in 1820, Henry Beechey joined his brother in a survey of the North African coast from Derna to Tripoli, and in 1835 published a three-hundred-page biography of Sir Joshua Reynolds. Twenty years later, he immigrated to New Zealand, bought a farm, and died there in 1862. Dr. Alessandro Ricci was both a valued physician (he saved the life of Mohammed Ali) and a skilled draftsman, as his work for Belzoni in Seti's tomb and the Bankes archive attests. Stung by a scorpion while at Thebes in 1832, Ricci became both physically and mentally ill and died in Florence two years later.[32] His contemporary, Linant de Bellefonds, was a better artist who spent most of his adult life in the Nile Valley and became the Egyptian minister for public works in 1869, and pasha four years later. Linant was one of the few of Sarah's contemporaries who outlived her. He died in Cairo in 1883.

Frédéric Cailliaud, whom Belzoni had derided as the explorer who did not find Berenice, was honored with the Cross of the Legion of Honor in 1824; he wrote several volumes describing his travels and treatises on the life and times of the ancient people of Egypt. His own life ended where it began, in Nantes, in 1869. Another contemporary, Giovanni Battista Caviglia, the Genoese ship's master whom Salt hired to work at the pyramids and Sphinx and with whom Belzoni declined to work, continued to excavate for Salt and others until retiring to Paris in 1837 and dying there eight years later.

Looming over these Franks throughout their careers was the puppetmaster Mohammed Ali Pasha, who, with his autocratic control of his country, secured Egypt's quasi-independence from Turkey, destroyed his Mameluke predecessors, built himself a navy, developed the cotton industry, and vigorously promoted corn exports to Europe and technological imports from the infidel West. He died in 1849 at the age of eighty, having spent his declining years on the edge of madness. He was replaced by his vicious stepson, Ibrahim, who conveniently died two months later.

Archaeological history is riddled with "what ifs." If Sir Joseph Banks had not been chairman of the British Museum's trustees, and had Henry Salt not been beholden to Lord Mountnorris, would he have entered the antiquities business? If Belzoni had not met Ishmael Gibraltar in Malta, or if his hydraulic system had been endorsed by Mohammed Ali, would he have taken the job of moving Young Memnon? If Lebolo had killed him at Karnak, what would have become of Sarah? The reality, however, is that, like Lord Mountnorris, whose earldom became extinct at his death, one by one the players have been forgotten. The burial chamber in the tomb of Ramesses III that gave Belzoni his famed granite lid has collapsed and is no longer open to the public. Seti's tomb (still known as Belzoni's) faces irreversible damage due to water-induced swelling and shrinkage of the marl and shale rock into which it was quarried.[33] The damage had begun much earlier at the hands of thieves and tourists. In 1895, less than eighty years after Belzoni revealed the tomb's pristine wonders, the British Museum curator Wallis Budge noted, "The mutilations and destruction which have been committed here during the last twenty-five years are truly lamentable."[34] Although museums are no longer able to chip away exhibitable samples, the exhaling of countless tourists has dulled the painted surfaces to the point that it is hard to appreciate the awe and wonder that Giovanni experienced at the moment of discovery.

Both in archaeology and in museology, context is the key to understanding. Popular though the mummy room is at the British Museum, we are seeing people out of place, their appeal less evocative than those who inhabit the Chamber of Horrors at Madame Tussauds wax museum. The fragment from a tomb wall that once showed huntsmen pursuing ducks and geese through a papyrus marsh has been stripped from the rest of its story and survives like a single scene from a lost two-hour movie. Giovanni Belzoni has been described as the greatest plunderer of them all, a rapist on the Nile, an archaeological vandal, and much else, but in truth he was no worse than his contemporaries and showed more serious interest in the context of the tombs and temples than did others. He did not, for example, propose to blow open Chephren's pyramid with gunpowder as did Drovetti, and as the British excavator Colonel Howard Vyse actually did to enter the Pyramid of Mycerinus.[35] Although one hesitates to imagine how Belzoni would have handled Seti's tomb if, like Tutankhamen's, it had escaped its ancient looters, the opinion of Howard Carter, who pioneered the science of on-site conservation, bears remembering. A century later he would write, "Belzoni's account of his experiences in Egypt, published in 1820, is one of the most fascinating books in the whole of Egyptian literature." Referring to the tombs Belzoni discovered and opened, Carter wrote: "This was the first occasion on which excavations on a large scale

Belzoni's name carved into the base of the statue of Amenophis III in the sculpture gallery of the British Museum (see also p. 2). (© Trustees of the British Museum)

had ever been made in the Valley, and we must give Belzoni full credit for the manner in which they were carried out."[36]

Giovanni Belzoni's accomplishments had nothing to do with his personal size or strength, but with his tenacity, common sense, and ingenuity employed at a time when carbon-14, DNA testing, spectrographic analysis, and virtually all the other scientific tools of modern archaeology were no closer than walking on Mars. One may hope, therefore, that visitors to the British Museum who cannot help but admire the heroic size of Young Memnon will pause long enough to stop at the smaller statue of Amenophis III to read the name carved beside its left foot, and whisper a word of gratitude to BELZONI—and, of course, to SARAH.

EPILOGUE

GIOVANNI BATTISTA BELZONI longed to be recognized as an archaeologist, and most of all by the gentlemen of the Society of Antiquaries. But he never was. Were he alive today, he would still be asking, Why not?

The reasons, in 1820, would have little to do with those that would prevent him from being recognized as an archaeologist today. Then, his class, entertainment background, and nationality determined that the man could be no antiquarian scholar. The wrangle with Salt over the Seti sarcophagus made him appear mercenary, and no gentleman openly talked about money. And he was a damned foreigner, probably no better than that cad Bergami. Besides, it was the trustees of the British Museum who carried the weight of acceptance or rejection among the fellows of the Society of Antiquaries, in which the late Sir Joseph Banks had been influential.

Belzoni's *Narrative* found both a scholarly and a popular readership, and belonged to a then well-received genre of travel books that coupled adventure with discovery. The book scored well on both counts, but it was his drawings (and those of Dr. Ricci, Sarah, and others) that gave his work enduring value.

Sitting with the famed Egyptologist Dr. Veronica Seton Williams at the entrance to the mastaba tomb of Mereruka at Sakkara,[1] I asked her to evaluate the contribution made by a skilled American draftsman who, in the 1930s had earned praise for copying that tomb's murals. I knew that he had claimed to be an archaeologist. This was her reply: "He was an excellent epigraphist, but he was not an archaeologist. If there is no interpretation, there is no archaeology." That was true also of Belzoni. Digging and finding without the knowledge to understand and interpret left his potential unfulfilled. Nevertheless, as I stressed earlier, Belzoni came on the Egyptian scene before archaeology in Seton Williams's terms existed, and the people from whom he learned—Burckhardt, Drovetti, and Salt—were, by her standards, no more archaeologists than was he. Burckhardt was an explorer, and Drovetti and Salt competing collectors, while in France, unbeknownst to Belzoni, Champollion was trying to open the door for future interpreters. At the British Museum, its trustees had no superior Egyptological experience, and relied on their self-proclaimed classical taste to assess the monetary and educational value of objects about which they knew nothing.

The illicit sale of Egyptian antiquities would go on for another century, indeed, as long as there were museums and collectors to buy them. When the supplies ran out, the busy craftsmen of Gournou stood ready to fill the void. The English travel writer Douglas Sladen offered this advice in 1907: "Ordinary antiquities from the tombs of ancient Egypt . . . are best bought at the Cairo Museum. They are far cheaper there, and they have the guarantee of the authorities, which would be accepted anywhere."[2] In sum, therefore, antiquities curators and collectors from London to Cairo deserve to be judged only in the context of their time.

As noted, Howard Carter said of Belzoni that he did the best he could with what he had, and Carter's is as fair an assessment as has been volunteered by a profession not renowned for its collegiate generosity.[3] In 1972, Warren Dawson, the compiler of the seminal *Who Was Who in Egyptology*, wrote that at the beginning of Belzoni's career he "was neither better nor worse than other contemporary figures, but he later evolved techniques for his work and acquired knowledge that raised him above the general level."[4]

In the twenty-first century, however, Giovanni's innate intelligence and skills as a hydraulic engineer would not open the door to a career in professional archaeology. Although neither class nor nationality would today raise barriers, it would be Belzoni's lack of a university degree that would forever override his many archaeological skills and deny him his place in the archaeological hall of fame.

Notes

Prologue

1. Magoffin and Davis, *The Romance of Archaeology*, 50.

1. Sampson and Sarah

1. Modern players of 6'9" are recognizably tall but are not described as giants. Charles Byrne, aged twenty-two, stood 8'4" when he died in 1783. The Multer Museum in Philadelphia has another skeleton standing 7'6" tall. In 1714, a French academic named Henrion theorized that there had been a significant decrease in human stature between the time of the Creation to the Christian era. Adam stood 123'9" tall, Eve 118'9", but Noah only 27', Abraham 20', and Moses a mere 12'.

2. Burton, "Giovanni Battista Belzoni," 37.

3. Belzoni, *Narrative*, vii.

4. General Menou to Napoleon, Alexandria, May 29, 1801, in Lloyd, *The Nile Campaign*, 114.

5. "Mungo" derived from his father's starring role in a popular play entitled *The Padlock*.

6. A Sadler's Wells playbill for May 9, 1803.

7. Chambers, *The Book of Days*, 2:652.

8. Ibid.

9. J. Smith, *A Book for a Rainy Day*, 1845, 176.

10. Chambers, *The Book of Days*, 266.

11. Although no record of her birth date is known to survive, it must have been in 1783. Her will of 1870 states that she was then eighty-seven. When consigning a mummy to the Brussels Musées Royaux d'Art et d'Histoire in the mid-1840s, Sarah identified herself as Madame Serah Belzoni-Banne (see chap. 17, n. 16).

12. Dickens, "The Story of Giovanni Belzoni," *Harper's New Monthly Magazine*, May 1851.

13. *Asiatic Journal* 24, no. 141 (1827): 313. The nose is now in the British Museum.

14. Chambers, *The Book of Days*, 2:652.

15. Information from Ms. Susan Broadwater, personal communication with the author, April 3, 2009.

16. Chambers, *The Book of Days*, 2:73: "In 1690, it was known as Miles's Music-house; to him succeeded Francis Forcer, the son of a musician, who introduced rope-dancers, tumblers &c."

17. Ward, *The London Spy*, 179. Ward later described "a youthful damsel" who wore "a holland smock and fringed petticoat, like a rope-dancer" (194).

18. Cited by Mayes in *The Great Belzoni*, 49.

19. Chambers, *The Book of Days*, 2:652.

20. Mayes, *The Great Belzoni*, 64.

21. Chambers, *The Book of Days*, 2:652.

22. Dickens, "The Story of Giovanni Belzoni," *Harper's New Monthly Magazine*, May 1851.

23. *Household Words*, no. 49, Saturday, March 1, 1851.

2. Mohammed's Man in Malta

1. Giovan Battista Belzoni alla luce di nuovi documenti, Padua, 1936 (Luigi Gaudenzio translation in Mayes, *The Great Belzoni*, 68–69).

2. Ibid., 70.

3. The 1755 earthquake was the most violent in western European history and destroyed most of Lisbon. But within a year, Portugal's prime minister, the Marquis of Pombal, was leading the speedy recovery effort.

4. Gaudenzio translation in Mayes, *The Great Belzoni*, 68–69.

5. Belzoni, *Narrative*, 2.

6. Turner, *Journal of a Tour in the Levant*, 2:326–27.

7. Ibid., 2:351. The "English servant" was the Irish James Curtin.

8. Ibid., June 30, 1815, 2:340.

9. Ibid., 2:342.

10. Like all Egyptian and Arabic names translated into English, variant spellings existed: "Joussef" was also spelled "Jousuf," and "Boghos" as "Boghoz."

11. Belzoni, *Narrative*, 4.

12. *Nagel's Encyclopedia Guide to Egypt*, 287.

13. Smyth, *The Great Pyramid: Its Secrets and Mysteries Revealed*, 511–12.

14. Belzoni, *Narrative*, 6.

15. Ibid., 7.

16. Quoted in Lloyd, *The Nile Campaign*, 67.

17. Belzoni, *Narrative*, 7.

18. Quoted in Lloyd, *The Nile Campaign*, 67.

19. El-Ezbekiya Square was deliberately flooded each August when the Nile reached a sufficient height to flow into it through a canal. The square then became navigable to shallow-draft boats.

20. Turner, *Journal of a Tour in the Levant*, 364.

21. Belzoni, *Narrative*, 12–13.

22. Ibid., 16.

23. Ibid., 20–21.

24. By the time he left office, Missett was partially paralyzed.

25. Belzoni, *Narrative*, 6.

3. Enter the Consul-General

1. It was a case of tit for tat, Napoleon's armies having looted objets d'art from Italy, Germany, Austria, and Poland in order to make Paris the artistic center of the world (Bazin, *The Museum Age*, 176).

2. Halls, *Life and Correspondence of Salt*, 1:428.

3. Salt to his sister, Malta, undated, ibid., 1:449.

4. Salt to William Hamilton, Alexandria, March 27, 1816, ibid., 1:451.

5. Salt to Viscount Valentia, Litchfield, July 19, 1815, ibid., 1:410.

6. Salt to the Earl of Mountnorris, Alexandria, December, 28, 1816, ibid., 1:468.

7. Belzoni, *Narrative*, 22.

8. Burckhardt to African Association, April 18, 1816, in Burckhardt, *Travels in Nubia*, lxxv.

9. Halls, *Life and Correspondence of Salt*, 1:485–86.

10. Belzoni, *Narrative*, 22.

11. Ibid., 22.

12. Halls, *Life and Correspondence of Salt*, 2:4.

13. Ibid., 2:3.

14. This is the mortuary temple of Ramesses II, and now known as the Ramesseum.

15. Belzoni, *Narrative*, 27.

16. Montulé, *Travels in Egypt during 1818 and 1819*, 99–100.

17. The term *reis*, or *rais*, had several meanings, but is essentially a foreman in control of workers, be they rowers or diggers. In the world of archaeology, however, there are ornamental *reises*, who take the money and do nothing but watch, and practical *reises*, who actually supervise the labor.

18. Though retaining the Englishness of her corset, at some unstated point Sarah began to dress in Arab clothes.

4. Moving Memnon

1. Denon's *Travels in Lower and Upper*

Egypt was translated by A. Aiken and published in London in 1802. His *Description de l'Égypte* was published in Paris in ten volumes between 1809 and 1825.

2. Ward, *The London Spy*, 41.

3. William Richard Hamilton was secretary to Lord Elgin, ambassador to Constantinople, and helped ship the Elgin Marbles to England (see Dawson, *Who Was Who in Egyptology*, 132).

4. Demotic identifies a cursive script that began to be used by the Egyptians in the later years of their pre-Roman history, while hieroglyphics continued to be used on monuments.

5. Belzoni, *Narrative*, 20. "Hermopolis" was the Greek name for the city named for the god Thoth and called "Khmunu" by the Ancient Egyptians. Thoth was the god of learning.

6. Belzoni had an apparently friendly exchange of letters with Drovetti, in which Belzoni called him "my friend" and told him about his waterwheel proposal. Before the arrival of Henry Salt, Belzoni posed no threat to Drovetti and was treated as an interesting fellow "Frank" who spoke Italian (see Mayes, *The Great Belzoni*, 81, quoting Giovanni Marro, *Il corpo epistolare di' Bernardino Drovetti*, vol. 1 [Rome, 1940]).

7. Ibid., 1:30.

8. Ibid.

9. Also spelled "káshif," a Turkish governor of a small district. For more details, see Lane, *The Manners and Customs of the Modern Egyptians* (1825–49), 129ff. "Deftardár" was the local name for a treasurer and tax collector.

10. An ancient settlement known to the Greeks as Hermonthis.

11. For "Negroes," read sub-Saharan Africans.

12. Belzoni, *Narrative*, 31.

13. Ibid., 40.

14. Ibid., 31.

15. Ibid., 32.

16. *Nagel's Encyclopedia Guide to Egypt*, 440.

17. Though long thought to be the only known portrayal of Mark Antony's Cleopatra, at least seven are now identified.

18. Belzoni, *Narrative*, 37.

19. The northern colossus was split in the earthquake of AD 27, after which, at dawn, it emitted a musical note that was considered a magical occurrence. The names of eight Roman governors are inscribed on the base, ranging from the reigns of Nero to Septimus Severus. In AD 199, the latter had the damaged statue repaired, after which it spoke no more.

20. Belzoni, *Narrative*, 39. This seated figure of Ramesses II is computed to have weighed more than 1,000 tons and one finger to be a yard long.

21. Ibid., 40.

22. Ibid., 41–42.

23. Now spelled "Armant."

24. Like most Egyptian place-names, Belzoni's "Gournou" has been spelled variously; other spellings include "Gournah," "Gourna," and "Gurna."

5. The Devil Made Them Do It

1. Belzoni, *Narrative*, 44.

2. Murray's *Handbook for Travellers in Egypt*, 4.

3. Belzoni, *Narrative*, 48.

4. Ibid., 52.

5. Bickerstaffe, "Strong Man; Wrong Tomb," 22–30; Habachi, "Setau, the Famous Viceroy of Rameses II and His Career," 51–68.

6. Others have called it "Bruce's Tomb".

7. Belzoni, *Narrative*, 51.

8. Montulé, *Travels in Egypt during 1818 and 1819*, 40. His drawing shows four of the eight side chambers that are unique to this tomb, KV11.

9. Belzoni, *Narrative*, 194–95.

10. It is not clear whether the boat's crew had been permanently laid off and another hired.

11. Belzoni, *Narrative*, 57.

12. Ibid., 58.

13. Possibly Anophis, the personification of evil.

14. Belzoni, *Narrative*, 62.

15. They were open in 1985 when I last visited the island but have since been backfilled. Around 1907, the travel writer Douglas Sladen complained that French excavators "have turned half the green island into a dust heap . . . and maintain a jealous secrecy even if they are only digging up the mummy of a cat" (Sladen, *Queer Things about Egypt*, 372–73).

16. Ibid., 65–66.

6. Staff Problems at Abu Simbel

1. Belzoni, *Narrative*, 66–67.

2. The god was associated with Isis, the patron goddess of nearby Philae, but chapels were dedicated by Ramesses II. The temple became a church in the Christian period and was moved to higher ground when Lake Nasser was created (see Arnold, *Temples of the Last Pharaohs*, 240–41).

3. When the new high dam was completed at Aswan in 1971, virtually the whole of arable Nubia was flooded to become Lake Nasser and necessitated moving the Abu Simbel temples to higher ground. It would prove one of the most difficult and ingeniously devised undertakings in archaeological and engineering history.

4. Burckhardt, *Travels in Nubia*, 85.

5. Belzoni gave his name as "Osseyn," but Captain Irby would call him "Hassan" and "the only honest man in the country" (Irby, *Travels in Egypt and Nubia*, 4).

6. Belzoni, *Narrative*, 81.

7. Ibid., 82.

8. Millet (Indian corn), the Nubians' staple food grain.

9. The exchange rate was approximately 72 piastres to the English pound. The smallest Egyptian coin was a *faddah*, which was made from the same alloy and was a fortieth part of a piastre, or akin to a quarter of an English farthing. Thus, two piastres for a day's work amounted to slightly less than five pence.

10. Moorehead, *The Blue Nile*, 206.

11. Belzoni, *Narrative*, 89.

12. Ibid., 91.

13. Sarah Belzoni, "Short Account of the Women of Egypt, Nubia, and Syria," in Belzoni, *Narrative*, 441.

14. Belzoni, *Narrative*, 100.

15. Ibid., 98.

7. A Present from Philae

1. Tompkins, in his *The Magic of Obelisks*, states that the Philae obelisk had already been found by Frédéric Cailliaud (there spelled "Caillard") and presented by him to Drovetti (168).

2. Belzoni, *Narrative*, 107.

3. Mayes, *The Great Belzoni*, 307 n. 15.

4. Belzoni, *Narrative*, 132.

5. Sarah Belzoni, "Short Account," in Belzoni, *Narrative*, 449–50.

6. Belzoni, *Narrative*, 134.

7. Belzoni to M. Visconti, in *Sydney Gazette and New South Wales Advertiser*, November 7, 1818.

8. Halls, *Life and Correspondence of Salt*, 1:472.

9. Ibid. Drovetti's offer to sell his first collection to France was refused, but the collection was bought by the king of Sardinia in 1824 for a princely 400,000 lire. A second collection was later bought by the Louvre, and a third purchased on behalf of the Berlin Museum (see Dawson, *Who Was Who in Egyptology*, 90).

10. Salt to Mountnorris, Alexandria, December 28, 1816, in Halls, *Life and Correspondence of Salt*, 1:465–74.

11. Ibid., 1:473–74.

12. Salt to Darwin, Cairo, June 2, 1819, ibid., 2:136.

13. Information provided by Sue Giles. The 5'8" croc was deaccessioned in May 1959.

14. Belzoni, *Narrative*, 135–36.

15. Salt to Lord Mountnorris, August 7, 1818, in Halls, *Life and Correspondence of Salt*, 1:494.

16. In 1615, Sandys published an account of his travels (in four books) titled *The Relation of a Journey begun an. Dom. 1610*. It included a relatively realistic woodcut of the pyramids and some not very good drawings of Egyptian gods.

17. Belzoni, *Narrative*, 134.

18. Ibid., 139.

8. Messing with Mummies

1. Burckhardt, *Travels in Nubia*, lxxxiv.

2. Belzoni, *Narrative*, 142.

3. Burckhardt, *Travels in Nubia*, lxxxiv.

4. Belzoni, *Narrative*, 143. Such an entertainment was known as a "fantasia" (see Duff Gordon, *Letters from Egypt*, 121).

5. Belzoni, *Narrative*, 143.

6. El Minya was located 153 miles upriver from Cairo.

7. Belzoni, *Narrative*, 145–46.

8. Ibid., 153.

9. Ibid., 155.

10. Ibid., 156–57.

11. This is the only occasion on which Belzoni referred to any deformity associated with his exceptional stature.

12. Belzoni, *Narrative*, 157.

13. Montulé, *Travels in Egypt during 1818 and 1819*, 107.

14. Herodotus, *The Histories*, 160–61.

15. Belzoni, *Narrative*, 167.

16. Ibid., 169.

17. Ibid., 157–58.

18. Wortham, *British Egyptology 1549–1906*, 16.

19. Andrews, *Egyptian Mummies*, 96.

20. I, myself, bought three hands (one wearing a ring) from a London curio shop in 1952 (see Noël Hume, *All the Best Rubbish*, 301).

21. Belzoni, *Narrative*, 161. They are now in the British Museum, Nos. 38212 and 38214.

22. Scamuzzi, *Egyptian Art*, pls. CIV–CVI, attributed to the Ptolemaic Period.

23. Much of the Luxor temple was then covered by the Arab township.

24. Belzoni, *Narrative*, 164.

25. Belzoni's reference to the temple's square pillars indicates that he may have been digging at the approach to the mortuary temple of Queen Hatshepsut (1503–1482 BC).

26. Belzoni, *Narrative*, 180.

27. Ibid., 184

28. This may be the head of Tuthmosis III, No. 986 in the British Museum Collection.

29. The vast temple was constructed in the reign of Ramesses III (1198–1166 BC), its entrance style borrowed from a Syrian fortress seen by the king during his campaigns in that region. Inscribed on it are accounts of those victories, as well as his defeat of invaders from the Mediterranean called the "Sea People." The Medinet Habu wall carvings include the earliest known representation of a sea battle.

30. Belzoni, *Narrative*, 189.

31. Ibid., 191.

32. Ibid., 198.

9. Return to Abu Simbel

1. Belzoni, *Narrative*, 193–94.

2. In 1978, I made a specifically focused tour of the Nile to record the graffiti, the most recent being the Russian "CCCP 1.1.1976" on a roof at Dendera.

3. The Arab word for "fifty" and also for the winds that usually last for fifty days.

4. Belzoni, *Narrative*, 195.

5. Ibid., 199.

6. Jefferson, *Notes on the State of Virginia*, 98–100.

7. Denon, *Egypt*, 46.

8. August 8, 1817, in Irby, *Travels in Egypt and Nubia*, 34.

9. Ibid.

10. Belzoni, *Narrative*, 201.

11. Ibid., 200.

12. Ibid., 21–22; Burckhardt, *Travels in Nubia*, lxxv.

13. Belzoni, *Narrative*, 202.

14. Finati gave the number as four men, as did Beechey (Finati, *Life and Adventures*, 2:195).

15. His Arab name was also spelled "Mahomet." For a biographical profile, see Burton, *A Pilgrimage to Al-Madinah and Mecca*, appendix 6.

16. One assumes that Yanni had been sent back to Esna on an errand. Esna has one late temple in the center of the town dedicated to the god Khnum, who created the world on a potter's wheel.

17. June 27, 1817, in Irby, *Travels in Egypt and Nubia*, 5.

18. Halls, *Life and Correspondence of Salt*, 2:9n.

19. Burckhardt, *Travels in Nubia*, lxxxiv.

20. The inscription is on the first pylon of the main temple (see *Bulletin of the Association for the Study of Travel in Egypt and the Near East*, no. 10 [October 2000]: 21–22). James Curtin died in London prior to 1830 (see Finati, *Life and Adventures*, 2:211n).

21. Sarah Belzoni, "Short Account of the Women of Egypt, Nubia, and Syria," in Belzoni, *Narrative*, 452.

22. Irby, *Travels in Egypt and Nubia*, 3. The reptile may have been a small Nile monitor. However, there are fifteen species of venomous snakes in the Nile River habitat.

23. Ibid., 12.

24. Belzoni, *Narrative*, 206.

25. For the complicated theogony of the cited Egyptian deities, see the glossary in this volume.

10. The Great Discovery

1. Irby, *Travels in Egypt and Nubia*, 24.

2. Ibid., 24.

3. Following in the footsteps of earlier epigraphists, in 1822, the French scholar Jean François Champollion finally was able to translate the Rosetta Stone's three passages written in Greek, Egyptian demotic script, and hieroglyphics.

4. When the sanctuary figures were later painted by Ricci, he showed them (from left to right) in yellow, blue, and reddish brown (Usick, *Adventures in Egypt and Nubia*, 96, pl. 56). The colors are no longer apparent.

5. Finati named Beechey as the central figure of the record keeping (Finati, *Life and Adventures*, 2:208).

6. Irby, *Travels in Egypt and Nubia*, 24. Six objects were listed in the original British Museum catalogue, Nos. 594, 595, 601, 602, 604, and 619. That they do not run consecutively is clear evidence that Salt had not listed them by site. The kneeling "female figure" was later identified as that of Pa-ser, Ramesses's governor of Nubia (Mayes, *The Great Belzoni*, 330). The ape who was sacred to the god Thoth, the inventor of writing, may be No. 619 in the British Museum Collection.

7. In 1851, in the Serapeum at Sakkara (the mausoleum of the sacred Apis bulls), the famed French archaeologist François Auguste Mariette found the three-thousand-year-old footprints of the priests who had entombed one of the bulls.

8. Finati, *Life and Adventures*, 2:208.

9. Belzoni, *Narratives*, 214.

10. Irby, *Travels in Egypt and Nubia*, 28.

11. Psammetichus II, Twenty-sixth Dynasty, 595–589 BC. A member of the British Expeditionary Force on his way to fight the Mahdi in 1898 also hoped to be remembered.

12. One must assume that Belzoni had forgotten these boots and mirrors when previously he had claimed to have no more gifts to give.

13. Belzoni, *Narrative*, 216.

14. These were the same men who had demanded baksheesh on Belzoni's voyage upriver (see chap. 6, p. 83).

15. The temple was dismantled and reconstructed in 1970 on higher ground thirty miles downstream when Lake Nasser was created behind the new High Dam (see p. 83).

16. Sarah Belzoni, "Short Account of the Women of Egypt, Nubia, and Syria," in Belzoni, *Narrative*, 452. Sarah wrote this work after her return to England during her husband's feud with Salt.

17. Duff Gordon, *Letters from Egypt*, 167, 183, 296. The house was said to have been built for Henry Salt in 1817.

18. Belzoni, *Narrative*, 218.

19. The vandalizing captains were soon followed by other memorialists who were there in 1819, 1830, 1834, and 1836, their names subsequently scraped off or written over. Why the captains' graffiti survived untouched (as did "K HUME 1836" on a pillar at Medinet Habu) remains a mystery.

20. In 1959, the author Stanley Mayes compiled a list of objects in the British Mu-

seum Collection attributable to Belzoni. Nos. 567 and 685 are thought to be the figures from the tomb of Ramesses I, although one of them was then dated to the Thirteenth or Fourteenth Dynasty (Mayes, *The Great Belzoni*, 330).

21. Belzoni, *Narrative*, 229.

22. Ibid., 230.

23. Wilkinson, *Manners and Customs of the Ancient Egyptians*, 1st ser., 2:269–83.

24. Belzoni, *Narrative*, 231.

25. In modern cataloguing terminology, the tomb is known as KV.17.

11. Enduring Achievements

1. Young published his first researches in his *Remarks on Egyptian Papyri and on the Inscription of Rosetta* in 1815. His article written for the *Encyclopaedia Britannica* in 1819 was reprinted as an appendix to the second edition (1821) of Belzoni's *Narrative*.

2. The reign brackets for Seti I (in his Greek form, Sethos) are those of the British Museum; other published sources attribute his reign to 1306–1290 BC.

3. Quoted by Harris and Weeks, *X-Raying the Pharaohs*, 103, citing T. Eric Peet, *The Great Tomb-Robberies of the Twentieth Egyptian Dynasty* (Oxford: Oxford University Press, 1930). The same papyrus is quoted by Leonard Cottrell in *The Lost Pharaohs*, but he gives a very different translation. In the Peet version, for example, the cited text refers to the burning of the wrappings, while Cottrell's substitutes "and set fire to their coffins" (146).

4. The name has also been spelled "Abdel-Rassoul."

5. Harris and Weeks, *X-Raying the Pharaohs*, 100.

6. The 1972 edition of *Nagel's Encyclopedia Guide to Egypt* noted that the tunnel had recently been investigated "and appears to lead nowhere" (512). See also Nigel and Helen Strudwick, *Thebes in Egypt: A Guide to the tombs and temples of Ancient Luxor* (Ithaca, N.Y.: Cornell University Press, 2004), 108.

7. University of California at Santa Bar-

bara to the author, e-mail, April 30, 2010.

8. Report from the Theban Mapping Project (see www.thebanmappingproject.com).

9. Reported in Past Preservers' blog, June 30, 2010.

10. Weeks, *The Lost Tomb*, 74–75.

11. Now spelled "Qena" or "Kenna," and adjacent to the Dendera temple of the goddess Hathor.

12. Belzoni, *Narrative*, 247.

13. Halls, *Life and Correspondence of Salt*, 2:51. The paintings that Salt admired but did not understand included those of the *Litany of Ra*, the *Book of David*, the *Book of Gates*, and the ritual of the opening of the mouth, all associated with the burial practices and its ceremonies. Salt was also unaware that the burial chamber's vaulted and painted ceiling was the earliest known.

14. Ibid., 2:54.

15. Salt's legacy from his father amounted to £5,000, which, coupled with his annual government salary of £1,700, left him relatively well off—providing he did not waste it on archaeology.

16. Salt to his agent Bingham Richards, undated, in Halls, *Life and Correspondence of Salt*, 2:40.

17. Halls, *Life and Correspondence of Salt*, 2:16.

18. Beechey to Halls, August 5, 1833, ibid., 2:26.

19. Ibid., 2:17.

20. Sarah's travels in Palestine are described in her appendix to her husband's book.

21. Belzoni, *Narrative*, 251.

22. Ibid., 251–52.

23. Ibid., 252–53.

24. Ibid., 257.

25. Halls, *Life and Correspondence of Salt*, 2:59.

26. Ibid., 2:54.

27. Belzoni would claim that it was he who had the door installed.

28. Duff Gordon, *Letters from Egypt*, 113 n. 1.

29. Ibid., 312. In December 1876, half the house collapsed into the temple below.

30. Belzoni, *Narrative*, 271–72. In this context, the word "lapicide" may mean only a stonecutter, though it could also mean one who cuts inscriptions on stones.

31. D'Athanasi, *A Brief Account*, 22.

32. Ibid., 24.

33. See chapter 15, pp. 206 and 207.

12. Confrontation in the Consulate

1. Belzoni, *Narrative*, 253. This was written much later, after he had incorrectly led himself to believe that Forbin had stolen his achievements.

2. Ibid., 254.

3. Ibid., 280.

4. Ibid., 252.

5. Quoted by Mayes, *The Great Belzoni*, 205, from Forbin's *Travels in Egypt*, 1820.

6. Ibid., 281.

7. Ibid.

8. The young visitor's name was Pieri, and he worked for the Cairo banking firm of Briggs and Walmas. How he obtained the opportunity to dig around in the sarcophagus is not recorded, but he did inspire Belzoni to delve further and find more bull bones (ibid., 275).

9. A full list of the British Museum's major antiquities attributable to Belzoni is included as an appendix to Mayes, *The Great Belzoni*, 329–32. In the British Museum's original acquisitions register, the coffin is No. 39 and the Sekhmet, No. 517.

10. Halls, *Life and Correspondence of Salt*, 1:487–88.

11. Ibid., 486.

12. The mother of all nine children was King William's mistress, Dorothy Jordan. Fitzclarence became the first Duke of Munster. He would commit suicide by gunshot in 1842.

13. George Fitzclarence, *Journal of a route across India, through Egypt to England in the latter end of the year 1817 and the beginning of 1818* (London: John Murray, 1819).

14. It is uncertain whether this was Drovetti's "gift" or the lid from the sarcophagus of Ramesses III, which Belzoni eventually donated to the Fitzwilliam Museum.

15. Halls, *Life and Correspondence of Salt*, 2:29–30.

16. Leonard Cottrell, *The Lost Pharaohs*, 168.

13. Over the Mountains and through the Passes

1. All that remains of the mortuary temple of Amenophis III of the Eighteenth Dynasty (1417–1379 BC).

2. Belzoni, *Narrative*, 290.

3. Ibid., 294.

4. Ibid., 295.

5. Salt to Hamilton, Cairo, May 4, 1819, in Halls, *Life and Correspondence of Salt*, 2:22.

6. Ibid., 2:316.

7. Belzoni, *Narrative*, pl. XXVI.

8. Salt to Mrs. H——N (Mrs. Hamilton?), Cairo, October 13, 1818, in Halls, *Life and Correspondence of Salt*, 2:131.

9. Although Sarah is credited with drawing a temple seen on the way to Berenice (pl. 16), she was not a member of the expedition.

10. Belzoni, *Narrative*, 309, Finati's journal, *Life and Adventures* (2:297) was equally enthusiastic about the drinkability of the Nile's water. Later European travelers would be less complimentary. But Edward Lane, author of the *The Manners and Customs of the Modern Egyptians* (1836), wrote that "the water of the Nile is remarkably good," but so, perhaps was the Ganges at the beginning of the nineteenth century (152).

11. Chambers, *The Book of Days*, 1:785.

12. Ibid, 1:324.

13. Ibid., 1:340.

14. Jean Baptiste Bourguignon d'Anville (1697–1782). The map was printed in 1766.

15. Chambers, *The Book of Days*, 1:332. *Nagel's Encyclopedia* gives the credit to American Colonel Purdy in 1873 (646).

16. Belzoni, *Narrative*, 346.

17. Halls, *Life and Correspondence of Salt*, 2:133.

18. Usick, *Adventures in Egypt and Nubia*, 151, 155–56.

19. Ibid., 22–23. The italics are Salt's.

20. Belzoni, *Narrative*, pl. XVII.

21. D'Athanasi, *A Brief Account,* 27.

22. B.A. 1808, M.A. 1811.

23. Finati, *Life and Adventures,* 2:206.

24. Ibid., 304n.

25. Quoted by Andrews, *Egyptian Mummies,* 7. Sir Ernest Alfred Thompson Wallis Budge, 1857–1934. An excavator himself, Budge appreciably enhanced the British Museum's collections.

26. Halls, *Life and Correspondence of Salt,* 2:23.

27. Belzoni, *Narrative,* 348n.

28. Ibid., 353.

29. Halls, *Life and Correspondence of Salt,* 2:309–10n.

30. Finati, *Life and Adventures,* 2:302.

31. Belzoni, *Narrative,* 351.

32. The Gebel Silsila quarries lie 38 miles north of Aswan and are the sites of shrines to river gods as well as to Amon-Rë, Khonsu, and Mut, the three deities of Thebes.

33. The crocodiles have now been moved to an on-site museum.

34. Belzoni, *Narrative,* 355.

35. Ibid., 355.

36. Ibid., 356.

14. Philae and the Grand Engagement

1. Belzoni, *Narrative,* 357.

2. Finati, *Life and Adventures,* 2:309.

3. D'Athanasi, *A Brief Account,* 39.

4. Finati, *Life and Adventures,* 309–10.

5. D'Athanasi, *A Brief Account,* 38–39.

6. In Jerusalem, the previously devoted James Curtin left Sarah and went into service with the English traveler Thomas Legh, who, with Captains Irby and Mangles, was planning a trip to Persia.

7. Belzoni, *Narrative,* 363.

8. Ibid., 365.

9. Burton, "Giovanni Battista Belzoni," 46.

10. Montulé, *Travels in Egypt during 1818 and 1819,* 46.

11. Ibid., 100–101.

12. Montulé's *Travels* were published in 1821 by Sir Richard Phillips and Co.

13. Montulé, *Travels in Egypt during 1818 and 1819,* 32.

14. Ibid., 41.

15. From the transcript made by Deborah Manley and Peta Rée, *Henry Salt,* 167.

16. Usick, *Adventure in Egypt and Nubia,* pl. 59.

17. Carter, *The Tomb of Tutankhamen,* 219.

18. Belzoni, *Narrative,* 372. He here claimed that the rain was limited to a few drops in five years.

19. At this writing in 2010, the tomb is closed to the public.

20. D'Athanasi, *A Brief Account,* 14–15.

21. Belzoni, *Narrative,* 372–73.

22. Also cited as "Turinga" by Salt (Halls, *Life and Correspondence of Salt,* 2:144).

23. Pearce, *Life and Adventures of Pearce,* 2:333–34.

24. It is unclear whether this was the Drovetti lid or the one from the sarcophagus from the tomb of Ramesses III.

25. D'Athanasi, *A Brief Account,* 40.

26. Belzoni, *Narrative,* 374.

27. "Fayyum" derives from a New Kingdom term *Pa-yom,* meaning the sea.

28. Herodotus noted that the sacred crocodile of Lake Moeris was fitted with glass or gold rings in its ears and bracelets around its front feet (Herodotus, *The Histories,* 156).

29. Salt's unattributed report, Alexandria, October 10, 1821, in Halls, *Life and Correspondence of Salt,* 2:24.

30. Belzoni, *Narrative,* 436.

31. Halls, *Life and Correspondence of Salt,* 2:24.

32. Bankes later renamed the house "Kingston Lacy."

33. The records are clear that the Seti sarcophagus was shipped aboard the *Diana,* but the Bankes obelisk may have been carried on a British navy transport named the *Dispatch* (see chap. 15, p. 211).

34. Belzoni, *Narrative,* 435.

15. Bingham Richards and the "Christie-Sort of List"

1. Halls, *Life and Correspondence of Salt,* 2:148.

2. Ibid., 2:147.

3. Manley and Rée, *Henry Salt,* 184–85.

The family had apparently arranged a marriage with an Austrian merchant whom Miss Pensa found not to her liking.

4. Salt's bride would bear him two children, but she died within a few days of giving birth to the second.

5. Salt to Lord Mountnorris, Cairo, March 2, 1820, in Halls, *Life and Correspondence of Salt*, 2:153.

6. Ibid., 2:157.

7. That the sarcophagus traveled aboard the *Diana* is proven by a letter from Belzoni to Richards, September 17, 1821, ibid., 2:328.

8. The historian Peter Clayton has informed me that the Paduan medal was acquired by the British Museum in 1872 from Frederick William Collard, who was said to have been a relative of Belzoni. There is no further information either about Collard or the transaction (Peter Clayton to the author, e-mail, March 23, 2010). I am indebted, too, to Peter Clayton for information relating to Thomas Murdoch (e-mail, July 11, 2010).

9. The inscription was copied by Burton, who might very easily have read the 8 as a 3 (Burton, "Giovanni Battista Belzoni").

10. Ibid., 44. His long article on Belzoni was intended to promote the casting of a more appropriate statue to be installed in a public park to be called the Piazzale Belzoni. That never happened, but there is still a street named Via Giovanni Battista Belzoni. It crosses via Marco Polo.

11. He was born "MacMurray" but dropped the "Mac" to avoid eighteenth-century English discrimination against Scots.

12. Chambers, *The Book of Days*, 1:822–23.

13. Halls, *Life and Correspondence of Salt*, 2:212.

14. Belzoni, preface to *Narrative*, v.

15. *Le Globe, The Philosophical and Literary Journal of Paris*, quoted in *Asiatic Journal* 24, no. 141 (September 1827): 316.

16. *Ackermann's Repository of Arts, Literature, Commerce, &c.* 3 (1810): 38–39, 314.

17. *Times* (London), March 29, 1821.

18. Quoted by Usick, *Adventures in Egypt and Nubia*, 196.

19. William Richard Hamilton was then under secretary for foreign affairs (1809–22) and had been responsible for wresting the Rosetta Stone from the French. He would later become a trustee of the British Museum (1838–58).

20. The Banks and Bankes families were not related, but William Bankes's father was a fellow trustee with Sir Joseph on the board of the British Museum.

21. In 1782, the celebrated artist John Zoffany painted a selection of objects from the collection displayed (just for the picture) in Townley's library, which appeared to house very few books (see Noël Hume, *All the Best Rubbish*, 2–3).

22. According to one unconfirmed source, the Townley Collection was then consigned to the museum's basement. However, the British Museum published a catalogue of the Townley Gallery in 1836.

23. Halls, *Life and Correspondence of Salt*, 2:302n.

24. A political meeting of the Manchester Patriotic Union on August 16, 1819, drew a crowd of sixty thousand or more that was attacked by cavalry of the local militia resulting in the death of fifteen demonstrators and the wounding of several hundred. The crowd had assembled in St. Peter's Field, hence the name "Peterloo," a parody of the still-recent Battle of Waterloo.

25. Halls, *Life and Correspondence of Salt*, 2:305.

26. Salt to Richards, May 26, 1822, ibid., 2:301, 311, 321.

27. Salt to Mountnorris, May 28, 1819, ibid., 2:311–14. Christie's, then as now, competed with Sotheby's as London premier fine-arts auction house.

28. The Rt. Hon. Charles Philip Yorke was a statesman who had held several high offices, was a trustee of the British Museum, and, as a friend of Henry Salt, was a strong advocate of the museum buying Salt's collection.

29. Banks to Charles Yorke, November 1, 1819, in Halls, *Life and Correspondence of Salt*, 317.

30. Ibid., 303n.

31. From the Foreign Office, August 30, 1821, ibid., 328.

32. Richards to Hamilton, September 12, 1821, ibid., 327.

33. Written from the Egyptian Hall, September 17, 1821, ibid., 328.

34. From Cairo, May 28, 1819, ibid., 308.

35. Theophilus Richards to Bingham Richards, September 10, 1821, ibid., 333.

36. Ibid., 340.

37. Letter of September 23, 1822, ibid., 341–42. William J.'s father was a trustee.

38. Croker (1798–1854) is best remembered for his anonymously published *Fairy Legends and Traditions of the South of Ireland* (1825).

39. The father of the future prime minister Benjamin Disraeli, Lord Beaconsfield.

40. The group had previously been enjoying a card game called "Pope Joan" that was popular in the early nineteenth century.

41. Chambers, *The Book of Days*, 2:652.

42. Redding, *Fifty Years' Recollections, Literary and Personal*, 1:138–39.

43. Anon., "Examples in the British Museum, Ashmolean, Fitzwilliam, and Birmingham Museums," in *British Historical Medals* 1, no. 969 (1987). The design is from a sketch by William Brockedon, whose portrait of Belzoni is in London's National Portrait Gallery. The medal was manufactured by Edward Thomason in Birmingham, probably early in 1821.

44. "The General Monthly Statement of Fashion," *Lady's Monthly Museum*, January 1822. This information was generously provided by the researcher Susan Broadwater.

45. Drawn by the London artist George Scharf (see Peter Jackson, *George Scharf's London*, 35). The painting on which the placard was based is part of the Wilson Collection in the Bristol City Museum, No. H44.

46. Salt to Richards, Cairo, May 26, 1822, in Halls, *Life and Correspondence of Salt*, 2:323.

47. Salt to the Trustees of the British Museum, May 10, 1822, ibid., 324–25.

48. Henry Bankes, father of William J.

Bankes, was a longtime Member of Parliament, and due to his fiscal parsimony as a British Museum trustee was known as "Saving Banks" (Usick, *Adventures in Egypt and Nubia*, 12).

49. Ibid., 374–75.

16. Hard Times

1. George Waddington and Barnard Hanbury, who in 1822 published their experiences in a *Journal of a visit to parts of Ethiopia*, presented an important mummy (now missing) and its sarcophagus to the Fitzwilliam Museum at Cambridge.

2. In a letter to his family, Belzoni explained the omission of Francesco from his will, saying that he had brought the trouble on himself, but did not specify the nature of the trouble (Mayes, *The Great Belzoni*, 283, citing *Giovan Battista Belzoni alla luce di' nuovi documenti*).

3. The Murray letters are cited in Mayes, *The Great Belzoni*, 273, and are there noted as being in the possession of that publishing house. The first was written on April 6 and the second on April 18.

4. Ibid., 273.

5. *Times* (London), June 3, 1822.

6. Mayes, *The Great Belzoni*, 318n, found that a Masonic jewel owned by Belzoni became the property of the Rev. Browne.

7. Browne to Richards, Ibbotson's Hotel, Vere Street, London, June 9, 1823, in Halls, *Life and Correspondence of Salt*, 2:365.

8. Browne to Richards, Cambridge, November 12, 1823, ibid., 2:367–68.

9. *Times* (London), April 3, 1823. The Fitzwilliam Museum curator, Dr. S. A. Ashton, advises that the mummy has long been missing, but that the still-exhibited coffin bears the name of Nepawashefy and dates from the Third Intermediate Period (ca. 1000–800 BC).

10. Dr. Ashton says that the lid's weight is closer to seven tons.

11. Belzoni to Richards, No. 6, Half-Moon Street, December 31, 1822, in Halls, *Life and Correspondence of Salt*, 2:349.

12. Quoted by Mayes in *The Great Belzoni*

(278), from a letter to John Murray of September 2, 1821.

13. Burton, "Giovanni Battista Belzoni," 42.

14. In 1788, the Gold Coast had trading bases for the Dutch, English, Danes, and the Duchy of Brandenburg. The map was engraved by J. Harrison of 115 Newgate Street, London, and published on February 11, 1788.

15. *Times* (London), April 26, 1824. Although Parisians had too little interest in Belzoni's exhibit, a generation later, at the Paris International Exhibition of 1867, an impressive reconstruction of the temple at Edfu, whose vast interior contained a miscellany of antiquities, drew a goodly crowd of top-hatted and parasol-protected visitors to stroll down its avenue of sphinxes. The *Illustrated London News* allowed it a full page (November 16, 1867, 548).

16. Burton, "Giovanni Battista Belzoni," 44.

17. Francesco was not named in the will. In "Giovanni Battista Belzoni" (48), Burton stated that the third share went to Theresa, the widow of Belzoni's brother Antonio, who had died in 1817 or 1818.

18. The will was published in the *Times* (London) for December 8, 1824.

19. Rice, *Burton,* 356. Burton had adopted the Muslim faith and espoused a lifestyle unacceptable to his Civil Service superiors.

20. Burton ("Giovanni Battista Belzoni," 48) stated that the will was divided into *three* bequests, one of them to Theresa, the widow of his brother Antonio.

21. *Times* (London), March 12, 1825. As the notice was credited to the *Cambridge Chronicle*, it is likely that the Reverend Browne was involved in the shared information.

22. The letter is a copy written by Sarah into a commonplace book now in the Belzoni Collection in the Bristol City Museum, U.K. Dated August 5, 1823, the copy was made by the museum curator, R. Stanton, on June 29, 1943, who noted that "The spelling and writing is very bad, and many words are doubtful."

23. Burton, "Giovanni Battista Belzoni," 42. The *Curlew* was almost certainly a slave trader. However, by the time of Burton's consular administration he was careful to note that "The export slave trade is totally stopped," wryly noting that the ban was "to the manifest injury of the slave, who was once worth eight dollars, and now hardly as many sixpences. Nothing," he added, "would be easier than to run a dozen cargoes of *casimir noir* [black fabric] out of the Benin river."

24. This inscription was contained in a letter written aboard the *Castor* at British Accarah (Accra), January 7, 1824. Almost certainly penned by William Fell, it appeared in the *Times* (London), May 1824. It was later reprinted in Chambers, *The Book of Days*, 2:653, where the wording had undergone several changes.

25. Burton, "Giovanni Battista Belzoni," 49.

26. Ibid.

27. *Times* (London), April 24, 1823, drawing on the *Cambridge Chronicle*.

28. *Times* (London), November 27, 1824.

29. On December 11, 1824, the *Times* (London) reported that "The chambers are preparing under the direction of Mr. James Courtine [Curtin], to whom the care of the tomb at Paris was entrusted by Mr. Belzoni, when he started on his hapless journey to Fez."

30. The letter now in the Sir John Soane Museum's archives is dated from 4 Lamb's Conduit Place, April 17, 1824.

31. The letter is in the above archive and dated April 13, 1824.

32. *Cambridge Chronicle*, December 11, 1824.

33. Father of William John Bankes.

34. Browne to Soane, Trinity College, Cambridge, February 9, 1825.

35. Soane to Browne, Lincoln's Inn Fields, February 10, 1825.

36. Soane to Henry Ellis, May 8, 1824.

37. *Times* (London), March 28, 1825. Mayes, *The Great Belzoni*, 290, stated that Soane gave three sarcophagus parties and inferred that they were to promote Sarah's Leicester Square exhibition. Mayes also implied that she was a guest at one or more of them. Unfortunately, he cited no documentation.

38. A contemporary handwritten copy of a column of November 2, 1825. From the archives of the Sir John Soane Museum.

39. Written in a hand that was not hers from her exhibition address at 28 Leicester Square, October 20, 1825.

40. *Times* (London), October 26, 1825.

41. Ibid., October 21, 1825, and November 15, 1825.

42. Ibid., December 8, 1825.

43. Ibid., September 12, 1828.

44. These prints included a splendid view of Kom Ombo, and all are now extremely rare.

45. One of the plates attributed to Sarah (Belzoni, *Narrative*, vol. 2, pl. XXI) shows the Greco-Roman temple at Dakke, which she visited with her husband on the first voyage to Abu Simbel. Even so, there is no proof that any of her artistic work was executed in the field.

46. Most of the published lithographs were the work of Antonio Aglio, whose autograph appears in a corner of Belzoni's otherwise uncredited view of his assault on Chephren's temple (see p. 157). It is tempting to deduce that Belzoni's original sketch was too rough and that Aglio had to work so hard on it that he signed it as his.

47. *Times* (London), April 27 and March 15, 1827.

48. First edition, 1821.

17. Saving Sarah

1. Sarah's age at the time she was contemplating leaving Brussels is derived from her scarcely legible commonplace book in the Bristol City Museum, U.K. (25).

2. *Times* (London), January 3, 1850.

3. See chap. 1, pp. 19.

4. In 1837, the British government awarded Lady Morgan a £300 per annum literary pension, twenty years before it gave Sarah Belzoni £100. Lady Morgan died in 1859.

5. In Sarah's entry in the *Dictionary of National Biography*, she declared herself to be "constitutionally inexact [and] avowed a scorn for dates," in which case it may be unfair to blame her editor.

6. *Lady Morgan's Memoirs*, 2:376. Such basket trays are still to be bought at Aswan.

7. In her *Memoirs*, Lady Morgan referred to her hosts "doing the honours by me as if I were a little queen!" (2:377).

8. Lady Morgan's letter to the editor of the *Athenaeum*, no. 312, dated October 20, 1833. In old age, she was described as "a little humpbacked old woman, absurdly attired, rouged and wigged" (*Dictionary of National Biography*).

9. That does not necessarily mean that Sarah's living space was restricted to a single room. Had it been, Lady Morgan would almost certainly have mentioned a bed. This room was more likely to have been set aside to keep Sarah's Belzonian memories alive.

10. Lady Morgan, *The Princess; or The Beguine*, 1:35.

11. John Wilson Crocker, in John Murray's *Quarterly Review* 25 (April–July 1821). Lord Byron called *Italy* "a fearless and excellent work." The *Examiner*, July 1821, 413, found it to be "the classic of tourist writing," but *Blackwood's Edinburgh Magazine*, no. 11, July 1822, 692–96, concluded that "Amusing it may certainly be called, for so are the ravings of the famous Knight of La Mancha." See also Badin, *Anglo-Irish Sensibilities and Italian Realities*.

12. Lady Morgan, *The Princess*, 1:35.

13. Identified by its hieroglyphics as Boutehamon (see note 20 in this chapter).

14. Lady Morgan, *The Princess*, 1:35. This and other Lady Morgan–related sources have been generously provided by the researcher Susan Broadwater of Charlottesville, Virginia.

15. Subsequently the Musées Royaux d'Art et d'Histoire.

16. Warmenbol, "Sarah Belzoni and Her Mummy: The Beginnings of the Egyptological Collections at Bruxelles," paper presented in the lecture series "Perspectives on Ancient Egypt since Napoleon," at the Institute of Archaeology, University of London, December 16–18, 2000.

17. I am indebted to Ms. Jeannine Johnson Maia in Brussels for tracking down Sarah's "priestess."

18. The drawing survives in the Belzoni Collection in the Bristol City Museum, H4451.

19. Dr. Dirk Huyge attributes the coffin to the Twenty-first Dynasty, although Dr. Ashton at the Fitzwilliam Museum notes that this type of laminated coffin was common throughout the Third Intermediate Period.

20. Dr. Ashton notes that Boutehamon, being a relatively common Egyptian name, might have belonged to the much later occupant. The Brussels curator Baudouin van de Walle, in discussing the attribution, noted that "L'Identification avec Boutehamon est contestable" (Van de Walle, *La Collection Égyptienne*, 22. The letter is a copy written by Sarah into a commonplace book now in the Belzoni Collection in the Bristol City Museum, U.K., 12 n. 13). Dr. Huyge, who does not claim to be a mummy specialist, replies only that his latest catalogue (1999) says that Sarah's is Ptolemaic. A possible means of getting at the truth may be by the carbon-14 dating process. While Dr. Huyge agrees, his museum does not have the money to authorize the tests.

21. Dr. Ashton has noted that bandaging of individual limbs occurred as early as the First Dynasty (ca. 3100–2890 BC) (Dr. Ashton to the author, e-mail, January 29, 2010).

22. Capari, "Le Cercueil & La Momie de Boutehamon," 11–13.

23. Van de Walle, *La Collection Égyptienne*, 11–12. In 1854, the sterling exchange rate for the franc was 9d.

24. Lot 1270. A Graeco-Egyptian male mummy from Thebes, the arms and legs each separately bandaged. £23.

25. The coffin donated by the Rev. Lansbury to the Fitzwilliam Museum in 1822 clearly shows how the arched head segment was attached and how easily it could break away if mishandled.

26. D'Athanasi, *A Brief Account*, 237. The coffin was said to have been made for a king named Enantoph, date uncertain.

27. The Porte de Hal was built in 1360 and was first used as exhibit space in 1835. In 1889, the collection began to be moved to a new pavilion in the Cinquantenaire Park.

28. Jean Capart (1877–1947), the internationally distinguished Egyptologist who in 1935 wrote the first study of Sarah's mummy and coffin. Among his many honors and appointments, he was made part-time honorary curator of Egyptology at the Brooklyn Museum in 1932 and retained that association until his death.

29. While the director of archaeology at Colonial Williamsburg, I dealt with a similar event when a mid-nineteenth-century iron coffin was broken by a trenching dragline. The well-preserved and well-dressed male slid out of it into the trench leaving his head in the coffin to roll out on its own several minutes later.

30. Salt to Mountnorris, Alexandria, December 28, 1816, in Halls, *Life and Correspondence of Salt*, 1:474.

31. Bankes to Byron, January 2, 1822, in Usick, *Adventures in Egypt and Nubia*.

32. This may have been the same house visited by Lady Morgan.

33. The reference in Weisse's book title to Commander Gorringe recalls the latter's moving the "Cleopatra's Needle" to Central Park, New York, in 1879. I have been unable to find a copy of the book, but Mayes, in *The Great Belzoni*, discussed the relationship between Weisse and Sarah Belzoni (295). See also Noakes, *Cleopatra's Needles*, 95ff.

34. Mrs. Joan Porter, Jersey Wildlife Preservation Trust, to the author, August 26, 1986.

35. See note 15 in this chapter.

36. Sarah Belzoni, commonplace book in the Belzoni Collection, Bristol City Museum, U.K., 23, n.d.

37. The census has her at Walcot, Somerset, a parish in the city of Bath. Another less likely Selina Tucker was born at Cheltenham, Gloucestershire, in 1850, and in 1881 was listed as a dressmaker.

38. The Report of the Bristol Museum Committee for the year ending September 30, 1900, said only that "From Mr. C. E. Wilson the committee received a number of original drawings and manuscripts, formerly the property of Belzoni the great Egyptian explorer." These drawings are of great importance, some of them apparently part of a type series of collars and plumes and suggestive of the educational mind-set of Alessandro Ricci.

39. In 1805, the physician Sir William Charles Morgan married a Miss Hammond, who died in 1809, leaving one daughter (*Dictionary of National Biography*).

18. Significant Others

1. Halls, *Life and Correspondence of Salt*, 2:261.

2. Salt to William Hamilton, Alexandria, October 4, 1824, ibid., 2:237.

3. Salt to Richards, April 10, 1826, ibid., 2:259–60.

4. Salt to Richards, probably from Alexandria, June 1825, ibid., 2:250.

5. Salt to Richards, Alexandria, June 18, 1825, ibid., 2:245.

6. Salt to Richards, Cairo, May 12, 1827, ibid., 269.

7. Santoni to Richards, Leghorn, April 12, 1826, ibid., 264.

8. Neither museum has volunteered to reunite them.

9. Salt to Alexandria Consul Lee, Cairo, April 26, 1822, Halls, *Life and Correspondence of Salt*, 2:185–86.

10. D'Athanasi, *A Brief Account*, 257, 247.

11. Ibid., ix.

12. Sotheby and Son, *Catalogue of the Collection of Egyptian Antiquities, the Property of the late Henry Salt, Esq.*, June 29, 1835, 103.

13. Dawson and Uphill, "Pettigrew's Demonstrations upon Mummies," 13.

14. D'Athanasi, *A Brief Account*, iiix.

15. Dawson, "Pettigrew's Demonstrations upon Mummies," pl. XXIII, following 177.

16. El Mahdy, *Mummies Myth and Magic*, 176.

17. This was the year that Viceroy Abbas I was assassinated in Cairo by two of his slaves.

18. Bankes had been the duke's aide-de-camp during the Peninsula campaign.

19. *Times* (London), June 12, 1833.

20. Usick, *Adventures in Egypt and Nubia*, 173–74.

21. The mansion was known as "Kingston Hall" until William J. Bankes's father remodeled it.

22. Usick, *Adventures in Egypt and Nubia*.

23. Bankes to Byron, January 2, 1822, ibid., 195.

24. Definition quoted in the *Encyclopaedia Britannica* under "Eugenics."

25. Sir William Matthew Flinders Petrie (1853–1942) was the foremost British Egyptologist of his era. However, he sold artifacts to museums to raise money for his excavations; thus his sending heads to Galton may have been mercenary rather than proof of an interest in eugenics (information provided by Dr. S. A. Ashton, Fitzwilliam Museum, December 15, 2009).

26. Salt to William Hamilton from Alexandria, October 4, 1824, in Halls, *Life and Correspondence of Salt*, 2:241–42.

27. Wortham, *British Egyptology, 1549–1906*, 61–62.

28. Like Nathaniel Pearce, in 1805 Coffin had accompanied Viscount Valentia on his Arabian and Red Sea survey and had been left in Abyssinia to study the native tribes and promote English interests.

29. Halls, *Life and Correspondence of Salt*, 2:215–16.

30. Ibid., 2:389–420.

31. Scamuzzi, *Egyptian Art in the Egyptian Museum of Turin*, pl. LXVI. Also many objects from the Drovetti Collection. An oil painting from 1881 includes a portrait bust of Drovetti exhibited alongside heads of decapitated mummies.

32. Patricia Usick, in her invaluable book *Adventures in Egypt and Nubia*, presents evidence suggesting that his death may have been caused by syphilis (199). Dawson and Uphill give the date of Ricci's death as 1832 (*Who Was Who in Egyptology*, 248).

33. Wüst and McLane, "Rock Deterioration in the Royal Tomb of Seti, *Engineering Geology* 58, no. 2 (November 2000): 163.

34. Budge, *The Nile*, 314.

35. The stigma of the colonel's martial penetration would be offset by his later contributions to pyramid archaeology.

36. Carter, *The Tomb of Tutankhamen*, 22.

Epilogue

1. Mereruka was a senior official and son-in-law of King Teti, the first king of the Sixth Dynasty, ca. 2340 BC.

2. Sladen, *Queer Things about Egypt*, 146.

3. Carter, *The Tomb of Tutankhamen*, 22.

4. Dawson, *Who Was Who in Egyptology*, 24.

Glossary

The English spelling of Arabic words varies both in time and hearing, while the never-heard hieroglyphic and hieratic translations are still debated and variously spelled.

Abydos: A great temple south of Asyut, dedicated to Osiris but largely built by Seti I.

Aga or agha: A town mayor, as at Aswan; a Turkish title.

Amon or Ammon: The principal god of Thebes and king of the gods beginning in the Middle Kingdom.

Amenophis II or Amonhotep: King (1450–1425 BC).

Amenophis III: King (1417–1379 BC).

Ankh: The symbol of life.

Anophis: Serpent god, enemy of Osiris.

Anubis: Jackal-headed god who presides over the preparation of the dead.

Apis: Sacred bull. *See* Serapeum.

Aswan: Town at the Nile's First Cataract.

Bahari or bahri. North.

Binbashi: A junior Turkish officer, a lieutenant.

Bes: A squat, animal-like god of motherhood and a protector against evil.

Bey: A Turkish title ranking below pasha.

Biban-el-Maluk or Bibân el-Malûk: Tombs of the Kings.

Bitumen: Mineral pitch, the Arabic word being *moumia,* which developed into the terms "mummified" and "mummy." The substance was identified by Herodotus (ca. 450 BC) as gum.

Cacheff or káshif: A Turkish governor of a small district.

Caimakan: A middle-level official akin to a major.

Cangia: A large, oared vessel.

Canopic jars: The embalmed viscera of the deceased were entombed in four jars capped by god-headed lids.

Cartonnage: Linen soaked in plaster and painted; used for masks and inner mummy coffins.

Cartouche: A round-ended rectangle enclosing the names of kings and gods.

Cataract: A stretch of a river where waterfalls and rocks impede navigation.

Coffin: The wooden burial container for the mummified dead, sometimes incorrectly called a sarcophagus.

Copt: A native Christian directly descended from the Ancient Egyptians; rulers of the country after the Romans and before the rise of Islam.

Dahabilah: A relatively comfortable Nile sailing vessel.

Dakke or Dahka: Greco-Roman temple in Nubia, since moved.

Deftardár: Treasurer, tax collector, and magistrate.

Deir: A Coptic (Christian) convent.

Deir el-Bahari: A natural amphitheater containing the mortuary temple for Queen Hatshepsut, begun one thousand years earlier for Mentuhotep I (Eleventh Dynasty), ca. 2050 BC.

Demotic: A secular Egyptian script superseding the hieratic.

Dendera: Temple dedicated to the goddess Hathor, largely Ptolemaic and Roman.

Dhoura: Millet (Indian corn).

Edfu: The temple of Horus. Most of the surviving temple was started in 237 BC but was not completed until 57 BC. Ritually associated with Hathor of Dendera.

El-Ezbekiya Square: The annually flooded center of Cairo.

Erment or Armant: A village north of Luxor known to the Greeks as Hermonthis.

Esna or Esneh: Site of ancient Latopolis, temple built by Tuthmosis III.

Faddah: A small coin then valued at about a quarter of an English farthing.

Faience: Composition of clay or soapstone covered with glass-based glaze, usually blue-green. *See* Ushabti.

Fantasia: An English term used to describe Arab dances, also used to describe a set of mounted evolutions by a troop of Arab cavalry.

Fayyum: A pseudo-oasis in the Western Desert, the location of Lake Moeris. Its agricultural usage developed in the Twelfth Dynasty with the construction of canals.

Fellah: A peasant.

Fellaheen: The peasantry.

Firman: An authorization, e.g., a permit or passport.

Ganja: An oared Nile passenger boat; also a preparation of Indian hemp. *See also* Cangia.

Gebel: Mountain and quarry, e.g., Gebel Silsila (Mountain of the Chain) north of Aswan.

Germ: A sailing barge.

Giza or Gizeh: Site of the Great Pyramids of Cheops, Chephren, and Mycerinus of the Fourth Dynasty, during which at least twenty-two pyramids were constructed.

Gournou, Gurna, or Gurnet: A village overlying ancient burial pits and located near the entrance to the Valley of Kings.

Hagg or hadge: The pilgrimage to Mecca and those who have performed it.

Hammam: A bathhouse.

Haram: Pyramid.

Hathor: Goddess of the sky and motherhood, depicted with cow horns. The consort of Horus, her principal temple is at Dendera.

Hatshepsut: Queen of the New Kingdom, Eighteenth Dynasty (1503–1482 BC).

Heliopolis: A modern extension of Cairo and the site of one of the oldest and most revered cities of ancient Egypt.

Hieratic: A script derived directly from hieroglyphics.

Horus: The son of Osiris and Isis, born after Osiris's death, foe of his father's brother and murderer, Seth.

Hypostyle hall or speos: Outer hall of a temple open to the praying public and having a roof resting on columns.

Isis: The Great Mother goddess, wife of Osiris and mother of Horus, depicted in human form, sometimes wearing the hieroglyphic symbol for a throne.

Janissary: A hired guard, guide, and translator.

Ka: The spiritual double of a living person.

Kádee or cady: Chief judge.

Khamsin or canseen: A violent wind that blows for fifty days.

Khnum or Knemu: Ram-headed god of Elephantine, lord of the cataract and creator of man on a potter's wheel.

Khom: An artificial mound.

Khonsu: The moon god, who wears the moon over his falcon's head. One of the city gods of Thebes.

Kikhyà: A pasha's deputy.

Kom Ombo: A town north of Aswan known for its temple to the crocodile god Sobek. Though built in the Ptolemaic Period, it remains an impressive ruin with three hypostyle halls.

Late Dynastic Kingdom: 1085–332 BC.

Lower Egypt: The kingdom of the Nile delta north of Cairo.

Maat: Goddess of morality and justice. She wears a feather on her head or is represented by the feather alone.

Mameluke or Mamluk: A powerful Egyptian military class whose sultans ruled Egypt from AD 1220 to 1517.

Mastaba: Arabic for "seat," but used to describe mud-brick structures built over tomb shafts in the Old Kingdom and Early Dynastic Period.

Medinet or medineh: A town.

Medinet Habu: The mortuary temple of Ramesses III in the Theban Necropolis.

Meretseger: Cobra-headed god.

Middle Kingdom: Ca. 2050–ca. 1786 BC, Eleventh and Twelfth Dynasties.

Min: Ithyphallic god of fertility, depicted wearing a feathered cap and holding a flail.

Montu: Falcon-headed, warlike god, guardian deity of the temple at Erment.

Mummy: The preserved body of a dead human, animal, or bird. Derived from *moumiya*, a Persian word for bitumen, which was thought to have been used in the bandaging process.

Mut: The wife of Amun, usually seen as a double-crowned female; the second of the Theban triad.

Natron: Salt from the western delta used in cleansing, purification, and mummification.

Necropolis: City of the Dead, a cemetery.

Nephthys: Sister of Isis, protector of the dead.

New Kingdom: 1567–1085 BC, Eighteenth to Twentieth Dynasties.

Nun: The god personifying the primordial waters and a lord of the Netherworld.

Obelisk: A tapering, monolithic pillar, usually inscribed with hieroglyphics.

Occale: A quarantined residence for Europeans.

Old Kingdom: 2686–2181 BC, Early Dynastic Period.

Osiris: God-king of the dead and the underworld, also of the inundation; depicted as a mummified king.

Osmánlee: A Turk.

Ostracon: Usually a potsherd used as paper in writing short messages.

Osymandias: Greek name for Amenophis III (1417–1379 BC).

Pasha or báshà: A man of high rank, like Mohammed Ali, who owed allegiance to the sultán.

Pharaoh: Originally meaning "house of the king," but from the time of New Kingdom, the word was applied to the king himself.

Philae: An island south of Aswan and the site of the Twenty-sixth Dynasty temple of Isis, since moved to higher ground.

Pronaos: A sacred precinct.

Psammetichus III: King who reunited most of Lower and Middle Egypt (595–589 BC).

Ptah: Creator god of Memphis, depicted as a mummy, patron god of craftsmen.

Ptolemaic Period: 332–30 BC, Alexander the Great to Cleopatra VII.

Punt: A rich, but unidentified kingdom, possibly on the Somali coast, that provided exotic trade goods to the New Kingdom.

Purse: 500 piastres, approx. £7 sterling in 1834.

Pylon: An ornamental gate structure.

Ramadan: The month of religious fasting by Moslems.

Ramesses or Rameses I: New Kingdom pharaoh, Nineteenth Dynasty (1320–1318 BC).

Ramesses II: Greatest of the New Kingdom pharaohs, Nineteenth Dynasty (1304–1237 BC).

Ramesses III: A militarily successful king of the Twentieth Dynasty (1198–1166 BC).

Ramesseum: The mortuary temple in the Theban necropolis of Ramesses II; also a shrine to Amon.

Re or Ra: The falcon-headed sun god, the supreme deity, city god of Heliopolis.

Re- or Rë-Harakhti: Falcon-headed god combining the attributes of Re and Horus.

Reis or rais: A crew leader or boat captain.

Rosetta: A port town east of Alexandria, archaeologically famous for the discovery in Fort Saint-Julien (Tabiet Rashid) of the Rosetta Stone.

Sakkara: South of Cairo, site of the Step Pyramid of the Third Dynasty and the burial place of King Zozer (or Djsosser), ca. 2600 BC.

Sarcophagus: The stone container that housed the coffin of the mummified dead. *See* Coffin.

Saquiah: Waterwheel.

Scarab: Representation of a dung beetle and symbolic of birth.

Sekhmet or Sakhmet: Lion-headed goddess, wife of Ptah, and destroyer of Re's enemies. One of the triad of Memphis.

Serapeum: Burial labyrinth of the sacred bulls at Sakkara; the animals (Apis or Hap) dedicated to Ptah and Osiris.

Seth: The evil brother and murderer of Osiris.

Seti or Sethos I: Father of Ramesses II, Nineteenth Dynasty (1318–1304 BC).

Shahdoof or shaduf: A primitive water-raising device.

Sheik: A native Muslim, a village elder.

Situlae: Holy-water containers.

Sobek: Crocodile god of Kom Ombo and Lake Moeris (Birket Kurun).

Sokar: A god worshipped in Memphis and a major player in the rituals of the after-life.

Solar boat: The boat in which Re, the sun god, traversed the heavens.

Stele: An inscribed stone slab, a gravestone.

Sultán: Ruler of the Ottoman Empire, of which Egypt was a province.

Thoth: Ibis-headed god of Hermopolis, associated with education.

Upper Egypt: The southern kingdom between Cairo and Nubia.

Ushabti: Wooden or glazed figure in the shape of a mummy placed in coffins and tombs to tend for the afterlife needs of the dead. *See* Faience.

Wadi Halfa: Town at the Nile's Second Cataract.

Wahhábees or Wahabees: A sect founded in the eighteenth century in central Arabia and, until 1811, a growing threat to Mohammed Ali and the Ottoman administration.

Young Memnon: The name mistakenly given to a sculpture of Ramesses II (1304–1237 BC).

Bibliography

Aldred, Cyril. *The Egyptians.* London: Thames and Hudson, 1961.

Andrews, Carol. *Egyptian Mummies.* London: British Museum Publications, 1984.

Arnold, D. *Temples of the Last Pharaohs.* London: Oxford University Press, 1999.

Atkins, Sarah (anon.). *Fruits of Enterprise Exhibited in the Travels of Belzoni in Egypt and Nubia.* 12th ed. London: Grant and Griffith, 1851.

Badin, Donatella Ablate. *Anglo-Irish Sensibilities and Italian Realities.* Bethesda, Md.: Academic Press, 2007.

Baumgarten, Monica. *Baedeker's Egypt.* Norwich, U.K.: Jarold and Sons, n.d.

Bazin, Germain. *The Museum Age.* New York: Universe Books, 1967.

Belzoni, Giovanni Batista. *Narrative of the Operations and Recent Discoveries within the Pyramids, Temples, Tombs, and Excavations in Egypt and Nubia.* 2nd ed. London: John Murray, 1821.

Bickerstaffe, Dylan. "Strong Man: Wrong Tomb. The Problem of Belzoni's Sarcophagi." *Ancient Egypt* magazine, no. 36, June/July 2006.

Bierbrier, Morris. *The Tomb-Builders of the Pharaohs.* London: British Museum Publications, 1982.

Bradford, Ernle. *Cleopatra.* New York: Harcourt Brace Jovanovich, 1972.

Brander, Bruce. *The River Nile.* Washington, D.C.: National Geographic Society, 1968.

Brown, Lawrence. *British Historical Medals.* 3 vols. London: B. A. Seaby, 1980–87.

Budge, E. A. Wallis. *The Gods of the Egyptians.* 2 vols. London: Methuen, 1904. Reprint, New York: Dover, 1969.

———. *The Nile: Notes for Travellers in Egypt.* 4th ed. London: Thomas Cook & Son (Egypt) Ltd., 1895.

Burckhardt, John Lewis. *Travels in Nubia.* London: John Murray, 1822. Reprint, Kessinger, n.d.

Burton, Richard F. "Giovanni Battista Belzoni." *Cornhill Magazine,* vol. 42, July–December 1880, 36–50.

———. *Personal Narrative of a Pilgrimage to Al-Medinah and Meccah.* London: Longmans Green, 1855–56.

Capart, Jean. "Le Cercueil & La Momie de Boutehamen." *Les Momies Égyptiennes.* Brussels: Bulletin Des Musées Royaux D'Art at D'Histoire, 1935, 111–13.

Carter, Howard. *The Tomb of Tutankhamen.* 1923–33 (originally published in three volumes). New York: Dutton, 1972.

Chambers, Robert. *The Book of Days: A Miscellany of Popular Antiquities.* 2 vols. London: W. & R. Chambers, 1862–64. Detroit: Omnigraphics, 1990.

Clayton, Peter. "Giovanni Belzoni, 1778–1823: Un pioniere dell' Egittologia." *Bolletino del Museo Civico di Padova,* Annata LXVII—1978 (1982): 3–17.

———. *The Rediscovery of Ancient Egypt. Artists and Travellers in the 19th Century.* Thames and Hudson, 1982. Reprint, 1990.

Cott, Jonathan. *The Search for Omm Seti.* New York: Doubleday, 1987.

Cottrell, Leonard. *The Lost Pharaohs.* 1961. New York: Grosset and Dunlap, 1963.

D'Athanasi, Giovanni. *A Brief Account of the Researches and Discoveries in Upper Egypt: Made under the Direction of Henry Salt (1836).* London: John Hearne. 1836. Reprint, Breinigsville, Pa.: Kessinger, 2009.

Dawson, Warrem R. "Pettigrew's Demonstrations upon Mummies: A Chapter in the History of Egyptology." *Journal of Egyptian Archaeology* 20 (1988).

Dawson, Warren R., and Eric P. Uphill. *Who Was Who in Egyptology.* London: Egypt Exploration Society, 1972.

Denon, Baron Dominique Vivant. *Description de l'Égypte.* 10 vols. Paris, 1809–25.

———. *Egypt: A Series of One Hundred and Ten Engravings . . . Descriptions and Explanations in French and English.* London: Charles Taylor, 1816.

Dickens, Charles. "The Story of Giovanni Belzoni." *Household Words,* April 1851. Reprinted in *Harper's New Monthly Magazine,* May 1851.

Duff Gordon, Lady Lucie. *Letters from Egypt 1862–1869.* Reedited, with additional letters, by Gordon Waterfield. London: Routledge and Kegan Paul, 1969.

Edwards, I. E. S. *A Handbook to the Egyptian Mummies and Coffins Exhibited in the British Museum.* London: British Museum, 1938.

———, ed. *Introductory Guide to the Egyptian Collections in the British Museum.* London: Trustees of the British Museum, 1971.

———. *The Pyramids of Egypt.* New York: Viking Press, 1972.

El Mahdy, Christine. *Mummies Myth and Magic in Ancient Egypt.* London: Thames and Hudson, 1989.

Fagan, Brian. *The Rape of the Nile.* New York: Scribner's Sons, 1975.

Finati, Giovanni. *Narrative of the Life and Adventures of Giovanni Finati, Native of Ferrara.* 2 vols. London: John Murray, 1830. Elibron Classics. Boston: Adamant Media Corp., 2005.

Forbin, Compte de, Louis Nicholas Phillippe Auguste. *Voyage dans le Levant,* Paris, 1819.

Fitzclarence, George. *Journal of a Route across India, through Egypt to England in the latter end of the year 1817 and the beginning of 1818.* London: John Murray, 1819.

Gardiner, Sir Alan. *Egyptian Grammar.* 3rd ed. Oxford: Ashmolean Museum, 1969.

Habachi, Labib. "Setau, the Famous Viceroy of Rameses II and His Career." *Cahiers d'histoire égyptienne* 10 (1967): 51–68.

Halls, J. J. *The Life and Correspondence of Henry Salt Esq. F.R.S. &c.* 2 vols. London: Richard Bentley, 1834.

Harris, James, and Kent R. Weeks. *X-Raying the Pharaohs.* New York: Scribner's Sons, 1973.

Hastings, Michael. *Sir Richard Burton: A Biography.* New York: Coward, McCann and Geoghegan, 1978.

Herodotus. *Herodotus: The Histories.* Translated by Aubrey de Sélincourt. London: Penguin, 1973.

Hornung, Erik, and David Lorton. *Ancient Egyptian Books of the Afterlife.* New York: Cornell University Press, 1999.

Irby, Charles Leonard. *Travels in Egypt and Nubia, Syria and the Holy Land and Asia Minor during the Years 1817 & 1818.* London: privately printed, 1823.

Jackson, Peter. *George Scharf's London, Sketches and Watercolours of a Changing City, 1820–1850.* London: John Murray, 1987.

James, Harry. "Howard Carter and the EEF." *Egyptian Archaeology: The Bulletin of the Egypt Exploration Society,* no. 2 (1992): 3–5.

Jefferson, Thomas. *Notes on the State of Virginia.* Chapel Hill: University of North Carolina Press, 1955.

Kaster, James. *The Literature and Mythology of Ancient Egypt.* London: Allan Lane; Penguin Press, 1968.

Kurlansky, Mark. *The Big Oyster: History on the Half Shell.* New York: Random House, 2007.

Lane, Edward W. *Manners and Customs of the Modern Egyptians.* Everyman's Library no. 315. London: J. M. Dent, 1966. Text of 1860 edition.

Le Feuvre, Cathy. "Does the Name Belzoni Ring a Bell?" *Jersey Evening Post* (Channel Island), October 30, 1986, 29.

Lloyd, Christopher. *The Nile Campaign, Nelson and Napoleon in Egypt.* New York: Barnes and Noble, 1973.

Magoffin, R. V. D, and Emily C. Davis. *The Romance of Archaeology.* New York: Garden City Publishing, 1929.

Manley, Deborah, and Peta Rée. *Henry Salt, Artist, Traveller, Diplomat, Egyptologist.* London: Libri, 2001.

Manning, Samuel. *Land of the Pharaohs.* London: Religious Tract Society, 1880.

Mansfield, Peter. *The British in Egypt.* New York: Holt, Rinehart and Winston, 1971.

Marlowe, John. *Spoiling the Egyptians.* New York: St. Martin's Press, 1975.

Mayes, Stanley. *The Great Belzoni.* 1959. New York: Taurisparke Paperbacks, 2003.

Mendelssohn, Kurt. *The Riddle of the Pyramids.* New York: Praeger, 1974.

Montulé, Edward. *Travels in Egypt during 1818 and 1819.* London: Sir Richard Phillips and Co., 1821.

Moorehead, Alan. *The Blue Nile.* New York: Harper and Row, 1962.

Morgan, Lady Sydney. *Lady Morgan's Memoirs, Autobiography, Diaries and Correspondence.* Edited by William Hepworth Dixon. 2 vols. London, William Allen & Co., 1862–63.

———. *The Princess or the Beguine.* 2 vols. London: Richard Bentley, 1835.

Murray, A. Margaret. *The Splendor That Was Egypt.* 1949. New York: Praeger Paperbacks, 1964.

Murray, John. *Handbook for Travellers in Egypt.* 5th ed. London: William Clows and Sons, 1875.

Nagel's Encyclopedia Guide to Egypt. Geneva: Nagel, 1972.

Nightingale, Florence. *Letters from Egypt: A Journey on the Nile 1849–1850.* New York: Weidenfeld and Nicolson, 1987.

Noakes, Aubrey. *Cleopatra's Needles.* London: H. F. & G. Witherby, 1962.

Noël Hume, Ivor. *All the Best Rubbish.* New York: Harper and Row, 1974.

Pearce, Nathaniel. *The Life and Adventures of Nathaniel Pearce; Written by Himself.* Edited by J. J. Halls. 2 vols. London: H. Colburn and R. Bentley, 1831.

Redding, Cyrus. *Fifty Years' Recollections, Literary and Personal.* 3 vols. London: Charles J. Skeet, 1858.

Rice, Edward. *Captain Sir Richard Francis Burton.* New York: Scribner's Sons, 1990.

Romer, John. *Valley of the Kings.* Edison, N.J.: Castle Books, 1981.

Salt, Henry. *Account of a Voyage to Abyssinia and Travels into the Interior of that Country . . . in the Years 1809 and 1810.* London: F. C. and J. Rivington, 1814.

———. *Essay on Dr. Young's and M. Champollion's Phonetic System of Hieroglyphics . . .* London: Longman, Hurst, 1825.

Scamuzzi, Ernesto. *Egyptian Art in the Egyptian Museum of Turin.* New York: Abrams, 1965.

Searight, Sarah, ed. *Women Travellers in the Near East.* Oxford: Oxbow Books, 2005.

Sladen, Douglas. *Queer Things about Egypt.* London: Hurst and Blackett, 1910.

Smith, John Thomas. *A Book for a Rainy Day.* London: Richard Bentley, 1845. Charleston, S.C.: Bibliobazaar, n.d.

Smith, Piazzi. *The Great Pyramid: Its Secrets and Mysteries Revealed.* Originally published as *Our Inheritance in the Great Pyramid.* London: W. Isbister, 1880. Reprint, New York: Crown, 1978.

Stead, Miriam. *Artists on the Nile.* London: Schuster Gallery, 1987.

Steegmuller, Francis, trans. and ed. *Flaubert in Egypt: A Sensibility on Tour.* Boston: Little, Brown, 1972.

Strudwick, Nigel, and Helen Strudwick. *Thebes in Egypt: A Guide to the Tombs and Temples of Ancient Luxor.* New York: Cornell University Press, 2004.

Tompkins, Peter. *The Magic of Obelisks.* New York: Harper and Row, 1981.

Turner, William. *Journal of a Tour in the Levant.* 3 vols. London: John Murray, 1820.

Urby, Charles Leonard. *Travels in Egypt and Nubia, Syria and the Holy Land.* London: First private edition, 1823.

Usick, Patricia. *Adventures in Egypt and Nubia: The Travels of William John Bankes (1786–1855).* London: British Museum Press, 2002.

Waddington, George, and Bernard Hanbury. *Journal of a Visit to Parts of Ethiopia.* London: John Murray, 1822.

Walle, Baudouin van de. *La Collection Égyptienne.* Brussels: Musées Royaux D'Art et D'Histoire, 1980.

Ward, Edward "Ned." *The London Spy: The Vanities and Vices of the Town Exposed to View, 1698–1703.* Edited by Arthur L. Hayward. London: Cassell, 1927.

Weeks, Kent R. *The Lost Tomb.* New York: William Morrow, 1998.

Weisse, John Adams. *The Obelisk and Freemasonry according to the Discoveries of Belzoni and Commander Gorringe.* New York: J. W. Bouton, 1880.

Wilkinson, Sir John Gardner. *Manners and Customs of the Ancient Egyptians.* 3 vols. London: John Murray, 1837. 2nd ser., 2 vols., and plates, 1841.

Wilkinson, Richard H. *The Complete Gods and Goddesses of Ancient Egypt.* London: Thames and Hudson, 2003.

Wortham, John David. *British Egyptology 1549–1906.* Newton Abbot, U.K.: David and Charles, 1971.

Index

Banks, Sir Joseph, 46, 61, 184, 212–14, 219, 225, 255; death of, 214; and Linnean Society, 226

Barre, Sarah (Mrs. Sarah Belzoni). *See* Belzoni, Sarah Barre

Bartholomew Fair, 13, 16–17

Bastinado, 112–13

Bedouins, 90, 103, 123; Moggrebyn tribe, 84

Beechey, Sir Henry William, 45, 100–103, 106, 110–11, 115, 119–20, 123, 135, 137, 158, 170, 173, 175, 179, 180, 184, 197, *208*, 223, 262; at Abu Simbel, 115; and Belzoni, 152; on the trail to Berenice, 171; and discovery of Karnak, 110; at Salt's wedding, 204; as secretary to Salt, 97

Bellefonds, Louis Maurice Adolphe Linant de, 184, 259, 262

Belmore, Lord. *See* Lowry-Corry

Belmore family, 150, 163, 165

Belzoni, Antonio, 5, 278

Belzoni, Domenico, 5, 227

Belzoni, Francesco, 5, 15, 18–19, 21, 23–34, 221–23

Belzoni, Giovanni Baptiste, 1, 3, *11*, 12, 15, 23–24, 31, 37, 40, 42, 44–45, 50, *52*, 54, 82, 85, 95, 103, 116, 123, 125, 136–38, 141, 156, 165, 167, 175, 179, 192, 199, 200–201, *245*, 263; birth of, 5; birthplace designated, 206; as celebrity, 206; and confrontation with Drovetti ("grand engagement"), 196; and confrontation with Salt, 191–92; death of, 220, 230; at exhibitions in London, 210, 217–18, 224, 247, *249;* at exhibitions in Paris, 226, 247; and hydraulic engineering, 6–7, 47; and map of the Valley of Kings, *153;* meets and marries Sarah, 15; and memorabilia, 252; and new contract with Salt, 181; as the "Patagonian Sampson," 12, *13*, 13–15, 22; and poetry, 225; in Portsmouth, 252; ring of Alexander of Russia presented to, 227; statue of (in Padua), *208;* will of, 227. *See also* Belzoni, Sarah

Barre; Burckhardt, John Lewis; Drovetti, Bernardino; Salt, Henry; *and individual artifacts and sites*

Belzoni, Sarah Barre, 15, 24, 26, 29, 34, 38, 51, 77, 82, 87, 90, 96, 119, 135, 164, 177, 199, 200, 221, 223, 229, 235; and African feminist history, 88; as artist, *48, 49*, 172; in Brussels, 237; death of, 222; departure from Cairo of, 101; as feminist, 4, 204; at Fez, 226–27; grave site of, 230; health of, 71; last letter to Giovanni, 230; and Leicester Square exhibition, 231; in London, 221; at Luxor, 94; marriage of, 15; and Lady Morgan, 238–43; mummy of, 241–50; nationality of, 240; new lithographs of, 235, 241; notebook of, 238; and ophthalmia, 96; in Padua, 206; in Philae, 83, 119–20; physical appearance of, 18, 20; and pilgrimage to the Holy Land, 154, 171; portrait of, 231; in Portsmouth, 252; and poverty, 234–35; published account of, 88; and role as mediator, 88; at Rosetta, 202; at St. Helier, 237; and Saving Sarah fund, 241; theater experience of, 15–16; will of, 250–51

Benin, 229–30; Bight of, *228*

Berenice, 171, 177, 179, 235; expedition to, 173, 180; map of trail to, *176;* temple in, *176*, 178–79; souvenir from, *179*

Bergami, Bartolomeo, 216

Biban el-Maluk. *See* Valley of Kings

Bickerstaff, Dr. Dylan, 74

bilharzias (hookworm disease), 174

billboard carriers, 218, *249*

Birnie, Sir Richard, 222

Blue Bear Inn, Oxford, 24

Boghos Bey, Joussef, 29, 32–33, 38, 40, 45

Bond Street, 216, 256

Bouchard, Pierre François Xavier, 10, 54

Boughton, Sir William, 142

Boulak, 29, 32–34, 38, 50–51, 96–97, 102, 154, 165, 200

Ottoman Empire, 35
Owenson, Robert, 240

Padua, 5–7, 44, 49, 206, 226, 239;
Palazzo della Ragione, 206–7; Piaz-
zale Belzoni, 276n10
Palazzo dell'Academia delle Scienze, 261
Palmersten, Lord (prime minister), 19
papyri, 107–8, 146, 149, 166, 181, 201,
255, 261, 273n3
Paris, 10, 224, 231; Belzoni's exhibition
in, 226, 247
Park, Mungo (explorer), 225–27, 230;
*Travels in the Interior Districts of
Africa,* 226
Parliament, British, 223
Pasha, Ibrahim, 55, 57–58, 262; and
army in revolt, 34
Patrick Street Theatre, Cork, 19
Peace of Amiens, 10, 25
Pearce, Nathaniel, 200, 205, 275n23
Pensa (father of Salt's wife), 204
Peterloo Massacre, 213, 276n24
Petrie, Sir William Matthew Flinders,
259, 281n25
Philae, 79–80, *80,* 82, 101, 117–18, 135,
179, 183–85, 190; damage by French
army at, 118; obelisk at, 92, 102,
183–84, *193,* 198, 200, 202, 206, 211,
231, 270n1; pedestal at, 192, 203,
256, 259; wall panel of Osiris at, 92,
119
pistols, 82–84, 90, 120, 130, 195, 196
Porte de Hal, Brussels, 249, 280n27
Porter, Joan, 250–51
Portsea, Hampshire, 252
Portugal, 21, 22
Project Memnon, 53, 68
Providence (ship), 229–30
Psammeticus, 134
Ptolemy, 142, 178
Ptolemy II, 171, 178
Ptolemy III, 185, *187*
Ptolemy V, 55
Ptolemy XII, *186*
Purchas, Rev. Samuel, 174

pyramids, 29–30, 156; Battle of the, 8;
of Cheops, 30–31, 99, 155, 218; at
Chephren, 155, *157,* 157–58, 163, 208;
at Giza, *161,* 164; interpretation of
Mycerinus *30,* 164, 263

Ramadan, 67, 72, 79, 122
Ramesses I, 139
Ramesses II, *63,* 74, 81, 83, *111,* 124, 130,
142, *208, 209,* 235, 269n20
Ramesses III, *74,* 74–76, 112, 224, 263;
sarcophagus of, 256; sarcophagus lid
of, *76*
Ramesseum, *63,* 66–67, *67,* 69, 70,
116–17, 197
Rë, 130
Red Sea, 168, 171, 200
Redding, Cyrus (editor), 217; on Bel-
zoni's height, 18
Reghellini, Martialis (antiquary), 243
Rë-Harakhti, *89,* 125, 130
Reis (defined), 268n17
reporters, role of in archaeology, 165
Reynolds, Sir Joshua, 262
Ricci, Dr. Alessandro, *147, 148,* 173, 180,
184, 199, 262, 281n38
Richards, Bingham, 212, 218–20, 223–
24, 231–32, 234, 254–55
Rifaud, Jean-Jacques, 86–87, *87,* 93–94
Robinson, Peter Frederick (architect),
21–22
Rome, 5–7, 44
rope dancer, 15–16, *16,* 267nn16–17
Rosetta 9, 9–10, 36, 97, 200–201; Battle
of, 184
Rosetta Stone, 55–56, *56,* 130, 142, 259,
276n19
Rosignani (Drovetti's excavator), 194,
202
Royal Geographical Society, 237
Royal Museum of France, 163
Royalty Theatre, 15
Russel, M. (French consul), 202

Sack, Baron, 179, 184
Sadler, Thomas, 10

Tucker, John, 252; sisters of, 252
Tucker, Sarah A., 252
Tucker, Selina Belzoni, 251
Turin Museum, 108, 244, 261
Turks and the Ottoman Empire, 35
Turner, William, 27–29, 31, 34, 37, 93
Tutankhamen, 141, 168
Tuthmosis, 142

University Club, 231
University College, London, 259

Valetta, 7, 25, 28
Valley of Kings (Biban el-Maluk), 137–39, *153*, 156, 164, 168, 193, 195, 198, 243
Venice, 5, 44, 258
Villena, Antonio Manoel de, 25
Vyse, Colonel Howard, 263

Waddington, George, 277n1
Wadi Halfa, 86–88, 121, 127

Wahhabis, 35–36
Ward, Edward "Ned," 16, 54
Waters of Nun, 147
Weisse, John Adam, 250; *The Obelisk and Freemasonry according to the Discoveries of Belzoni and Commander Gorringe,* 250
Wellington, Duke of (Wellesley, Arthur), 21, 25, 211, 258
Westminster Abbey, 3, 216
Wilkinson, Sir John Gardner, 139
Williams, Dr. Veronica Seton, 265
Wilson, C. E., 252
Wilson, William Rae, 234, 252
Woodlark (ship), 45

Yorke, Charles Philip, 214–15, 276n28
Young Memnon (statue of Ramesses II), 41, 45, 47, 50–51, 56–57, 61, 63, 69, 71–72, 93–97, 118, 166, 167, *209, 239,* 263
Young, Thomas, 142, 260

Also by Ivor Noël Hume

Non-Fiction

A Passion for the Past: The Odyssey of a Transatlantic Archaeologist (2010)
Wreck and Redemption (2009)
Something from the Cellar (2005)
If These Pots Could Talk (2001)
In Search of This and That (1996)
Shipwreck! History from the Bermuda Reefs (1995)
The Virginia Adventure (1994)
Martin's Hundred (1982)
English Delftware from London and Virginia (1977)
All the Best Rubbish (1974)
A Guide to Artifacts of Colonial America (1970)
Historical Archaeology (1969)
1775: Another Part of the Field (1968)
Here Lies Virginia (1963)
Great Moments in Archaeology (1957)
Treasure in the Thames (1956)
Archaeology in Britain (1953)

With Audrey Noël Hume

The Archaeology of Martin's Hundred (2001)
Handbook of Tortoises, Terrapins and Turtles (1954)

Fiction

Civilized Men (2006)
The Truth About Fort Fussocks (1972)
The Charleston Scheme (1971)

Play

Smith! Being the Life and Death of Cap'n John (2007)